The Methuen Drama Anthology of
Testimonial Plays

Also available from Bloomsbury Methuen Drama:

The Methuen Drama Anthology of Irish Plays

The Methuen Drama Book of Naturalist Plays

The Methuen Drama Book of New American Plays

The Methuen Drama Book of Plays by Black British Writers

The Methuen Drama Book of Plays from the Sixties

The Methuen Drama Book of Post-Black Plays

The Methuen Drama Book of Royal Court Plays 2000–2010

The Methuen Drama Book of Suffrage Plays

The Methuen Drama Book of Twenty-First Century British Plays

Modern Drama: Plays of the '80s and '90s

Not Black and White

Producers' Choice: Six Plays for Young Performers

Six Ensemble Plays for Young Actors

Theatre in Pieces: Politics, Poetics and Interdisciplinary Collaboration

The Methuen Drama Anthology of Testimonial Plays

Bystander 9/11

Big Head

The Fence

Come Out Eli

The Travels

On the Record

Seven

Pajarito Nuevo la Lleva: The Sounds of the Coup

Edited and with an introduction by
ALISON FORSYTH

BLOOMSBURY
LONDON · NEW DELHI · NEW YORK · SYDNEY

Bloomsbury Methuen Drama

An imprint of Bloomsbury Publishing Plc

50 Bedford Square	1385 Broadway
London	New York
WC1B 3DP	NY 10018
UK	USA

www.bloomsbury.com

Bloomsbury is a registered trademark of Bloomsbury Publishing Plc

First published 2014

British Library Cataloguing-in-Publication Data
A catalogue record for this book is available from the British Library.

ISBN: PB: 978-1-4081-7652-8
ePub: 978-1-4081-7653-5
ePDF: 978-1-4081-7654-2

Library of Congress Cataloging-in-Publication Data
A catalog record for this book is available from the Library of Congress.

Typeset by Newgen Knowledge Works (P) Ltd., Chennai, India
Printed and bound in Great Britain

Contents

Acknowledgements

I would like to express my thanks to all the contributors of this volume. These include Meron Langsner, and JAC Publishing/JulieAnn Govang who should be contacted if somebody intends to produce *Bystander 9/11*; Denise Uyehara and Kaya Press who first published *Big Head* in *Maps of City & Body: Shedding Light on the Performances of Denise Uyehara* in 2003; Alecky Blythe, the Recorded Delivery Theatre Company and Camilla Young for helping to arrange the interview with Alecky and for introducing me to the text of the hitherto unpublished *Come Out Eli*; Christine Bacon and Noah Birksted-Breen of ice&fire theatre company; Tim Etchells and Forced Entertainment; María José Contreras Lorenzini and her colleagues, Ornella de la Vega, Milena Grass and Nancy Nicholls at the Universidad Catolica de Chile, as well as Camila Le-Bert for agreeing to translate the commissioned transcription of the performance text, *Pajarito Nuevo la Lleva*, for this volume; Dr Caroline Wake, postdoctoral fellow at the Centre for Modernism Studies in Australia at the University of New South Wales for conducting such an insightful interview with Alicia Talbot of Urban Theatre Projects. In addition, thanks go to Alicia Talbot, Raimondo Cortese and Lina Kastoumis for transcribing the performance text of *The Fence* for this anthology – a work which was originally devised by Alicia Talbot with Helen Dallas, Richard Green, Vicki van Hout, Kelton Pell and Skye Wansey; Michael Callahan of Josef Weinberger Ltd for allowing me to discover the play, *Seven*.

Furthermore I would like to extend a special note of gratitude to my commissioning editor, Mark Dudgeon, who has been most supportive and incredibly patient during the various peaks and troughs that have occurred during the preparation of this volume.

Alison Forsyth
Aberystwyth, 2013

Introduction:
Testimony in Performance: Memory in Action

Alison Forsyth

Testimony is usually taken to mean the intentional expression of an individual's memories and recollections about a given event in the past, and it has been traditionally associated with a mode of speech used within the context of the courtroom – that is, words uttered in the witness box and under oath. However, as noted by Robert Audi, over recent years, testimony has acquired a wider, more general definition and application beyond its usual legal connotations, whereby 'formal testimony differs from the informal kind in the conditions of its expression . . . [it does] not necessarily in credibility.'[1] Theatre provides a platform from which one such 'informal' kind of testimonial expression can be aired, and it is the purpose of this volume to illustratively explore the various ways in which testimony is utilized in the making and execution of a range of plays and performances since 2001.

During the last two decades there has been a marked multiplication of dramatic works which utilize testimony (verbatim theatre, Tribunal plays, documentary theatre) leading one critic to note that 'mere dramatic fiction has apparently been seen as an inadequate response to the current global situation.'[2] This pronounced focus on testimony in drama over recent years is perhaps reflective of an increasing appetite to gain a deeper personal, even more intimate, insight into the world we inhabit over and above the seemingly ceaseless yet perhaps superficially depthless access we have to rapid-fire, mass-circulated news' stories and journalistic reports via 24-hour television and radio, the internet and social media.

The potential to gain a more profound insight into recent or more distant historical events and experiences of which we may or may not be already familiar is made available in testimonial theatre by dint of the form's capacity to present information about such events *differently*. Instead of placing an emphasis on testimony as a means of accessing data on a purely cognitive level (as is arguably its purpose in a court of law or news stories) theatre consciously engages its many performative and creative tools when utilizing testimony, in order to move us beyond a merely fact-bearing exercise. Thus, rather than merely relaying the bare facts of an historical event in an almost evidentiary manner, testimonial theatre strives to engage the spectator on an emotional and affective level so that the particular circumstances of the past may be illuminated by, for example, more intimate, personal and even conflicting perspectives which, in turn, highlight the complexities of any one given historical event as well as sometimes exposing the fallible mnemonic foundations of testimony. In a way, one could say that the most challenging testimonial theatre takes us further away from easily digestible and discrete factual narratives, and instead brings us closer to an understanding of the complicated and even irreconcilable truths of a past event, and indeed it could even be a form which makes us interrogate the way we consign, oftentimes prematurely, historical events to 'the past' when in fact that past may be still shaping our present, and potentially our future. Testimonial theatre's potential to let us know about historical and/or past personal events *differently* does not, therefore, necessarily equate with knowing about historical and/or past personal events definitively; on the contrary, this form of theatre can prompt an interrogation of our often all too easy acceptance of the supposed inviolable relationship between fact and truth. Indeed, Alessandro Portelli's excellent summation that 'the credibility of testimony does not rely on its slavish adherence to facts, but rather in its departure from it' highlights the way testimony, and by extension, testimony in performance, can create the potential for us to *know differently*.

When quizzed by Robert Martin about the historical accuracy of his work, Arthur Miller retorted that '. . . well a worship of fact – by fact, I mean in the crudest sense – is always an obstruction if one is looking for the truth. There is a difference between facts and the truth; the truth is a synthesis of the facts.'[3] Here, with reference to his own stagecraft, Miller encapsulates the way performance can creatively mediate and thus expand upon and even interrogate received fact. As distinct from the courts' or journalists' evaluation of testimony, often gauged against a rigid benchmark of proof or evidence, testimony is valued in theatrical practice for its potentially complicating insights into how individual people involved in past events interpret these events and their implications. Although mindful of Rinaldo Walcott's perceptive caveat that '[I]n many quarters, personal testimony has taken on the spectre of transparent truth-claims whereby questioning them suggests a kind of vulgarity on the part of the questioner'[4] it is crucial to acknowledge that once testimony is consciously demarcated in dramatic practice from either the notion of being little more than a dry and incontestable record of fact, or a rather crass method of eliciting spectator sympathy towards a given perspective, it can actually provide the very means to expose, to subvert, to complicate, to emphasize and to question a past that has not yet been mastered, and to use Max Stafford-Clark's description of his own project when using testimony, to delve deeper and 'find the story within the story'.[5] (Hammond, 2008, 58) With this in mind, testimonial theatre need not imply work that is little more than a testimony-filled superimposition onto a narrative arc which, to use David Mamet's phrase, follows a 'dramatic urge'[6] – a reductive device which flattens out complexity, nuance, subtlety and indeed contradiction to allow us to stage life as a series of simplistic and easily digestible exempla which in turn serve to allay our anxieties about the real world. Indeed, recent examples of testimonial theatre do successfully counter Mamet's concerns, often reflecting an increasingly more self-reflexive approach about, for example, the relationship between witness and listener/spectator, far removed from the presentation of sense-dulling and descriptive monologues in the service of reductive and possibly tendentious authorial viewpoints. With this in mind, this selection of plays endeavours to provide an insight into how much recent testimonial theatre utilizes and incorporates other people's words in order to be affectively engaging, provocatively critical and even transformative.

Bystander 9/11 (2001) is based on Meron Langsner's own experiences of being physically caught up in the horrifying events of the attacks upon the World Trade Centre on 11 September 2001. Interestingly, throughout this autobiographical work, Langsner does not identify himself as 'Narrator' – suggestive perhaps of his desire to convey how the scale of the event overwhelmed his sense of identity, as well as placing the event, as opposed to character, centre-stage. From within the play itself, we learn that Langsner started to record his thoughts and fears almost immediately, as and when the catastrophe was unfolding. The overlay of immediate testimony (from e-mails and messages sent contemporaneous with the events of that fateful day) with the Narrator's subsequent memories some weeks later, dramatically illustrate how witnesses to traumatic events do not fully realize the significance of various sights and sounds until later, in keeping with Cathy Caruth's observations that '[T]he impact of the traumatic event lies precisely in its belatedness, in its refusal to be simply located.'[7] The timeframe of the play and its expression of testimony at different intervals from the events of 9/11 (some being recollections of secondary 'choric' type voices) thus provide a fascinating glimpse into the way memory can become *the subject as well as the source of testimony*, particularly in relation to trauma. One particularly harrowing insight into the way *Bystander 9/11* captures the sense of trauma as existing beyond the event and more from within the 'structure of its experience' after the event (p. 4, Caruth) is when the 'Narrator' recounts seeing

> . . . things falling from the towers. I didn't know what they were. I thought it was some kind of debris. I heard later about the people

throwing themselves from the burning floors. I try not to think about that now, even though the little falling specks play through my mind a lot.

9/11 and its aftermath is further explored in Denise Uyehara's *Big Head* (premiered in 2003). This is a highly physical, multi-media and interactive one-woman exploration into the relationship between memories and identity, and in particular, how family and personal memories can come into conflict with, distort and destabilize one's sense of national identity. By making links between the xenophobic hate crimes which proliferated in the United States after 9/11 and the experiences of her Japanese-American grandfather who was labelled and subsequently interned as a potential 'alien' security risk during the Second World War, Uyehara performatively explores the issue of postmemory – an intergenerational mnemonic phenomenon which Marianne Hirsch identifies as '[T]he relationship . . . to powerful, often traumatic, experiences that preceded their [earlier generations'] births but that were nevertheless transmitted to them so deeply as to seem to constitute memories in their own right.'[8] This play interweaves personal memories about the hateful xenophobic atmosphere which was made manifest immediately after the 9/11 attacks with family testimony about the incarceration of Japanese Americans during World War Two. By juxtaposing two past events, one recent and one distant, which are deeply relevant to the author's own sense of identity as a Japanese-American, *Big Head* explores the complex plasticity and volatility of memory, showing how recollections of more recent events can suddenly and unexpectedly coalesce with events from one's own familial history to instigate further questions about concepts such as citizenship and multiculturalism in the present.

A variety of documents and media are used in *Big Head* to highlight the many ways testimony can be expressed – through voice, writing, home movies, action – and also to illustrate how individual and collective memories overlap, intersect and sometimes collide. Private letters and family home movies are presented alongside oft-recited national oaths such as the Pledge of Allegiance and carefully constructed tape-recorded interviews about societal issues – a compelling testimonial interweaving which reminds the spectator of the family within the state, the individual within the nation, the personal within the public. Just as the title 'Big Head' refers to the brain disease encephalitis which can result in severely impaired mnemonic functions, this play also raises the issue of the fallibility of memory and the way the human mind is open to actually distorting, confusing and appropriating memories about past events – a fallibility highlighted towards the end of the play when Uyehara's sister insists that it was *she* and *not* the author who suffered a burn from a sparkler firework during a July 4th celebration when they were children. The work's exploratory interplay between both the fragility and the resilience of memory defies any sense of resolution, not only foregrounding how precariously an individual's idea of their past sits alongside and within a received and established sense of national history, but also putting into stark relief just how unstable the foundations upon which we construct our identities can be. For a work replete with testimony – recorded, filmed, written, recollected – *Big Head* provocatively complicates rather than resolves the issue of how personal and national identity and their relationship to private recollections and state memorialization can collide, and somewhat fittingly it ends with a doubt-filled but searching question:

> Maybe I even got the facts wrong, (*Looks at hand*)
> Or did I?

Childhood and intergenerational memories are also the focus of *Pajarito le Nuevo Lleva: Sounds of the Coup* (2008), but with a particular focus on recollections of what it felt like to be a child at a time of sudden, confusing societal and political change.[9] This collaborative and devised laboratory work focuses on the experiences of children during the 1973 military coup in Chile and subsequent events under the dictatorship of General Augusto Pinochet, as recollected by adults living in current post-Pinochet Chile.

The initial fieldwork for *Pajarito le Nuevo Lleva: Sounds of the Coup*, labelled 'the recuperation stage', involved conducting interviews and collecting testimonies from across social classes and the political spectra, with a specific focus placed on the interviewees' memories of childhood and growing up in Chile during the military coup which commenced on 11 September 1973 and under the dictatorship between 1983–7. One of the motivations the group cite for working on memory was the fact that even though the military dictatorship has not been in official power since the plebiscite in 1988, its legacy continues to raise issues that are pertinent for Chile today and in the future – not least, the question of social memory and its articulation. Indeed many critics have cited a relative state of amnesia in Chile, attributed in part to the hangover from the draconian censorship under Pinochet's dictatorship, and also contributed to by a distinct lack of will on the part of Chile's recent neoliberal regimes to confront the traumatic national past. Thus, as opposed to an emphasis being placed upon the recitation of fluent, discrete testimonial transcriptions about past events in Chile, the group purposively focused on performatively conveying just how incomplete, faltering, fragmented and self-censored are the witnesses' long-suppressed perceptions of Chile at that time from the standpoint of one of the most often overlooked, ignored yet fundamentally important sections of society – children. The performance of these memories not only recaptures the children's disorientation and bewilderment at a time when state censorship operated alongside fearful parental silence, but it also evokes the linguistic limitations common to young children when trying to articulate their thoughts and feelings. Thus, rather than retrospectively narrating a rationalized and over generalized Chilean 'past', mnemonic traces, usually recounted in the form of open-ended anecdotes, are sequentially juxtaposed in a manner which evokes the children's confusion at that time. In addition, the performance's focus on the diverse multiplicity of childhood perspectives is enhanced by the use of a number of soundtracks, of which only one is selected at random by individual audience members prior to the commencement of the performance – a staging device which fittingly acknowledges Chile's past as a far more complicated and opaque phenomenon than the mono-dimensional grand narrative one can retrieve in the national historical archives. Another fascinating dimension to the work is that this disjointed and fragmentary testimony – comprising half-heard comments, unsubstantiated rumours and incomplete stories – is embodied by performers from a much younger post-Pinochet generation who 'play' the witnesses as children – a generational interplay in performance which well suits the work's themes of memory, post memory and the underlying but potent desire which drives the work – a gradual movement towards a greater future national cohesion. The group seek to create a performance that eschews any perceived form of evaluative elitism, such as the disproportionate legitimacy and status often accorded to first-hand and well-articulated verbal and written witness accounts, which in turn might diminish and even drown out the potential voices of the illiterate, the poor, the disenfranchised and indeed, children. As explained in more depth in María José Contreras's prefatory essay, it was the intense and often painful workshops between the group members (comprising performers, practitioners, socio-linguists, theatre academics, historians) and the witnesses which prepared the ground for the performance of what she has described elsewhere as the 'asphysxiated'[10] traumatic memories of the subjects. This arduous collaborative process facilitated the partial transfer of these sense-based mnemonic traces from the bodies and mouths of the witnesses into the bodies and mouths of the performers to form an impressionistic loosely structured story which had been hitherto suppressed and repressed. Karen Malpede discusses such a process when discussing her own practice with:

When the rehearsal scenes are presented back, the original
testifiers become, not just the subjects of, but the witnesses to this

transformation. Thus the usual therapeutic dyad is altered: the listener takes in the memory in order to perform it; the testifier gives the memory in order to receive it back as crafted image – an artefact now placed outside the self.[11]

As mentioned, the sense memories which are performatively recreated in *Pajarito le Nuevo Lleva: Sounds of the Coup* are often incomplete, fragmentary and disjointed, and the decentring of narrative structure this creates is extended by the choice of soundtracks which the spectator arbitrarily makes at the beginning of a performance. The fragmentation of a core and centred narrative structure has the effect of casting the audience members in the role of co-constructors of meaning during the performance, an experiential engagement which may, in turn, elicit a transformative affect. It could be suggested that works like this, which demand the proactive co-construction of meaning by the spectator, can make for a far greater sense of responsibility or to use Felman's insightful terminology when analysing testimony, 'response-ability'[12] on the spectator's part, for it is the spectator's own proactive response to making sense of the testimony which engenders a sense of ownership (and thus responsibility) with regard to the issues raised in the work. In a similar vein to the devised laboratory work of Contreras et al., Urban Theatre Projects' *The Fence* (2010) is based upon intensive collaborative consultation with witnesses from the play's inception to its first performance. As Malpede suggests with reference to her own devising processes, such concentrated and often long collaboration between performers and witnesses could be seen as facilitating a therapeutic effect for the latter:

> Artistic representations of stories normally told in the consulting room add an additional dynamic to healing. If therapy can help turn a victim into a survivor, the theatrical process can help turn a survivor into a creator, no longer a victim of culture, but a contributor to a new vision of collective life.[13]

However, just as the witnesses who provide the fabric for a testimonial play could be viewed as potentially benefitting therapeutically from a dramaturgical process which eventually transforms them from survivor into creator, so too the spectator to such work may undergo an edifying transformation. Works which refuse to guide spectators through clear narrative and elucidatory structures – such as *Pajarito le Nuevo Lleva: Sounds of the Coup* and *The Fence* – invariably prompt the spectator to potentially co-construct meaning, with the effect that he/she is drawn into a more intense degree of engagement with, and even a sense of vicarious implication in, the torrid issues raised in the plays.

Urban Theatre Projects' *The Fence* (2010) avoids the standard reiteration and recitation of testimony to convey a particular slant or to factually inform audiences in the present about the circumstances of a past event. Indeed, on first seeing *The Fence* or on first reading the script (which like *Pajarito la Nuevo Lleva: Sounds of the Coup* was especially transcribed into a textual format for this volume) one may well be forgiven for questioning as to where and how testimony is used in this play? There are neither lengthy descriptive monologues dedicated to voicing the injustice of the Australian government's policy of forcibly institutionalizing children, nor identifiable real-life witnesses within what appears to be a seemingly fictional work about a group of people at a drink-fuelled barbeque. However, as the play progresses one becomes aware that a preponderance of pauses, sharply truncated sentences and confusing non-sequiturs are affectively displacing any clear, lucid and simplistically descriptive statement of the plight of the indigenous Aboriginal and non-indigenous children who were forcibly removed from their natural parents, and who have been subsequently and respectively labelled 'The Stolen Generations' and 'The Forgotten Australians.' Indeed, as the play unfolds, the cumulative oblique conversational references made by various characters about their own or others' disrupted childhoods (all of whom have 'evolved' as a result of a long collaborative and consultative process between real-life survivors of the state-driven institutionalization of children and the Urban Theatre Projects' ensemble) begin to form a discernible, albeit muted, pattern. The deafening testimonial silence which suffuses *The Fence*, albeit set against the characters' often awkward and hollow banter, listless and repetitive actions and a number of eclectic musical interludes, has the effect of, to use Alicia Talbot's words, 'opening' rather than 'containing meaning' in relation to the horrifying state policies which took place, for the most part, from the 1930s right up until the 1970s. Conscious of the ongoing memories and trauma suffered by those who were forcibly institutionalized, *The Fence* concertedly avoids hastily retrieving, re-presenting and thereby further 'containing' traumatic stories about these past events, for to employ such a narrative strategy could risk the erasure of the continuing traumatic experiences it seeks to evoke. Instead, through the concerted observance and use of testimonial silence and site specificity *The Fence* takes the time, care and respect to acknowledge the victims' *ongoing* trauma and to explore what Diana Taylor identifies as '. . . the transitional space between remembrance and future project'.[14] As a result, this site-specific performance, appositely played out beneath the shadow of a derelict and empty shell of a building which once housed a notorious children's orphanage, does not insensitively and erroneously consign these events to a distant historical 'past'; rather it observes the still unresolved presence of a transitional space through which the incessant but muted refrain of 'if walls could speak' continues to reverberate in a palpable and meaningful way.

Alecky Blythe's first, yet hitherto unpublished, play *Come Out Eli* (first performed at Arcola Theatre in 2003) is an example of her distinctive 'recorded delivery' approach when utilizing verbatim testimony in her work. As opposed to actors learning a script based on verbatim interviews, the copious recorded transcripts which provide the foundations for the eventual play-script actually become (after a period of rigorous editing) an intrinsic and a seamless part of the performance, as headphone-wearing actors meticulously repeat the words and, more crucially, the sound patterns of the words, uttered by the interviewees/witnesses they are representing in performance. *Come Out Eli* is a lively representation of a local community's response to what was to become the longest siege in British history when armed Eli Hall barricaded himself and a 'hostage' in a house in Hackney, London, over the Christmas period of 2002. Using interviews collected at the time from the diverse range of people gathered around the police cordon (which remained in place for 15 days) and further material retrieved in the aftermath (the house was destroyed in a subsequent fire and it is generally reported that Eli Hall died either from a self-inflicted gunshot wound or was overcome by fumes) Blythe's play gives an insight into how the local people responded to the disruption and chaos which suddenly descended upon their neighbourhood during the festive period, besides providing a fascinating insight into Blythe's own experience with the hostage who managed to escape the house before the end of the siege. Forty-one characters are played by five actors with the effect that the sound and content of the actual testimony is emphasized over and above characterization, with '. . . every um and argh, every vocal tic, every train of fuzzy thinking transmitted by actors who are frequently of a different nationality, even gender, to the interviewees in the play'[15] (Oliver Jones, Review, *What's On*, 17/9/03). This form of testimonial theatre is distinctive not only in its use of headphones in performance, and a purposive resistance to actors learning lines and thereby diluting the original words and speech patterns of the witnesses, but also in the overarching serendipity to the play's inception and initial construction. The play evolved out of Blythe's self-set broad remit to investigate the theme of fear through general interviews and field work – a relatively aimless but inquisitive process which ultimately brings a refreshingly unconstructed lightness and honesty to the work, even when dealing with the most tragic of events. Perhaps it is this distinct lack of premeditation to Blythe's process which limits any sense of an overbearing authorial viewpoint or over-earnest retrospective investment in an event that has passed? Ultimately, *Come Out Eli* evokes a grassroots sense of spontaneous present-tense conversational authenticity, while also accommodating the juxtaposition of moments of raucous hilarity next to poignant interludes in a wholly credible manner.

Another serendipitous, less agenda-driven approach to testimonial theatre is further exemplified by Forced Entertainment's *The Travels* (2002), a work which evolved from the ensemble's exploration of the A–Z atlas of British roads and streets. The testimony in this work is generated by the ensemble members themselves, as they recount their various solo journeys to diverse locations which were chosen as destinations because of their intriguing and resonant names. The participants' thoughts about their future destinations (usually imaginative ruminations based on the street names' associations) intermingle with their own reflections on arriving at their agreed geographical targets in a series of testimonies, to create what Tim Etchells describes as 'a strand of distorted, intimate and even fictional documentary'.[16] These testimonies (delivered during the devising process as individual 'reports' which were subsequently worked up and edited into a script) are presented to the audience via a news conference set-up, during which the various witnesses/performers are sat side by side at a long table, speaking into microphones. Although the various witnesses/performers read out their testimonies from what appear to be pre-prepared transcripts, they often appear to playfully digress, extrapolate and chat to each other in between taking sporadic gulps of bottled water, giving an improvisatory and more spontaneous edge to their delivery – an interesting variation and expansion of testimony in performance which, whether ultimately scripted or not, draws attention to the various levels of creative mediation that may occur when performing, presenting or indeed communicating. In this way, the line between performance and non-performance, artifice and reality, character and witness, is blurred in *The Travels* with the effect that the testimonial basis of the work is open to question. As Alex Mermikides points out '[W]e can only see through each performer's subjective – possibly exaggerated, maybe even outright false perspective. This gives the performers a strange sort of power over us – and the more "banal" the performance and stories, the more sinister the power.'[17]

Juxtaposing the process behind the work – something as simple and even banal as picking out interesting street names in an A-Z atlas – with the rather official atmosphere of a news conference setting during the performance, draws our attention to issues pertaining to the associations we make with respect to *not only words* (as with street names, for example), but also with regard to *certain modes of address and the various contexts within which we hear/listen to stories.* Does the lecture theatre or news conference format lend more authority and even a sense of greater authenticity to the testimony we hear? Will we listen more intently to those speaking at a news conference than to the words taken from the recording of an everyday conversation with an anonymous member of the public who happens to be standing at a police cordon? Do we give more credence to the words of the real-life witnesses than we do when watching and listening to actors who play out the experiences and stories of other people? Do the more intimate, seemingly spontaneous, digressions and asides during *The Travels* capture our attention more than the prepared narrative components of the ensemble members' testimonies? In this respect, *The Travels* is a highly inventive and self-reflexive testimony-based performance *about* testimony, which is as much, if not more, an exploration of the ways in which we recall, confide, announce, tell, inform and, most crucially, listen to other people's words as it is about the conceit upon which the performance is based – the various individual journeys taken by the ensemble members across the length and breadth of the British Isles.

Not only is *On the Record* a testimonial play, but it also focuses on journalists from across the globe whose major source material during their own work *is* testimony and first-hand witness statements. Unsurprisingly, ice&fire self-consciously address issues of censorship (whether at a state managed or cultural level) and the concomitant dangers of attempting to speak out and disseminate information. Bringing together testimony from journalists working in Sri Lanka, Russia, United States, Israel and Mexico, undoubtedly the play relies on the cumulative effect of verbatim testimony from disparate areas of the globe for much of its hard-hitting impact. However, alongside testimonies (which have been already adapted and to an extent altered during the process of translation), there are instances of what could be termed fictionalized truths, whereby, for example, a constructed, personal back story gleaned from but beyond the actual verbatim interviews are added to the stage representation of a real-life witness, such as Zoriah, who features in the play. Such creative latitude is neither duplicitous or misleading, but rather it is an acknowledgement of the imaginative space around and within any expression and reception of testimony, which, as discussed earlier, creates just as many questions as it does answers and may well prompt the spectator or as in this case, the writer, to co-construct and even imaginatively 'fill in' with well sourced and credible further information. In this respect, and as discussed during the prefatory essay by Christine Bacon and Noah Birksted-Breen, ice&fire's initial aim to make a strictly verbatim example of theatre evolved into a much looser form, '. . . moving from a text which solely used real testimony into a play which is both dramatized *and* also intimately rooted in truth.' The creative process used by ice&fire when constructing *On the Record* reflects the challenges of not only gaining a meaningful insight into the work of journalists on the basis of interviews with subjects who operate in often clandestine and perilous circumstances, but it also highlights the problems of providing an authentic sense of the person behind the verbatim transcripts that recount the trials and tribulations of his/her everyday professional activities. To overcome these challenges, ice&fire quite openly admit to embellishing the journalists' stories with words which cannot be sourced from verbatim interviews, but which are nonetheless 'rooted in the truth' of the dramatists' own first-hand knowledge of the subjects' lives. Arguably, the approach adopted by ice&fire could be construed as entering 'the story-space of people interviewed with the purpose of expropriating it'[18] (as remarked by Derek Paget in response to a similar creative process behind gathering and shaping testimony for David Hare's *The Permanent Way*) – but it is instructive to note that all the witnesses who participated in the making of *On the Record* were consulted about the inclusion of such dramatic embellishment and did consent to the final script, with some of them even welcoming the insertion of what could be labelled fictionalized truths about their own experiences and personal lives.

Another fascinating approach to constructing a play from testimony is revealed in the play, *Seven*. This work is multi-authored (Anna Deavere Smith, Paula Cizmar, Ruth Margraff, Gail Kriegel, Carol K. Mack, Susan Yankowitz and Catherine Filloux) based upon interviews with seven extraordinary women from Russia, Nigeria, Pakistan, Guatemala, Northern Ireland, Cambodia and Afghanistan. Although the seven discrete interviews were conducted in isolation from each other, they share a foundational aim and focus – namely to provide testimonial examples of the transformative power of women's leadership. Only *after* the seven interviews had been edited into seven discrete dramatic monologues in their own right, were the testimonies dramaturgically interwoven by the seven dramatists into one faithful verbatim play titled *Seven*, in which testimonies overlap, intersect and fade in and out of each other, with the use of culturally specific music and props. In this way *Seven* not only reflects the various distinctive regional, cultural and national communities from which the testimonies emanate, but also through the cumulative power of presenting the women's stories of overcoming injustice and hardship side by side, a wholly credible, cohesive and most crucially, inspiring celebration of international sisterhood across continents is created.

Notes

1   Robert Audi, 'The Place of Testimony in the Future of Knowledge and Justification', *American Philosophical Quarterly*, 34(4) (1997), pp. 405–22.

2   Stephen Bottoms, 'Putting the Document Back into Documentary: An Unwelcome Corrective?, *TDR*, 50(3) (2006), pp. 56–68.

3   Robert Martin, 'In Conversation with Arthur Miller', in Matthew C. Roudane (ed.), *The Creative Experience of Arthur Miller*, University of Mississippi Press, 1987, pp. 177–87.

4   Rinaldo Walcott, 'It's My Nature: The Discourse and Experience of Black Canadian Music', in Joan Nicks and Jeanette Sloniowski (eds), *Slippery Pasttimes: Reading the Popular in Canadian Culture*, Waterloo, ON: Wilfred Laurier University Press, 2002, p. 265.

5   Max Stafford Clark, 'David Hare and Max Stafford Clark', in Will Hammond and Dan Steward (eds), *Verbatim, Verbatim: Contemporary Documentary Theatre*, London: Oberon Books, 2008, p. 58.

6   David Mamet, *Three Uses of the Knife: On the Nature and Purpose of Drama*, New York: Vintage, 1998, p. 6.

7   Cathy Caruth, 'Trauma and Experience: Introduction', in Cathy Caruth (ed.) *Trauma: Explorations in Memory*, Baltimore: Johns Hopkins University Press, 1995, p. 9.

8   Marianne Hirsch, 'The Generation of Postmemory', *Poetics Today*, 29(2) (2008), pp. 103–28.

9   See Marianne Hirsch's 'Projected Memory: Holocaust Photographs in Personal and Public Fantasy', in Mieke Bal, Jonathan Crewe and Leo Spitzer (eds), *Acts of Memory: Cultural Recall in the Present*, Hanover and London: University Press of New England, 1999, pp. 3–23 for an interesting perspective on the especially charged effect the child witness elicits upon the viewer/spectator because 'The adult viewer sees the child victim through the eyes of his or her own child self.'

10 I first encountered the phrase 'asphyxiated memories' when I attended a conference paper by the Chilean practitioners/academics who devised *Pajarito la Nueva Lleva/Sounds of the Coup* at IFTR (International Federation of Theatre Research) Lisbon, Portugal in 2009.

11 K. Malpede, 'Chilean Testimonies: An Experiment in the Theatre of Witness', *Journal of Comparative Psychotherapy*, 29(4) (1999), pp. 307–16.

12 S. Felman and D. Laub, Testimony: *Crisis of Witnessing in Literature, Psychoanalysis and History*, London: Routledge, 1992.

13 K. Malpede, 'Chilean Testimonies: An Experiment in the Theatre of Witness', *Journal of Comparative Psychotherapy*, 29(4) (1999), pp. 307–16.

14 D. Taylor, 'Trauma as Durational Performance', in James M. Harding and Cindy Rosenthal (eds), *The Rise of Performance Studies: Rethinking Richard Schechner's Broad Spectrum*, Basingstoke: Palgrave Macmillan, 2011, pp. 237–47.

15 Oliver Jones, *What's On*, 17 September 2003.
16 T. Etchells at Forced Entertainment's website, www.forcedentertainment. com/page/144/The-Travels/111#-readmore.
17 A. Mermikides, 'Forced Entertainment – The Travels (2002) – The Anti-Theatrical Director', in Jen Harvie and Andy Lavender (eds), *Making Contemporary Theatre: International Rehearsal Processes*, Manchester and New York: Manchester University Press, 2010, pp. 101–20.
18 D. Paget, 'The Broken Tradition of Documentary Theatre and its Continued Powers of Endurance', in Alison Forsyth and Chris Megson (eds), *Get Real: Documentary Theatre Past and Present*, Basingstoke: Palgrave Macmillan, 2009, pp. 224–38.

Meron Langsner Interviewed
by Alison Forsyth

AF *Bystander 9/11* is based upon personal experience. Could you give me some background as to how and why you came to write this play?

MS *Bystander 9/11* started to take shape only days after the attacks. Its origins are from a mass email I sent when I got to the relative safety and calmness of the Performance Studies department at NYU (New York University) not very long after the second tower had fallen. A close friend and sometime artistic collaborator who was in rabbinical school in Jerusalem at that precise time was one of the recipients of that email. In it I detailed my experiences that morning from the subway up until hitting 'send'. He told me that I should record my experiences and 'kick some playwriting ass'. I cannot say that he was the only reason I started writing the play, but the encouragement helped.

Writing this play seemed to have been a form of therapy. I began with the email I'd sent and my journal entries, and then started shaping it into something that I felt could be performed. It was all very raw. I am fairly certain that I finished most, if not all, of my first draft by the end of that September. I definitely had the time. The first week after the attacks my job in the Financial District was shut down (I was working for Goldman-Sachs at the time), so I had time on my hands immediately after the experience. One of the things I did was to write everything down. This became the raw material of the play.

AF Although the 'Narrator' is not identified, it does seem he/she is closely based on you and your own personal experiences. Why did you decide to obscure your identity as the witness, the testimony-giver?

ML Though the Narrator is closely based on my own experience, I obscured my identity because I wanted the central character to be a sort of Everyman. 9/11 was a huge event that was broadcast and replayed over and over around the world, but in New York City it was experienced by individuals. The personalization of the events on stage addresses the reality of the experience. That said, so many things that I saw, smelled, and heard, I experienced alongside throngs of other people. Anyone stepping into the Narrator role is telling one person's story, not the story of the city or the country. But that person's story has a lot in common with anyone else who was nearby. When I wrote it, it was important to me that whoever played any of the characters was not playing me. I should say also that though I have directed performances of this piece, I have never performed any of it myself. Nor had it ever occurred to me to do so. I was told by a colleague after one of the early performances of this play that the actor playing the Narrator had done a fine job capturing the cadence and intonation of my own speech, which was shocking as I did not direct that particular performance and had only met the actor in passing prior to the event.

Though the majority of the experiences recorded are my own, again I must emphasize that I did not want the character to be me. This was mostly to universalize the experience, as well as the very practical matter of wanting the text to be shared by multiple actors, and not necessarily be gender-specific. On another level, with the exception of the first performance at Brandeis in 2002, this play has always been difficult for me to watch. That particular performance was incredibly cathartic. Since then I've always found this piece incredibly awkward. I tried to sublimate my identity so as to create enough distance from myself for me to apply craftsmanship to it. As the experiences are largely my own, I wanted to maintain authenticity without feeling like it was a confessional. I try to avoid discussing my experiences in the towers too often, but I know that when I do I use some of the same phrasing that is in the play.

I admit to having some survivor guilt even years after the attacks. As close as I was, there were many who were far closer. I can't say if this had anything to do with my choice to make the narration anonymous. There is a moment in the play in which the Narrator encounters a woman who feels the need to tell anyone who would listen to her about her experience, and I have the Narrator say 'in a way I am doing that now' in terms of the act of recounting the events on stage.

AF   As you mention earlier, during the play the Narrator encounters a woman who 'would tell anyone who would listen to her' about her experiences and the Narrator goes onto to admit that 'in a way I am doing that now'. Could you explain and expand upon this compulsion 'to tell' and 'to recount'?

ML   For me this ties in with Dori Laub's work on bearing witness to trauma. Laub theorizes that there is a need among survivors of trauma to recount the event, to have the event heard and to have the experience understood. As I said before, the experience was traumatic. And I was lucky. There is a lot of work on trauma theory out there, and I cannot pretend to be anything of an expert on it, but I believe that there is something healing about being able to recount the narrative, and about knowing that the account is being heard and understood. I should maybe stress again that this is a play that I am not very comfortable seeing. When it was first performed in 2002 it was cathartic. Later performances became more and more uncomfortable for me. The last time I saw a performance was at Tufts University in 2008 (directed by my good friend Tom Fish). By then I was becoming fairly detached from the play and could see it again from an emotional and artistic distance. There were a few performances in 2011 that I could have attended but I could not bring myself to see it again. I am grateful that they happened, but it felt healthier for me not to spend 11 September 2011 dwelling on 11 September 2001.

AF   There is a compelling sense of immediacy and urgency to the play in which the audience are almost placed in the position of listening to characters as and when the towers are hit and when the towers fall one after the other. These are juxtaposed with sudden reflective moments when you make it clear that some weeks have passed. Could you explain why you decided to structure the play in this way?

ML   I edited and rewrote the play several times between the years 2001–3. Some of the sections were almost directly from journal entries and emails that I'd written within 24 hours of the attacks themselves. As I was processing the events and living in the immediate aftermath, other passages grew around them. Some stories I heard in the following months were added in during this process.

The challenge for me as a playwright was to take my very raw immediate reactions and turn them into something that could play on stage. Remember that as I was working on the first few drafts, the site of the attacks were still smoking and I was going to work having to pass by crowds of tourists taking pictures of the fenced-off remains of the World Trade Centre. 'Ground Zero' was just beginning to take on the specific layer of meaning it had in relation to the former site of the towers. I was writing as I was processing my own traumatic response to the attacks, and as news was still coming in.

Some of my later work also deals with 9/11, but far less directly. I began to write a play the following year called *B'Shalom* in which an Israeli immigrant and a Palestinian-American enter into a tumultuous friendship in New York City in the summer of 2002. Some of the raw material that did not make it into *Bystander 9/11* was used for that play, and some of the imagery of the documentary drama was further processed and then fictionalized into the later work. *B'Shalom* won several awards and a piece of it is included in Applause Theatre Books' *DUO!: Best Scenes for Two for the 21st Century*. I began writing that play in 2003 as an exercise when taking a course on Israeli film at Brandeis University. One of the indirect effects of the attacks on my own life was that their impact on my employment prospects in New York made me reconsider returning to graduate school, which led me to an MFA in playwriting at Brandeis University (and later a PhD at Tufts University). A significant portion of my work in this period involved me processing what I believe was my post-traumatic stress disorder (PTSD) from 9/11. It was in the elective course on Israeli film that made me most able to deal with the experience. As this later play was far more fictionalized, I was able to deal with the repercussions of the events, as opposed to what to me felt like stylized reportage in *Bystander 9/11*.

AF   Are the encounters with the various strangers on that day based in fact? Did you have those exchanges? I suppose the memories of certain words and short conversations continue to be very vivid?

ML   The exchanges with strangers are all based in fact. I eliminated profanity as I began to realize that the play would be done as a form of remembrance. Not that there was very much, but for instance, the man whose binoculars I borrowed uttered a far more colourful lament than is portrayed in my play. I also left some images that were counter to the spirit of the play. My most notable omissions were my own observations of people celebrating the attacks, as well as reports I heard from others about seeing similar behaviour. These instances were rare, but profoundly disturbing. There were also brief flashes of information that hit the airwaves and then were barely heard of again, such as reports of explosives being found in the locker area of a bus station and so on. Paranoia was very high and did not need to be staged.

Many conversations and experiences of the day remain vivid, such as the old man ordering everyone to go home. The girl from New Orleans who said that this sort of thing does not happen where she is from, only a few short years before the floods after Hurricane Katrina; the woman in the token booth under the towers yelling at me to get out of there; conversations with my friends and family once we were able to speak.

AF   Besides the awful and poignant sights on that day, the sounds of 9/11 are very pronounced in the play, and most of all the overwhelming sound of voices. Could you comment upon the sense memories which feature in the play perhaps?

ML   When I began working on the play I knew that my primary tool would be voices. Most performances of the play are fairly still physically. This is unusual for my work as I see playwriting as a physical art and I have a whole other life as a fight director (I often think of the Edward Gordon Craig quotation about the dramatist being the son of the dancer rather than the poet). Since voices were to be my primary tool, I made an effort to use evocative language. I have other work that experiments with testimony in a far more physical way, including a collaborative piece in progress based on the lives of American servicemen in Iraq and Afghanistan (co-written with Chris Mandia, a former US Marine and Iraq War veteran). I wonder if *Bystander 9/11* feels static to me because the attacks themselves forced people to either run (away or towards) or be spectators. Something that is hard to imagine is the scale of the towers, and how much they dominated the southern part of the Manhattan skyline. Watching the monoliths burn was one sort of spectacle. When they fell it was another.

The play is a crystallization of a version of the experiences of being in Manhattan that day. Of being under the towers themselves when they first began burning and of being disturbingly close by when they fell. It also recounts the immediate aftermath, which although imprinted with the inciting events, takes up far more cognitive space than the attacks themselves. During a reading of an early version of the play that took place in Buffalo the following May, someone said to me 'I saw it live'. By this he meant that he saw it on television as it was happening. My immediate reaction to this was 'Yeah, me too – in 3D'. Many people said that the event itself was 'like a movie'. Because we have seen recorded images of the towers falling so many times and because exponentially more people have seen the towers fall on a screen than were even in New York at the time, the value of accounts of seeing it happen in person become more important. Less than a year later, in Boston, I remember walking into a room where the end of *Fight Club* was being shown. If you recall, the film ends with the destruction of New York City, including, of course, the towers. I remember thinking 'That's not what that looks like. They got it all wrong.' As I type that, I think to myself that it may be read as being flip about the attacks, but please do believe me when I say it was not meant in that way.

Actors performing this play now have easy access to footage of New York at the time, as well as other written testimonies. I like to believe that the play itself provides enough background to be its own source of research (though I wonder too how much of it is now a period piece).

The relationship between the actor and the testimony in a case like this is deceptively simple. When called upon to clarify or give advice I mostly tell actors to remember that parts of it are (or should be) funny. Humour is a survival mechanism. Having the Narrator identify as Israeli-American allows for a fairly dark sense of humour. I have a personal theory that theatre audiences rarely cry if they have not already laughed. I feel that this play would be nearly unbearable without humour.

AF   Why do you only have three actors (a narrator, a female chorus and a male chorus) even though there are far more than three 'characters' involved in the play?

ML   I have three as the minimum amount of actors, though the cast can be expanded. So long as the words are said in the right order, I am fine with seeing the cast increased. In fact, there was a production in Alaska with 11 performers. Several productions have also had a female narrator. I wrote it for three because at the time I was working with a lot of Off-Off-Broadway theatres with no budgets, very little space, and often limited time. It was originally pretty much a practical matter.

AF   Although short, the play takes the spectator on an emotional rollercoaster ride (shock, fear, astonishment, sadness, confusion, relief, gratitude and pathos-driven humour at times). However, it seemingly ends on a very pronounced and unified sense of patriotism. Could you explain this further?

ML   The play was written in the immediate aftermath of the attacks when New York City, and the United States, really pulled together. Rebuilding and healing were important priorities in those months that followed. Many people rose to the occasion. One thing about being in New York at that time was that many of the police and firefighters helping put the city back together were from hundreds of miles away. I remember seeing police cars from states in the Midwest. Which means that a police officer from someplace like Ohio or Kansas drove for days to get to New York to help my city get back on its feet. To put that in context for Europeans, think about driving from Munich to Lisbon at a moment's notice.

How could we not be grateful that so many people were coming from so far away to help us? That was amazing. As I'm writing this I'm wishing that I had put that in the play. Remember also that this play was first written before the United States entered a decade of two unpopular wars. The focus was inward, on reconstruction and healing. It was an immediate reaction both to being attacked, and to seeing the city around me pull itself together. The sense of community in the immediate aftermath was amazing, and lasted for quite some time. When I wrote the play I was not really thinking beyond 2002. Many parts of it read as very strange as I write this essay in 2012.

AF   Do you consider the play, which is based on your testimony (which in turn incorporates the remembered words of other people you encountered and communicated with that day) as an act of remembrance? If so, would you say that this was your impetus at the time you wrote the play? Has your relationship with the play changed, in other words?

ML   The play is absolutely an act of remembrance. When I wrote the play it was an act of testimony and a form of catharsis. I think I knew that it would be performed as a remembrance as I was working on it. The first two performances of the finished play took place on 11 September 2002; one at the Episcopal Actor's Guild in New York, the other at Brandeis University just outside Boston, where I had just begun my MFA in Playwriting. For me, seeing it a year after the events it recorded was a step forward in my own recovery from PTSD. My relationship to the play has changed drastically since that time. It was performed several times in the early part of the last decade, and each time it became harder for me to watch.

It's an odd play for me because it has little in common with my other writing. This play feels too much like my journals being put on stage and too little like an act of artistic creation. I'm glad that it is getting attention, but my own feelings on it are mixed. When I look at it now, I think a lot about what has happened since. There are the many clichés about how the world changed forever that morning. I've written elsewhere and in another context that cliché is where truth goes to die. I do not feel at this moment that we live in a better world than we did then. Looking at the play now, I feel like it can help us resurrect the truths of where we were at the time, and maybe immediately before. And maybe in doing so help to actually bring ourselves to a better place. There is a concept in Judaism called *Tikun Olam*, literally 'repairing the world', that I had in mind as the play moved away from being a form of therapy and towards becoming a performable script. In the years immediately following the attack, my intention was that this play would be an act of remembrance that would help not only me, but also help others make sense of the world. My hope for the play now is that the play might instil a sense of compassion.

Figure 1 Courtesy of JulieAnn Govang.

Bystander 9/11:
A Theatre Piece Concerning the Events of September 11, 2001

Meron Langsner

Production History

An early version of *Bystander 9/11:* A Theatre Piece Concerning the Events of September 11th, 2001, had its first public reading on May 28, 2002, at the New Phoenix Theater in Park in Buffalo, NY as part of the Buffalo Ensemble Theatre's 'Playreadings and Such' program. On September 11, 2002, in commemoration of the events of the year before, the play was given readings in both New York City at the Episcopal Actors Guild (co-produced by Polaris North) and at Brandeis University at the Shapiro Student Center Atrium. The director of the NYC reading was William Kevin Young, the cast was Kevin Makely, Danna Call and Paul Knowles. The cast of the Brandeis reading was Yari Sigal, Sarah R. Moon, and Noah Smith. The play was given a production at Brandeis University in the Shapiro Center Theater on September 11, 2003 under the direction of Tina Snell. The cast was Jake Sher, Angie Jepson, and Willie Teacher. The production was designed by Sean Sliney. The play has also been produced at Tufts University and the University of Alaska at Anchorage. The UAA production had a cast of 11 performers.

Narrator – Male, Mid 20s to early 30s
First New Yorker – Female Chorus
Second New Yorker – Male Chorus

The *New Yorker* characters switch functions constantly, sometimes taking the roles of various people the *Narrator* encounters, sometimes acting as a Greek chorus.

It is possible to cast the *Narrator* as female, so long as appropriate gender references are adjusted accordingly (Him/Her, 'Hey Buddy' becomes 'Hey Sweetie', etc.) or to expand the cast by dividing and distributing parts among additional performers.

As the audience enters, the Narrator and chorus characters are standing onstage, perhaps holding lit candles, as in a vigil. The Narrator wears an American flag in some way, either as a pin or a patch or a ribbon, as in the style popular in NYC after the September 11th attacks. After all are seated, they simultaneously blow out the candles and discard them.

First New Yorker   Emergency Service Helpline.

Second New Yorker   My mommy and daddy both worked in the World Trade Centre and haven't come home yet, what should I do?

Narrator   Emergency Service Helpline.

First New Yorker   My husband is missing, he works downtown in Tower 2.

Narrator   Emergency Service Helpline.

Second Narrator   My wife is a police officer, no one's heard from her since she went in, is there any word yet?

(*Narrator steps forward.*)

Narrator   I have this story I tell a lot. Lots of people have a similar story, and everyone saw my story on TV to one extent or another. If you lived or worked in New York City in September of 2001, you've been asked to talk about it a lot too. This is just one person's story. Individual experiences get lost in the spectacle and the chaos of the towers coming down. This thing happened to me on the way to work back then. The story starts there anyway. Most people stop at the point of getting home, maybe getting laid. When I tell it it goes on longer, up to a week and change later when we all went back to work in the post-apocalyptic Financial District.

Second New Yorker   We're still living the aftermath.

First New Yorker   But now we have the benefit of hindsight.

Narrator   As I was saying, this thing happened to me on the way to work. Happened to a lot of people actually, some more than others. All things considered, I'm one of the lucky ones.

First New Yorker   Is it true you were really there?

Second New Yorker   So what happened?

Narrator   I work, or worked rather, in the financial district in New York City. People don't necessarily realize that a lot of the grunt work of Wall Street is done by artists of some kind. At the time I was one of those. An actor and a writer by night, and a corporate grunt by day. Big business supports the arts in more ways than you realize. Sometimes the receptionist you see preoccupied with work is doing something far out of the realm of the corporate world. Every morning I would wake up way too early and take the A train to Chambers Street under the World Trade Centre, then get out and walk a few blocks to work where the investment banking industry would give me a new appreciation for Kafka. On September 11th, 2001, I overslept a little.

Second New Yorker   A little?

Narrator   Ok, so I was late to work again. Nothing worthwhile ever got done in the first hour or so anyway. So there was this rumble in the subway . . .

Second New Yorker   Hey Buddy, you hear something?

First New Yorker   What are you a tourist? This is the subway. How you gonna tell one rumble apart from any other?

Narrator   I thought nothing of it. Sometimes I think I remember it only in retrospect. I got out of the train and took the stairs up one level. In that station, that meant I was still underground where the A and the C, and the 1 and the 9 trains all met, not far from where the E terminated. The newsstand that supplied my morning candy was not far, near the entrance to the mall that was directly under the towers. As I went through the turnstiles, I saw a crowd of people running toward me. There is a very specific kind of fear that comes from a screaming mass of people headed right at you. But that was only the beginning.

First New Yorker   Run! Get out of here!

Second New Yorker   What happened?

First New Yorker   A plane just crashed into the World Trade Centre!

Narrator   People were running everywhere. It was chaotic. I heard the words 'plane crash' and thought some idiot in a single propeller plane tried to pull a stunt and was gonna make me even later for work than I already was.

In the chaos of the station, I didn't know whether I was safer going up to the streets or down to the trains.

Second New Yorker   Hey Buddy, you'd best move on.

Narrator   I went to the lady in the token booth to find out what was happening and if I should head up or down. What's going on?

First New Yorker   Go back down! Get out of here!

Narrator   That woman may have saved my life, because until I spoke to her, I was going to head for the streets. I would have been right under the towers. I hope she got out herself while there was still time.

I got into an uptown train. Being that it was still rush hour, trains were easy to come by. At that point, subways weren't affected yet. When I asked the conductor what was going on, he didn't know.

Second New Yorker   I heard something about a plane crash, but that was from you guys. If it doesn't affect us, we don't hear anything.

First New Yorker   Do you know how bad it is?

Second New Yorker   Hey, like I said, all I know, I know from you guys. If something just happened now, I won't know anything till they radio us, and that's only if it affects us.

Narrator   I took it one stop uptown to Canal Street, and got out just east of Broadway. At the staircase where I got out onto the street my view of the towers was blocked by a building. I was clued in that the situation was far more serious than I had originally thought by the clouds of black smoke overhead.

When I turned the corner onto Broadway and saw both towers in flames, I was in disbelief.

What happened?

First New Yorker   I dunno man, they said a plane hit.

Second New Yorker   Did you see it?

First New Yorker   No, I just got out of the subway.

Second New Yorker   How did one plane do that to both towers?

First New Yorker   Someone said it was two planes.

Second New Yorker   No way – two planes messed up that bad.

First New Yorker   I don't think it was an accident. I think it's terrorists. It's gotta be.

Narrator   When did the second plane hit?

Second New Yorker   Maybe there was no second plane. Look at it. Maybe the plane hit and spun off and then hit the next building.

First New Yorker   I'm no expert, but I don't think planes do that.

Narrator   At this point you have to realize that I was still trying to get to work. You also have to realize that we in the streets knew less of what was going on than people at home watching TV. Part of me knew that things were really bad, but it hadn't hit me that I was watching a whole lot of people die until later. I just kept looking at the towers and trying to get downtown. I was going against most of the foot traffic, most people who were in the streets were either staying where they were or going uptown. Most people going towards the towers had uniforms on. Cops, people in FBI jackets, and a couple uniforms I haven't seen before. There were lines a dozen people long at all the payphones.

(*First and Second New Yorkers trying cell phones.*)

First New Yorker   Hey, any luck with that thing?

Second New Yorker   Would I be on this line with you if I were having any luck?

Narrator   After a couple dozen tries I managed to get through to my family's answering machine. *Speaks as if into a phone* 'Mom, whatever you're seeing on TV, I'm safe, I'm ok, and I'm on the way to work.'

I'm safe. I'm ok. And I'm on the way to work.

I kept going down Broadway. The sidewalks were crowded, but like I said, more people were heading uptown or standing still than going my way, the streets themselves were a steady stream of cop cars, ambulances, fire trucks, and these things that looked like spaceships on wheels, mobile command centres I think they're called. At this point I could see things falling from the towers. I didn't know what they were. I thought it was some kind of debris. I heard later about the people throwing themselves from burning floors. I try not to think about that now, even though the little falling specs play through my mind a lot.

I kept trying to get further downtown. I tried reaching work on my cell to tell them I was running late for obvious reasons. The cell of course was worthless. I started to have my doubts. People on the streets were talking to each other in an almost friendly way.

This is looking pretty bad.

Second New Yorker   Yeah, but you gotta give respect to them architects, cause them buildings are still standing!

First New Yorker   They shoulda learned when they tried to blow it up a few years back that it wasn't coming down.

Second New Yorker   That's right! We build 'em strong here. But all those people! That's just wrong. How'd the pilot screw up that bad?

First New Yorker   I heard it was two planes.

Narrator   It's terrorists. It has to be.

First New Yorker   How do you know?

Narrator   I'm Israeli.

Second New Yorker   Heh, that's right. You people are used to it.

Narrator   No, you never get used to it.

At that point, no one in the street had any clue the buildings would come down.

First New Yorker   I wonder how long that'll take to fix.

Second New Yorker   At least a couple of years. What a shame. All a them people . . .

Narrator   We were all in for a rude awakening.

A couple of things I saw made me reconsider my walk downtown. A woman walked by me like a zombie. Tracks of dried tears on her cheeks, and her face blank. Another one was sobbing uncontrollably, being guided by a friend. All the people with cameras took me aback, but these days that sort of thing is expected. What I was seeing was slowly beginning to hit me. Not because of the spectacle of the burning towers, but because of the few people in tears I saw walk by, whose stories I didn't know, but whose reactions I felt as they passed me by. I started to whisper the Kaddish as I kept looking at the buildings.

(*First and Second New Yorkers begin to murmur the Kaddish.*)

For those who don't know, that's the Jewish prayer for the dead. In terms of religious law, I am not sure that was the technically correct response, but I am not a religious person. It somehow seemed the only response that fit.

I started to make my way uptown.

Second New Yorker   That's an act of war, whoever did this. We're at war now.

First New Yorker   But at war with who?

Second New Yorker   We'll find them.

Narrator   As I got further north, every now and then there would be someone with a radio and a cluster of people around them. We heard about the Pentagon, we heard about planes crashing in Pennsylvania, and we wondered what more to expect that day.

(*Narrator faces upstage, First and Second face towards audience.*)

Second New Yorker   Holy . . .

First New Yorker   Oh my god!

(*First and Second freeze for a moment, as Narrator continues.*)

Narrator   I heard gasps and the beginnings of a crashing sound, and every head in my view turned to face the towers. Or one of them rather. I spun around to see a sight that's going to stay with me a long time.

The two towers fell in very different ways. The first, from where I saw it happen, exploded out from the corners, floor by floor and then folded in on itself once the corners weren't there to support it. You have to understand the scale of these things to understand what I saw. From where I was that tower seemed to take up almost my whole field of vision. It was big enough that though each floor exploded and burst out fast, the whole thing took some time to come down. From the street you could still see it happen piece by piece. I was a good enough distance away to see the huge clouds of dust and debris swallowing up everything they passed, but far enough away to be a bystander.

Second New Yorker   I saw one man around my age collapse and sob before the tower had finished falling.

First New Yorker   I saw people frozen in disbelief in the middle of the street.

Narrator   There was an old man in a business suit, very dignified, very serious, marching uptown on Greene Street and shouting orders.

Second New Yorker   Go home!
Get out of here!
Don't stay here!
Go home!

Narrator   That man woke a lot of people up. My walk uptown took on some urgency, as did many others. Not panic, but urgency. New Yorkers do not stampede.

First New Yorker   That's it, no more Twin Towers. There's just one now. My kids are gonna ask me what it was like with two.

Second New Yorker   This is horrible, but this is history. This is like being at Pearl Harbour.

Narrator   As I got further uptown, closer to New York University, I stopped to listen to the radio of a jeep that was parked along the street. There was a man in his late 20s or early 30s standing at the open door, looking at the remaining tower with binoculars. There was nothing being said on the radio that I hadn't already heard or seen for myself.

Can I borrow your binoculars?

Second New Yorker   Here ya go buddy.

Narrator   What I saw was that the flames had gotten bigger, and were spreading further. I was lucky in that, by that point I wasn't going to see people throwing themselves from the windows anymore, and would not have to learn about that till later. I watched a helicopter come close to the tower, hoping to see it spray something that would put out the fires, hoping the fires wouldn't spread anymore than they did, and praying against all logic that I wouldn't have to see this tower come down too.

Do you think it'll stay up?

Second New Yorker   I hope so man.

A shame. Such a shame. All them womens. All a' them beautiful womens I'm never even gonna meet now. Such a shame.

Narrator   I walked up through SoHo to NYU. Now there were crowds of students mixed in with the business people now, and though we could still see the one remaining tower and the growing flames, we bystanders didn't feel as much in harm's way anymore.

First New Yorker   That changed fast.

Narrator   There was still one tower up, Tower 1, the one with the antennae. It had been hit closer to the top. It still stood, but you could see the flames getting higher and larger even from a few miles away, just north of Houston Street.

We thought that since the hole seemed to cover less area the tower might weather the damage. Little did we know.

I was facing away from the tower. You could only stand and stare so much at once. I had my cell phone out again. Maybe my mother was home, maybe she'd be there to get the call this time. I dialled. There was the pause I was already familiar with when the phone tried to connect and was most likely going to fail. This time though, instead of the quiet beep that signals a call failure, I got a loud, high-pitched feedback sound. I heard screaming all around me, and all anyone would look at was right behind me.

First New Yorker   Oh god not the other one . . .

Second New Yorker   No . . .

Narrator   I said before that both towers fell in very different ways. I turned around to see the second one fall.

Second New Yorker   From where we were standing, it was like dominos falling downwards.

First New Yorker   Starting from the top, a floor would collapse onto the floor underneath it, which it would combine with to collapse a story lower and so on.

Second New Yorker   There was this horrible rumbling sound and the cloud of debris that expanded outward as it followed the collapse of the tower downwards. Unlike the first tower, I didn't see this one go all the way down, I was spared that sight by the buildings in my immediate view.

First New Yorker   But just like the first one, when something that big comes down, it doesn't happen instantly, we had to watch it happen, piece by piece until the other buildings blocked our view.

Narrator   A woman turned to me and told her story. She had to talk, she was very pale and seemed like she would need to tell everyone who would listen what happened to her. Later on I would be the same way. In a way I'm doing that now.

First New Yorker   All my neighbours are still under there. I lived near there, everyone in my building was watching it happen from the roof. I told them that it wasn't safe, that they should get away. They said I was crazy. They're all still there. Oh G-d, they're all still there . . .

Second New Yorker   Don't worry lady, I'm sure they got evacuated.

First New Yorker   Oh G-d I hope so. I don't believe they stayed. When I got to the street I just ran. I didn't slow down until a few blocks away, and then the other one came down . . .

I was running and running and I saw this kid, sorry, to me anyone in their 20s is a kid, and I don't know if you know this about people in suits, but when they eat, they throw their ties over their shoulders. Well, he was throwing up, and his tie was about to slip down his shoulder. I pulled the tie back and put my arm around him, and well, he finished, and he got up and put his arm around me and I said 'Are you OK?' and he said, 'Yeah, are you ok?' and I said yes and then we both started running again . . . But everyone in my building is still on the roof, they were watching it burn . . .

Second New Yorker   I'm sure everyone got out safe, let's get you somewhere inside, you're in shock.

Narrator   (*aside to Second New Yorker*) Do you really think they all got out?

Second New Yorker   I hope so kid. I hope so.

Narrator   I heard later about how everyone in the area was evacuated by the police and fire departments. I was glad to know that guy was right, whether he knew it at the time or not.

I fell in momentarily with an older businessman and a student.

Second New Yorker   Hey buddy, I'll give ya five bucks if I can use that cell phone to call my wife.

Narrator   If this thing worked I'd give it to you and not even think about taking your money. You're welcome to try it, I've been trying to call home since all this started.

Second New Yorker   I've gotta get through to my wife. She hasn't heard from me since before we were evacuated.

Narrator   I think we should try to get to a land line.

First New Yorker   Listen, I live in the dorms right here, you guys can come in and use the phone if you want.

Second New Yorker   Thank you so much.

First New Yorker   I've only been in New York for three weeks. We don't get this sort of thing at home.

Narrator   We normally don't get this sort of thing in New York either. Where are you from?

First New Yorker   New Orleans. Were you guys close?

Second New Yorker   I was a couple blocks away.

Narrator   I was in the subway station underneath.

First New Yorker   Wow. I'm glad you guys are ok at least. Come with me, I've got a phone and there's a big TV in the lounge, we can find out what's going on.

Narrator We started to follow her into a building. There was this huge crowd around a TV.

Second New Yorker In an apparent terrorist attack, both World Trade Towers have been destroyed and the Pentagon is on fire.

Narrator I watched for a while. The hallway was mostly filled with students, though a few people seemed out of place in the crowd of college kids. I was hoping the TV would tell me something I didn't already know, but that close to the fact what they knew didn't have a lot to offer. Eventually, I lost the people I had walked in with in the crowd. I realized that I still had someplace to go where I could get to a phone. I walked to the arts building. There is a lounge on the first floor. Contingency plans had already been put in place apparently. There was a big TV monitor surrounded by students. The café in the lounge had a sign up that student affairs was picking up the tab for coffee, tea, and water.

Second New Yorker There were about as many of us in the lounge as on Broadway in front of the Tisch Building. The view from the TV was a variation of the view from Broadway. On TV, you could see the disaster from cameras, on Broadway, you could see a pillar of smoke rising from a few short miles away.

First New Yorker Some professors tried to continue teaching class as though nothing had happened, but eventually everyone realized that something big was up, and we all were trying to find out what was going on.

Second New Yorker My dorm was on Water St, not far from Ground Zero. Pretty soon I was going to get the news that I was gonna be homeless for a while.

First New Yorker I didn't think to call my family in California till much later, when I got home and there were a ton of messages on my machine. I hadn't been anywhere near it, so I didn't think anyone would be that worried. Of course, this was before the paranoia and bomb scares of the next few days and weeks.

Second New Yorker At this point, all we were trying to do was find out what was going on. We still couldn't grasp what was happening only a few miles away.

Narrator Not seeing anyone I knew in the lounge, I took the elevator to a mostly empty office.

First New Yorker   Can I help you?

Narrator   Hi. I'm alumni. I was at the towers when they were being hit. I just want to use the phone.

First New Yorker   Come here, use this line. Do you need anything else?

Second New Yorker   Are you alright? Were you really close?

Narrator   I'm about as alright as I can expect to be. Thanks so much. I was in the subway underneath as it was happening. I couldn't get above ground, probably lucky. I went uptown one stop and got out and saw it all from the streets.

First New Yorker   Thank God you're ok.

Narrator   They were wonderful to me. I realized then that I had this unbelievable need to tell people I was there, to talk about what I saw.

The landlines were worthless too, all phones were still dead. Though, to my surprise, I could access the internet. There were already emails from friends around the country making sure I was alive.

Second New Yorker   You'd better be ok. Call me in Chicago Now!

First New Yorker   Please check in, I'm watching the news and I know you work around there. I just want to know you're alive.

Narrator   I emailed everyone I could think of.

'I was there. I am alive. I am shaken up. But I am ok.'

I emailed some of my co-workers who do not share my habit of sleeping in and would have been a few blocks away at the office. I heard from them later, they had had adventures of their own that day. Some time later I saw some of them and heard their stories. I was there for almost an hour. I got some messages back almost right away. One from a close friend came as I was growing restless.

First New Yorker   I'm at the Arts Building in the University, in the studio on the third floor. Come see me.

(*They hug.*)

So good to see you. How is your family? Are they all ok?

Narrator   I left a phone message when both towers were still up. I've been trying to call and can't get through, and they didn't answer my email. I emailed a friend in DC who was trying to call them for me. I don't know if he got through yet.

First New Yorker   Come into the studio. We have food and coffee and there are a bunch of computers, you can try and reach everyone from there.

Narrator   How about you? Is everyone accounted for?

First New Yorker   My friends who temped downtown emailed me that they're ok, everyone else would have been far away.

Narrator   It was so unbelievably good to see a friend. The kindness of strangers is one thing, but in crisis you want the people who are close to you to be there.

I spent most of the afternoon in the design studios at New York University. It felt calm and quiet and safe as compared to the streets. I had coffee and water and an internet connection to follow the news and keep in touch with the rest of the world. I exchanged emails with everyone I could reach and read the news as it was coming in. I got in touch with my family, found that everyone was accounted for. My father was supposed to be flying back from a business trip that day, it was a big relief to know that his plane was grounded.

Everyone on my end was accounted for. Later, I would hear some scary stories and near death experiences. But then and there, I knew the people close to me were safe.

It wasn't till the middle of the afternoon that we left.

First New Yorker   When was the last time you ate?

Narrator   You know, with all this going on. I forgot I was even hungry. I didn't even have breakfast yet.

First New Yorker   Let's go then.

Narrator   While we were eating, someone managed to get through to me on my cell phone.

Second New Yorker   Oh thank G-d you're alive! You scared the hell out of me! I was so worried that you were trapped underneath. Are you ok?

Narrator   Well, obviously I am unemployed, but otherwise I'm ok.

Second New Yorker   Unemployed?

Narrator   Yes.

Second New Yorker   How can you joke?

Narrator   I'm joking 'cause I'm still alive. Though I really am pretty sure I watched my job blow up a few hours ago.

The next few days I got a lot of calls like that. There were other worries besides the job though. I had deposited my last pay-check in a bank machine on the ground floor of the World Trade Centre after business hours the day before. That was something that was going to need to be dealt with later on as well. At the moment though, all I could think about was the food in front of me.

First New Yorker   I'm supposed to go meet my boyfriend up at a friend's house in Hell's Kitchen. You should come with me if you don't have anywhere to go. Maybe we can try to give blood on the way up.

Narrator   No one would have our blood. All the blood banks were filled to capacity within hours of having been opened up. It would be like that for weeks.

We walked uptown 50 blocks. The streets were empty of cars. This does not happen in New York. There were police everywhere and I was glad to see them. Behind us, there was still that huge pillar of smoke. We spent some of the afternoon with other friends, and later, when the subway worked, I went home to shower. My cell phone was active again. It took me five minutes to hear all the messages and I almost wore out the battery answering them all. One was from a friend who did not want to spend the night alone. She worked in a hospital uptown and spent the whole day waiting for victims that never came.

I didn't want to be alone either.

I went home to shower before I went to see my friend. My cell phone rang a few times more. More calls like the last one, making sure I was alive, seeing if I was ok, wanting to hear what I saw. It was evening by the time I got onto a subway at Columbus Circle, almost halfway up the island from where I had originally gotten out under the towers. The gates were open, free rides for all. It wasn't crowded, but there were people everywhere, all very quiet and sombre. I decided to go home and change before going to my friend's apartment. There was a fireman in the subway station, in full gear, covered with dust, and looking unbelievably tired. It was obvious where he had been. I wanted to come up and shake his hand, thank him for his work, for his bravery. But something in his face at that moment said that he just wanted to be left alone.

Second New Yorker   The next day, the streets were still empty of cars.

First New Yorker   You couldn't get milk in the grocery stores, because no trucks could cross the bridges.

Second New Yorker   Of course, there are no cows in Manhattan.

First New Yorker   I am sure you remember the covers of all the newspapers.

Second New Yorker   They look a lot like what we saw from the streets.

First New Yorker   No one could talk about anything else.

Second New Yorker   Lots of businesses were closed.

First New Yorker   There was a long, long line outside Red Cross headquarters.

Second New Yorker   Again, you had to wake up really early to give blood. And if you wanted to volunteer, forget about it. They were turning doctors away. Doctors!

Narrator   Most of us couldn't do much the next day. I woke up in my friend's apartment. She was already working at the hospital by then. I went to the Red Cross, was told they had as much blood as they could take that day, and filled out a volunteer form. From uptown you couldn't see the smoke, though for weeks there would be a pillar of smoke marking where the towers used to be. On my way home, there were already pictures of the missing hanging in every public place. Those pictures would be everywhere for a while, some places were shrines in memory of the missing. Eventually they got taken down, though in a few places they were up for months. I got home early in the afternoon and gave in to the exhaustion of the day before. I slept till late the next morning. It didn't even occur to me to check in at work. Everything below 14th street was sealed off.

I stayed uptown in Washington Heights most of the next day. Everywhere I went all anyone could talk about was the towers. I live far enough uptown that I couldn't see the smoke, but the images of the day before were still playing through my head. And then, there were still the bomb scares that kept happening. None where I live, but they kept coming through on the radio and internet.

First New Yorker   There was one at the Empire State Building almost right away, and that became a regular occurrence. Rockefeller centre too.

Second New Yorker   General paranoia was high. There was a fake Nostradamus prediction circulating about 'The Next Great War' and 'Twin Brothers Falling', and 'The Great City in Flames'.

First New Yorker   Ooo . . . Spooky.

Second New Yorker   Wanna hear spooky? I read that Nostradamus says you owe me money.

First New Yorker   You'll get nothing from me.

Second New Yorker   In all seriousness though, I jumped at every siren I heard.

First New Yorker   In New York, you hear a lot of sirens. If you jumped at every one you must have had plenty of exercise.

Second New Yorker   How about you when you heard a plane overhead a week later?

First New Yorker   Let's not talk about that. You know, this would all be easier if there was something we could do.

Narrator   Towards evening on the 14th, I received a very welcome call from an old friend.

Second New Yorker   Hey! You still want to get on a volunteer crew?

Narrator   He worked for the Red Cross. All their employees were drafted to work on the relief crews. Volunteer positions were hard to come by, the supply of volunteers was unbelievably high in proportion to the jobs available, even for people with specialized skills.

Second New Yorker   We spent the entire night below the 14th street line.

First New Yorker   Going downtown in the middle of the night on September 14, 2001 was a quick drive. There was still no traffic.

Second New Yorker   But once we got downtown there were layers and layers of security barricades. Though of course, no one was going to stop a Red Cross vehicle.

First New Yorker   The owner of a couple of Starbucks had donated lots of time and coffee to the cause. The canisters were going to be distributed to rescue workers.

Second New Yorker   The kid at the coffee shop said he would 'brew his ass off' for us.

First New Yorker   We made coffee until about 5 a.m.

Second New Yorker   Just doing something, anything, to help made us feel so much better.

Narrator   At maybe 3 a.m., a man walked up to the coffee shop with a poster.

Second New Yorker   Hey, I'm looking for my partner, can I put up a flyer here?

First New Yorker   Sure.

Second New Yorker   Thanks buddy. Listen, if you see him, call the number, everyone's really worried.

Narrator   Much of the city was wallpapered with posters like that. Walls and walls of missing people. Many walls had candles and flowers, as well.

When the truck was full, there was a murmur among my crew about wanting to see Ground Zero.

Second New Yorker   What do you want to see that for? It's off limits anyway.

First New Yorker   I need to see it. Or at least try to.

Narrator   Me too. I say we go for it. I was there. I saw them fall. I want to see.

First New Yorker   The worst that can happen is that we get turned away.

Second New Yorker   Ok, but for the record, I'm against this.

Narrator   On the drive down, I noticed a box of teddy bears and stuffed dogs in the truck.

Who are we feeding the teddy bears to? Or are these for kids?

Second New Yorker   Kids and adults. They're for the people in the shelters. If you just had your home blown up, you take what comfort you can get.

Narrator   The little stuffed dogs didn't look quite as silly to me after that.

The closer we got to Ground Zero, the more it started to look like a demilitarized zone. Getting below 14th Street was just police. Lots of police, and police from all over the country, but now there were soldiers mixed in with the police. And military vehicles. And the closer we got to the place itself, the more we knew we were beyond civilian territory.

First New Yorker   We got really close. Almost to the gates.

Second New Yorker   There was this massive pillar of smoke, and that smell that we were all learning to get used to and trying not to get used to got stronger; sort of sour, like burnt concrete with something else mixed in that you didn't want to think about.

First New Yorker   We were able to see debris and remains of the lower walls of the towers through the smoke.

Narrator   We were stopped by a police officer near the gates.

Second New Yorker   What are you doing here?

First New Yorker   Delivering coffee. Would you like some? Fresh brewed.

Second New Yorker   You can pull in over there with the other support crews.

Narrator   We drove by the other crews, made inquiries and found that there was no shortage of coffee at that part of Ground Zero at the moment, and headed back to the Red Cross to deliver our eighty plus canisters of fresh coffee for redistribution. The crew I was working with was dissolved and I got home at about eight am.

Later that week, I got a call from my employer. All the niceties of the situation were observed, that is, verification that I was in one piece physically and emotionally, and seeing if I had lost anyone in the attack. Not that these niceties were not heartfelt, but the state of the city was that it was just good manners at the time to check vital signs.

It seems Wall Street was to reopen that coming Monday. The day arrived and I got ready to return to work. It seems I was to be closer to the aftermath than I had thought. When the train reached the empty Chambers Street-World Trade Centre station where my story began, it passed through slowly and without stopping, everyone on the train became very quiet, and we all passed through in silence.

(*beat*)

There were two kinds of uniforms all over the financial district when I got there on the morning of the 18th. One army was in camouflage, the other in corporate casual.

Second New Yorker   There was a sombre and determined mood in most offices.

First New Yorker   A lot of stories of the week before were exchanged.

Second New Yorker   We were only a few blocks away. We found out via the intercom, then stopped working and saw the whole thing on television from the company cafeteria.

First New Yorker   Not long after the buildings fell, we decided we couldn't stay. We wrapped handkerchiefs around our mouths so we could breathe.

Second New Yorker   I saw a new Mercedes abandoned on the street covered with dust and debris. We walked home in shock, not even stopping to rest until we were in midtown. My main office was in One Liberty. I couldn't go back and get my things, they were still worried that it might collapse.

Narrator   One Liberty would dominate the skyline in most cities. It's about half the size of one of the towers, which is saying a lot. Early on you couldn't get anywhere near it. I remember spending most of September 10th there. Eventually it was reopened.

Second New Yorker   Some people didn't come back to work that Monday. They said they would never be able to go to the Wall Street area again. A few that said that came back within a few days, others moved out of New York.

First New Yorker   Pictures of the missing were plastered everywhere.

Second New Yorker   It was heartbreaking. A lot of people went past hope into denial, still thinking they would hear from their missing loved ones.

First New Yorker   There were also posters about ethnic violence.

Second New Yorker   One thing that sticks out in my mind that just infuriates me as an American was a Sikh man standing at Penn Station handing out flyers explaining his ethnicity. It's bad enough they had to deal with bigotry, but the hate-mongers should at least get their ethnicities straight.

First New Yorker   In America today, that should not be necessary.

Second New Yorker   It's embarrassing. I apologized to him on behalf of the rest of the country.

First New Yorker   What did he say?

Second New Yorker   He just smiled.

Narrator   One vivid irony was the reversal of the situation between my friends and family here and in Israel. Just this once everyone over there were calling here to see that we had survived the terrorism rather than vice versa.

First New Yorker   Some of us that came back to work started getting sick.

Second New Yorker   The phrase, 'World Trade Centre Cough' entered our vocabulary.

First New Yorker   Think of going to work every day where not only are there unbelievable amounts of industrial waste in the air and fires still burning underground, but thousands of bodies decaying not far away.

Second New Yorker   Many people wore masks. There was that definite smell in the air that wouldn't go away for a while.

First New Yorker   I could smell it in Brooklyn on some days, depending on the wind. I could also still see the smoke coming up for a long time after the fact.

Second New Yorker   Who knows what was in that smoke.

First New Yorker   One day after coming back to work, I got dizzy.

Second New Yorker   You got pale too. Sit down, are you ok?

First New Yorker   I think I need to go home . . .

Narrator   She was back to work in a couple of days. There were a lot of things in the air, in different combinations every day. One day it could just be the wrong combination for your body type and then you could just drop. Some firemen working on Ground Zero ended up retiring not long after from being disabled by what they inhaled.

We all went back to work though. The best treatment for us all was to rebuild. Those who could anyway. Some companies were hit hard, they stayed in business, but had to let most of their employees go.

Second New Yorker   I was one of them.

First New Yorker   Me too.

Narrator   People found ways to keep going though. I for one am staying in New York. I live through crime and pollution and ridiculous rents to be here, damned if some terrorists are going to scare me away.

Second New Yorker   We still have the best pizza in the world.

First New Yorker   And I could never give up going to the theatre here.

Second New Yorker   And the hot dogs on the streets, you can't forget the hotdogs. Where else are you gonna get a hotdog like that?

First New Yorker   And the nightlife.

Second New Yorker   Still no place like it.

First New Yorker   I'm staying.

Second New Yorker   I'm with you.

Narrator   History came knocking really loud on everyone's door on September 11th. I had a really close call. I still tell that story a lot.

First New Yorker   I was there.

Second New Yorker   I got away.

Narrator   I am shaken up, but ok.

(*Indicates the American flag he is wearing.*)

This is the flag of my country. I did not choose it. It was chosen for me by my parents not very long before I was born. I love my country. I have another country, and another flag. But the beauty of being here is that there is no conflict of interest in me saying that. I had a really close call because some people take issue with what this flag stands for. Some men I never even met tried to kill me, and throw my country into chaos. They didn't kill me.

First New Yorker   They did kill a lot of other people.

Second New Yorker   Lots of kids saw things from classroom windows that they shouldn't have seen.

First New Yorker   Some of those kids are still waiting for a mommy and daddy or brother or sister who's never going to come home.

Narrator   I came home clean.

Second New Yorker   Other people lived, covered in dust and debris that would wash away far sooner than the shock and trauma.

Narrator   Other people had closer calls than I did. I was just a bystander really.

First New Yorker   Not long after, some people were scared to leave their houses, some people are so scared they are thinking of leaving New York.

Narrator   I will not leave.

Second New Yorker   I will live my life.

First New Yorker   I will rebuild.

Second New Yorker   We will mourn the dead, and heal the injured.

First New Yorker   We will have justice, and we will have peace.

Narrator   The term 'And Justice for All' has implications that cannot be ignored here.

Second New Yorker   I hear you there.

Narrator   I will NOT live in fear.

First New Yorker   WE will live our lives.

Second New Yorker   WE will rebuild.

All   WE will NOT live in fear.

An Essay

Denise Uyehara

Those of us living in a post-9/11 United States have reached the New Big Normal. And yet, is anything 'normal' in the United States? At the time of this writing, Obama has just been re-elected for a second term, much to my relief. He was kept in office by an array of voices – women, people of color, gay/lesbian/bisexual voices, white allies – not by the white men of privilege who would prefer to keep the wealth and power for themselves. Still, I remind myself: Obama is a politician. His job is to make the choices to keep the machine moving – hopefully in ways that help those without voice – at home and abroad. We shall see in the next 4 years what unfolds. Meanwhile, nothing is really 'normal' in the US, except that its people continue to respond, refuse and resist. Even in small ways.

Looking back, the months following the events of 11 September 2001 were completely shocking. I was thrown off-balance while watching the towers fall into rubble in Manhattan. 'Could this really be happening?' was my response to not only how New York responded but also to the way our country reacted. Hysteria, hate crimes, the best and worst of emotions rising to the surface. Like many Japanese Americans, even as I watched the Twin Towers fall in New York, I remembered the days following Pearl Harbour, the xenophobia that followed, leading to our country's incarceration of over 110,000 Americans of Japanese descent. But this time, Japanese Americans wouldn't be the target, someone else would.

In the greater scheme of things, the attack on the World Trade Centre was not more significant than the thousands washed away in a tsunami in Thailand, or dying in a war in Africa, or an attack on the London Underground. To paraphrase Noam Chomsky, what *was* significant about the attack on 11 September 2001 is that it happened on United States soil. This fact opened a floodgate of opportunity for the United States to go to war, to send its citizens into a frenzy and to establish a secret prison in Guantanamo. It also allowed our government and many of its residents a chance to create a new 'enemy' at home: Middle Easterners, Muslim Americans, Arab Americans and South Asian Americans.

My performance, *Big Head*, examines this post-9/11 world. Interestingly, I began research on it a year *before* the attacks on the World Trade Centre. In 2000, I was considering the parallels between the mistreatment of Japanese Americans during World War II and those perceived as 'the enemy', in particular Arab Americans. In the early 1990s, members of these two communities formed a small but strong coalition to speak out against the mistreatment of Arab Americans. 'Somebody should create a performance about this', I thought. I even suggested to fellow artists that it might be an interesting project they could pursue, but no one took me up on it. Eventually I realized that was because *I* was supposed to do it. I was weary of 'camp plays', that is, theatrical productions about the US Government's incarceration of Japanese Americans during the war. While I knew these plays were important historical and theatrical pieces that provided a voice for those who had been imprisoned, it was difficult for me to make an emotional connection to that past. I began to consider the nature of my role as the generation who had watched these plays. What could we learn from artists who came before us? I decided my way of honouring those who were interned, including my older relatives, was to help fight for the rights for others in current times. As an artist, the act of writing/performing/witnessing what is happening now is a first step toward making sure it is remembered.

When I started researching this project, I knew very little about the Arab American or Muslim communities, and I still consider myself a novice. I knew even less about the crisis in the Middle East. How could I take on such a large topic? I'd be found out as a fraud for sure. But I realized there was no better place from which to begin: I was an average American citizen with an average amount of information (i.e. very little) about current events. I would have to educate myself, even if it was by taking small steps. I became my own experiment: What could I do as an average citizen? Where would I find answers? Would I ask the difficult questions?

I remembered the small coalition of Japanese American and Arab American groups who had fought against the potential plan to intern Arab Americans. This intrigued me. I called Guy Aoki of Media Action Network for Asian Americans, who had been in that early coalition, and also activist/writer Martín Hernandez. Their conversations eventually led me to Michel Shehadeh who was at the time with the American Arab Anti-Discrimination Committee (ADC), and who mailed me a document: the 'Alien, Terrorist and Undesirables: A Contingency Plan', a 1986 INS document made public through the Freedom of Information Act. One of the items in this plan was the imprisonment of 'aliens' in the recently opened Oakdale, Louisiana processing facility in order to house and isolate this population. I couldn't overlook the fact that this shit had happened before: over the years, our government has systematically imprisoned Native Americans, African Americans, Latinos and Asian Americans for their beliefs or simply because of the colour of their skin. Citizens commit hate crimes (assaults, rape, murder) against people of colour, women, queer-identified people on a daily basis. Still, I was a little overwhelmed by the potential breadth of the project. I was also a bit intimidated because I felt I wasn't a history scholar, and at the time I had left my demonstration years behind me. So who was I to speak out?

In the days following the attacks on the World Trade Centre I was cleaning my studio. News of the terrorist attacks, body counts and impending war blared from the radio. I came across my great uncle Masamori Kojima's dusty folder, which contained letters he composed on his twentieth birthday while incarcerated at Rohwer Relocation Centre in Arkansas during World War II. He had written them to friends on the outside and had the foresight to save a carbon copy – blue letters imprinted on fragile yellow paper. I had been holding onto these letters since his death in the late 1980s, certain they would make good subject matter for a project 'somebody' could take on, somebody, but certainly not me. Suddenly the letters I held in my hands made sense to me: Masamori knew he was living through historic times and he knew he needed to document what was happening to him. The dusty folder contained other documents, which gave a record of him leaving the camp before the war's end, and with help from the Quakers, going on to attend Haverford College. After the war he helped form the Chicago Resettlement Committee to assist thousands of Japanese Americans released from camps. He led an early series of broadcasts opposing the Vietnam War on Pacifica's KPFK, was a labour organizer, and joined Mayor Tom Bradley's staff as a chief liaison to various communities. Here was one of my own relatives who had experienced oppression and then stood up to fight for others. Suddenly history was getting personal. I knew it was my turn to step up.

'Vigil' [see Figure 2] is inspired by footage edited by John Esaki for the Japanese American National Museum (JANM), which shows a candlelight vigil hosted by the Nikkei Civil Rights and Redress (NCRR), Japanese American Citizens League (Pacific Southwest District), the Muslim Public Affairs Council (MPAC), the American Arab Anti-Discrimination Committee (ADC) and JANM in Little Tokyo, Los Angeles. The organizations paid tribute to the victims of the World Trade Centre and condemned the terrorist attack, but also spoke out against the US Government incarcerating individuals with no formal charges. During World War II, the Museum had been a Buddhist Temple that started being used as gathering site from which thousands of Americans of Japanese

Figure 2 Courtesy of Marcel Schaap.

ancestry would be packed off to 'assembly centres' and their 'relocation centres.' Since that vigil in the fall of 2001, our government has imprisoned over 2000 people, mostly non-citizens, who were living in the United States at the time of the attack on the World Trade Centre. They have been held in secret, most without formal charges brought against them and without the right to a public defender, many secretly deported. Some are still imprisoned and as we go to press, names of most of the incarcerated have still not been released to the public. They were simply 'disappeared', the way people disappeared in Chile and Argentina. Meanwhile, John Ashcroft quietly proposed his desire to institute camps for those US citizens he deems to be 'enemy combatants'. In December 2002, hundreds of men from Muslim countries were arrested and held after they dutifully came in to comply with the INS' new registration program.

In addition, hate crimes against anyone too brown or too Muslim or just too 'other' have risen to disturbing proportions post 9/11. I believe that turning to look the other way is also a type of hate crime. At the very least, we can bring it up in conversation. One crime in particular stays in my mind: a group of East Asian Americans beat a South Asian man in Anaheim, CA. The suspects thought he was Middle Eastern. After I read the news, I stood in my living room and created a dance in response to the news. As I moved, I wondered what were we doing to each other? We Asian Americans are just as susceptible to beating our neighbours in xenophobic rage. It could have been Denise Uyehara who broke Sundeep's jaw. Slowly I began to think of it as a clay animation figure. When you hit someone, it is a three-dimensional violence that leaves a mark. I created a clay man sequence using my digital video camera on a tripod on my kitchen table. It was a quietly horrific process to create a clay man and then tear him apart. How does the body respond to blows? What happens to my fist if I hit person? What does it take to hate a body? I became both the attacker and the attacked [see Figure 3].

During 2001–2 it was difficult for me to move forward with the project. The amount of information pouring in was immense, and I didn't want to capitalize on people's situations just to further my art. I was acutely aware, that even with all our rights to freedom of speech, it's difficult to speak out while living in the most militarized country in the world. I never knew how people would act or react during that time of crisis. A white, middle-class man yelled at my neighbour that it was because of 'liberals' that 11 September 2001 happened, and 'it was a good thing we put those Japanese in camps'. These are people I see every day, walking down the streets of

Figure 3 Courtesy of Pete Lee.

Santa Monica. Then came the flags. Within weeks of 11 September 2001, SUV owners began attaching flags to their vehicles. When I walked down the streets I felt like I was living in pre-war Germany: fall in line, no discussion. My partner Marcel Schaap, who is from the Netherlands, still finds America a surreal experience.

But coupled with the surreal is the real. In a post-9/11 world, a community of artists and activists were willing to speak out, and this encouraged me to do the same. Small artistic events began to take place in Los Angeles, even in Santa Monica. A group of Butoh-style artists walked down Third Street Promenade shopping centre carrying a stretcher on which a mannequin lay, gagged with the American flag. A South-Asian artist collective held an open mike session of song and poetry at a local dojo/comedy centre. Others performed Augusto Boal-style theatre on the Venice Beach boardwalk. Danielle Brazell of Highways brought together local artists to perform *The Gathering: An Alternate Response to Recent Events*. Japanese Americans from the NCRR and MPAC came together to break fast at Ramadan at Senshin Buddhist Temple. They discussed not only our differences in terms of culture and religion, but also our common struggle to fight for peace and tolerance at a real, grass roots level. The next year they repeated the event for packed crowds. Meanwhile, in simple solidarity, some of us resident artists at the 18th Street Arts Centre made black T-shirts emblazoned with the words 'Our Grief is Not a Cry for War', a phrase that sprung out of the art actions taking place in New York that had made their way to us via the internet. Grassroots groups that brought together artists, activists, concerned citizens such as the Artists Network of Refuse and Resist, A.N.S.W.E.R., Not in Our Name, The South Asian Network, Indo-American Cultural Centre and Cafe Intifada continue to galvanize people with their strong, collective energy. Even Pacifica Radio managed to reboot itself in the midst of its own turmoil to give a voice for peace. And most importantly, across the nation, thousands (and across the globe, millions) took to the streets to demonstrate.

The community of advisors for *Big Head* were the NCRR, Michel Shehadeh, Ketu Katrak of University of California – Irvine, Kamal Abu-Shamsieh of MPAC, with additional support from artists Michelle Berne, Jude Narita, Teresa Conrow, Chay Yew, Keith Mason, the UCLA Department of World Arts and Cultures. Tamadhur Al-Aqeel has been invaluable as dramaturge to the project. She herself is a performer, playwright and former KPFK co-host of *Middle East in Focus*. We interviewed members of the aforementioned communities so that their voices would inform this interdisciplinary performance and its focus on the theme of memory: *How will we remember these times? What will we do? What will we tell our children?* So many things in history get re-written. The least we can do is continue to voice it, to perform it, to create a forum to remember what happened here. For me, *Big Head* is like typing a letter to send out into the world. Its resonance, like the blue lettering of carbon paper, remains for my posterity.

In the years following the *Big Head* production I've continued to link the experience of my community with others, even when I do not articulate this linkage directly in the project. Currently I reside in Tucson, Arizona. Tucson is a mere 70 miles from the United States/ Mexico border. It is the home to many undocumented workers, families and students. I've been collaborating with Jason Aragon and Pan Left Productions to create a new work, *Bus Stop Dreaming*, inspired by interviews with those most affected by the recent deportations. Our community resources for this project include Derechos Humanos and Las Promatoras, who have provided stories and insights into the harsh realities of living undocumented in the city. Jason is part of Copwatch, a group of activists who rush out to videotape the South Tucson Police as they conduct 'routine' traffic stops, ask for documentation and then call in Border Patrol to begin the deportation process. The title *Bus Stop Dreaming* comes from an incident in which a woman was waiting at a bus stop when the police approached her. She fled into a nearby grocery store and was chased and apprehended by police. They demanded that she show proof of residency. When she could not they called in Border Patrol and began the deportation process – simply because she was brown and waiting for the bus. I worked with video designer Adam Cooper-Terán and dancer Yvonne Montoya, to weave together video projection onto a moving body, an installation and written/aural testimony.

Initially we were going to create a one-night, outdoor performance at the sites of deportation in the city, but soon realized this was problematic. Many local residents were afraid to drive at night, let alone congregate outside. They too feared deportation. When the Supreme Court upheld the 'documents please' condition of Arizona's anti-immigration law SB1070, things worsened. Instead, we as artists adjusted to meet the needs of the community. Our plan shifted to the grass-roots social justice center where people felt it was safe to gather. We needed to go to *them*, not the other way around. As our project continues, I often think back to how *Big Head* challenged me to create work that responded to these unheard voices, but I had to find a way to go beyond the literal into new terrain which made the body a central site of performance. It is an effort, my effort, to add a human face to those most at risk.

Big Head

Denise Uyehara

with the additional words

of Edina Lekovic, Masamori Kojima,

**Tamadhur Al-Aqeel, Lulu Emery, Shady Hakim
and Lillian Nakano**

Production History

Big Head premiered at Highways Performance Space February 21, 2003 with the support of the California Civil Liberties Public Education Project. It was developed at Highways and the Mark Taper Forum's Asian Theatre Workshop Reading Series. Select performances: The Japanese American National Museum, the Dokkyo University Performance Studies Conference, Tokyo, Tigertail Productions, Miami, Florida.

The stage is clear except for a white screen on which to project images and a black box on stage right. A small mound of red clay sits on the box.

Prologue

Lights rise on Denise. Her right hand raised to shoulder height, palm facing out to audience.

When I was five, I burned my hand by reaching for the hot end of the sparkler. It was the Fourth of July. I remember my complete shock as the hot-cold pain shot through my palm, up my arm, then strangely up into my armpit. My mother dropped her fireworks and held my wrist up in the glowing light of the street lamp. My hand looked as if it had been X-rayed: ghostly white where I'd touched heat, and soft, normal flesh everywhere else.

Coincidentally that same evening, a fire raged throughout an apartment on the other side of the complex. We were told the fire was contained, so my mother, sister, brother and I stayed inside. While my mother dressed my hand with a milky ointment, my siblings craned their necks out the window to try to catch a glimpse of the fire.

I didn't actually see the fire, but I remember it clearly because my father filmed the entire event on our family's Super 8 camera:

(*Peers through her hand which makes the shape of a camera lens.*)
Giant flames licking at a two-story building. Trucks, ladders, water. Firemen pushing us back.

(*Walks stage right*)
Weeks later, we kids ventured into the burned-out apartment to survey the damage.

'Wow . . . Was it arson?' I asked.

(*Pointing up to the sky*)
'A stray firework!' My brother said. 'Maybe someone threw a streaming Roman Candle up into the sky until it landed on the rooftop!'

'Dad says a man fell asleep in bed while smoking,' my sister said.

'Nah-ah! That's stupid. How can you smoke and sleep at the same time?'

My sister explored the outside of the building. 'Hey, come here and look at the Ice Cream Bricks!'

(*Points at an imaginary wall*)
And there stood a wall with melted, bubbled, blistered, bricks, each dripping down to its neighbour. Fudgesickles in the sun.

(*Calling*)
'Ice Cream! Ice Cream! Chocolate, strawberry, peach, vanilla, banana, pistachio, peppermint, lemon, orange, butterscotch ice cream!'

'Look what the fire made!'

'Look what the fire made!'

'Ice Cream mixed with fire.'

(*Suddenly serious. Beat.*)

'A Baked Alaska!'

(*Laughs*)
'Chocolate, strawberry, peach, vanilla, banana, pistachio, peppermint, lemon, orange –'

She moves along the wall, pointing out different flavours until she spies something behind the wooden box and stops. She picks up two small American flags and a special black headband. She places the headband on her head, and attaches the flags to each side of her head.

She becomes the driver of a giant sports utility vehicle (SUV), careering through space, while talking on a cell phone, making Fuck You hand gestures at other drivers, etc.

An assistant enters holding up an electric fan. Denise stands in the fan's breeze until the flags are blowing dramatically behind her. She smiles wickedly to audience. Suddenly she crashes, rolls over, recovers, continues. Assistant places fan on the box next to the clay. Denise continues to be slowly blown by a eerie wind, as if on a deserted moon landscape. Lights change to a dim, ghostly blue. She moves in slow motion, as if in outer space. She struggles to keep reaching forward, finally makes it to the table on which sits a mound of red clay. Still fighting the imaginary wind, she moulds it into several shapes: a heart, a rocket ship, a human. She tears the head off the human figure and it blows away slowly. She takes the flags off from her head, and after much effort, she manages to lift the flag and mount it into the red clay, which now resembles a mountain top. The fan blows the flag in a perpetual wind. She holds her hands up, one at a time, to reveal red palms. She looks at her palms, then wipes them on cloth.

The Fourth Grade Book Report

Throughout the scene, the flag continues to blow in the fan's breeze.

She picks up an oversized white sheet of paper and becomes a fourth grader, speaking with great enthusiasm.

'The History of the Pledge of Allegiance'

By Denise Ya-hara. Fourth Grade.

Many of us know how to say the Pledge of Allegiance, but few of us *con-tem-plate* its history. The Pledge of Allegiance was written in 1892 by Francis Bellamy, a Socialist Baptist Minister from Boston who was later kicked out of his church for preaching too many socialist ideas. Francis Bellamy's cousin, Edward Bellamy, was the author of many *u-to-pi-an* novels. Francis and Edward often gave speeches about how the middle class could create a planned *e-co-no-my* with *po-li-ti-cal*, social and *e-co-no-mic* equality for all. These ideas became part of the Pledge of Allegiance.

It is interesting to note that today, the United States and the Philippines are the only nations to have pledges to their flags.

The words of the Pledge have changed over the years. For example, the words 'under God' were added in 1954 under the reign of President McCarthy.

Now I will perform the Pledge the way it was originally intended in 1892 to *com-mem-orate* the 400th Anniversary of Columbus's discovery of the United States of America.

For this part I need two volunteers from the audience to help me hold these signs.

(Assistant enters with handmade signs with the pledge of allegiance written on them. Audience hesitates.)
Don't be scared, I'm only in fourth grade.

(Audience members volunteer, come onto the stage and hold signs.)
These are the original words to the Pledge. Please read along silently while I read out loud.

(*Hand on heart*)
Ready, begin:
I pledge allegiance
(*outstretches arm, palm facing upward*)
To my Flag
And the Republic for which it stands
One nation indivisible
With Liberty, and Justice for all.
(*drop hands militantly to sides*)

– One country! One language! One Flag! –

It is interesting to note that during World War II,
(*hand outstretched, palm upward*)
The pledge position was changed from this
(*hand over heart*)
to this
(*hand outstretched*)
because this looked like a Nazi asking for a hand-out.

Also, during World War II, my grandparents and great-grandparents often recited the Pledge of Allegiance while in the Japanese American internment camps!

Now please join me in reciting the Pledge of Allegiance the way it was originally intended in 1892.

Please rise.

(*All rise*)

Assume the position!
(*Audience raises their hands to heart*) Ready, begin:
I pledge allegiance
(*Audience outstretches their arms, palm facing upward*)
To my Flag
And the Republic for which it stands
One nation indivisible
With Liberty, and Justice for all.
(*All drop hands*)

– One country! One language! One Flag! –

Thank you. You may be seated.
(*Volunteers return to their seats*)

Let's give a round of applause for our volunteers.

(*Applause. She turns off fan and holds up flag waving it in the air.*)

That concludes my report on the Pledge of Allegiance, thank you.

She accidentally drops flag audience gasps. She panics and salutes it as it lies on the ground. Upbeat 1940s music plays.

Masamori Kojima

Walks to soft white light, stage left.

Throughout the sequence, she dances forward and back on a diagonal, her movements citing hand-over-heart, hand-extended, and salute gestures.

November 1, 1942 – Rohwer Relocation Centre, Arkansas

Dear Fred,

This letter no doubt, is a real surprise, coming from someone for whom you must have despaired of long ago.

Today is my birthday; I am twenty. I should feel elated, getting out of the teens, to be regarded less a boy and more a man, and all that sort of thing. Maybe I do.

I received that letter you wrote on the outside and copied to many of us on the inside, urging: 'Do not for one minute let the American public forget the Nisei or the Issei. Write a continual flow of letters out into the world.'

So this is what has been happening to me since we saw each other last:

The first week was spent in trying to achieve a semblance of home in our barrack unit. I have not adjusted myself to evacuation as well as I had thought. I miss the intellectual companionship readily accessible to me in Santa Anita – Sets, Bob Fuji, Eddie Shimano, Joe Oyama. Our books were not to be enjoyed alone, but in each other's company where their contents were freely exchanged. But I lost them all – books and friends – in the relocation.

They interrogated my neighbour, old Mr Sumida:

- What do you think of the statement in the Japanese constitution that the emperor is a sacred god?

- Well, I believe in it the same way the Englishmen regard the statement that the king can do no wrong.

- I never heard that interpretation before. Who would you rather see win the war?

- I like this country very much and like it happens in a boxing match, I would prefer a draw.
- What would you do if a Japanese parachute landed and the soldier came to your back door and asked for food?
- I would invite him in and take him to the dining hall.
- But wouldn't that be treason?
- Gentlemen, time and time again tramps and beggars have come to our back door asking for food and I never refused them. This Japanese is a human and I will feed him.

(*She hits an invisible wall, tries to break through, but cannot.*)

Fred, what are your plans for the immediate future? I know as little about you at the present as you do about me. Eventually, I'd like to get out of this place, I hear the Quakers have a program so that we could return to college. Haverford, the East Coast, things are different out there. I know there's a slim chance of this happening, but I can dream, can't I?

(*She tries to break through again*)

I have your books still, and what an aid they are. I think I would have died long ago if I didn't have them.

(*She stops trying, composes herself, puts her hand on her heart.*)

And your health Fred? Is all well on the home front?

Send this letter out into the world.

(*She gestures out with her hand*)

Your friend,

Masamori Kojima

She picks up flag, puts it in the red clay again.

Edina Lekovic

Walks to centre stage.

Throughout this sequence she moves a white, blank sheet of paper between her hands and over her body, interpreting the voice of Edina.

My name is Edina Lekovic. I was the editor of the UCLA paper, the Daily Bruin, and that put me in a unique position, especially for a young Muslim woman in this nation.

I started at the Bruin my freshman year. I wasn't outwardly Muslim until my sophomore year, so people that I got to know saw me go through – I don't know if I'd call it a transformation – but an *evolution*. They watched me figure out what I was doing with my life, my own identity. So as I worked my way up and through the staff, people already knew me, it wasn't that big of an issue. But when I was a candidate for editor-in-chief, I'll never forget, we held a staff hearing, which is when the staff endorses a candidate.

And a Japanese American man asked me, directly, 'So what effect is you being Muslim going to have on the job that you do here?'

And I was extremely offended.

But I tried to handle it as politely and courteously as possible and I said:

'Beyond the fact that I'm going to be praying five times a day which will take a few minutes here and there, and that I'm a moral person who believes in ethics, and that will benefit the newspaper – beyond that, I don't think this has anything to do with anyone else.'

I was upset with myself that I let it upset me. I think that was the first time I saw what the road was going to be like, because you sort of get insulated. And dealing with the outside community, a lot of people were surprised when they walked into the office and saw me as the person who was running an operation with over 100 staff and a million dollar budget, that wasn't what they were expecting to see. But I think it also empowered me. It prepared me for real life. I had more good experiences than bad so I can't complain, but it was definitely eye-opening.

And then, shortly after September 11th –

(*She drops paper suddenly, watching it fall to the ground. Beat. She recovers, picks up paper, holds it to her chest.*)

I randomly ran into that same guy at UCLA. It was so insane. I had gone back to speak at an event that connected the Japanese American experience with the Muslim American experience. I was talking about the connections between the internment camps and the Patriot Act, and all these infringements on our civil liberties, and I was making a point that this whole 'never again thing' is unfortunately in our time sort of a joke because it happens over and over again.

And this guy who had sort of called me out a few years ago walked up to me – he was on campus doing something with his transcripts –

And he said, 'I'm so glad I ran into you because it's really been bothering me that I treated you badly those years ago, especially with everything that's going on, it's one of my real regrets in life and I wanted to apologize to you. I don't know why we ran into each other today but I'm grateful that I had this opportunity.'

I said, 'Oh I have nothing to be upset about, I'm sorry that I even held a grudge against you.'

But inside, it humbled me. It made me want to go and apologize to other people (*laughs*).

Because it had been one of those experiences that hurt so much when it happened. Because I'd felt I'd made so much progress and that people who knew me knew who I was and that they wouldn't sink to that level, so when that happened I thought 'What am I really doing? Have I really made any progress? Is this all for nothing?'

I guess God has his ways. It's amazing how things came full circle and sort of took care of themselves. Because this guy was obviously so affected by his own actions.

Denise slowly turns in a circle with paper floating through the air.

She moves to stage left and holds the paper in the light of the projector until it catches video footage images of an evening candlelight vigil. It is a gathering of Arab Americans, Japanese Americans, and Muslims, holding candles. It is the silent footage of speakers, flashes of signs, faces from the very old to the very young, holding tiny flickering lights. A quiet ballad on amplified guitar plays under the various voices from the community.

(*Male voice*)

A day or two after that, the grocer in San Gabriel was killed. And he goes to my parents' church. And that's when fear began to be a bigger part of my life. Because suddenly it hit real close to home. Where a member of my immigrant community had been killed. And we weren't sure whether it was just a random act of violence, or a hate crime. I hadn't even thought about my personal safety at all until I got to work. And the next couple of days, my co-workers – at the time I was working for another small, progressive, faith-based, non-profit – and they were saying, 'hey, please be careful out there'. And I was going, 'why?' I didn't really think about it until the American flags started popping up everywhere. And then, every time I would drive on the freeway and see a flag or see a bumper sticker I would wonder, what does that mean to that person? Does that flag mean they want me dead? Or does that flag simply mean they're expressing their solidarity and sympathy for those who died on September 11th? So many different things that it could mean. You're almost driving with your head down because you're not sure what the person next to you is thinking. Luckily my hair kind of, I mean, most Arab Americans don't wear their hair in (dread) locks, so I didn't feel like I was ever an obvious target.

– Shady Hakim
Pasadena, California

(*Female voice*)

I'd like them to remember the power of grassroots activism. No matter how little you are, how insignificant you are, you still have a say, whatever you say will have an effect. And even if you talk to your next door neighbour and educate them about whatever it is – if it's about your country, about your rights, about peace issues, no matter how – you don't have to be this famous person, you don't have to be an artist, you don't have to be an author, you don't have to be a poet, you can be this average person. And grassroots activism has been an extremely powerful factor in kind of keeping things in line. And sometimes we get very, very discouraged and say 'what's the point?' You know, 'where are we going with all this? Nobody is listening'. But no matter what, at the end of the day, it does make a difference. And that's I think my suggestion to future generations. Don't give up your rights of speaking up. Every little thing helps.

– Lu Lu Emery
Canyon Country, California

(*Female voice*)

I'm Arab-American, and I'm thinking of changing my name. I'm afraid to travel. Not because I'm afraid of terrorists, but because I'm afraid that a fellow passenger, or maybe a flight attendant, will get spooked by my looks or my name, and I'll be humiliated and ordered off the plane. At least I'm not afraid to leave my house anymore, like I was for a while after September 11th. Will there ever be closure for the September 11th attacks? Probably not. But one thing's for sure: there is no closure for being the target of racism. It's like how I felt when I watched the towers fall. It was just as shocking and horrifying to watch the 50th time as it was the first. Being the target of racism is like that. It's shocking and painful and somehow incomprehensible the first time, and every time after that. I'm always waiting and wondering: who out there, with the careless or intentional remark or action, will send my pain and anger crashing through me? It could be anyone.

– Tamadhur Al-Aqeel
Los Angeles, California

(*Denise's voice reading the words of Lillian Nakano.*)

What would I say to Arab Americans and Muslims right now? If they could only remember that there are many people who will support them – even in the white community, the progressive ones – and that progressive groups throughout the United States are watching the government, and certainly if anything like the camps or mass incarceration or any kind of blatant type of injustice happens, we'll be out there. If it comes to a mobilization to stand up to the government, I will be out there, and thousands will be out there, to support them.

(*Denise begins to fold paper until it becomes a small letter.*)

Because they're facing so much unjust treatment – it's racism, when you really come down to it, it's racist. And they have to persevere. Because it won't stop. Unfortunately, there's always people like that in the government and outside our government . . . but we can't let them break us. I just hope that they will go through all this and still remain strong, because they have a lot to be proud of. They have all the rights, like all the rest of the citizens in this United States. It is their right, and they have to fight for it, and we will fight for it too.

Lillian Nakano
Incarcerated during World War II

(*Vigil video ends. House lights rise slightly.*)

(*Denise walks into audience with the folded letter. She speaks to an individual in the audience.*)

Could you do me a favour? Could you keep this for me until the end of the war?
(*She gives them the letter*)
Thanks.

As if on a departing train, she raises her hand to wave good-bye and returns to the stage.

The Nerve

Centre stage.

Someone has the nerve to call me at eight a.m.
I ignore it.
It's a sleepy September morning.

They call again at nine.

- Hello?
-Oh, you *are* there.
- Hi Mom –
-We thought maybe you were on a plane.
- Is everything OK?
- Turn on the television.
- Oh my god. All those people. What's going to happen to the Arab
Americans, the Muslims? Things are going to get a little weird.

When I get off the phone
I do what any respectable Westsider does in times of crisis:
I go shopping.
I go grocery shopping at Trader Joe's.
Trader Joe's is Los Angeles' specialty store
with all the finest domestic and imported
food and wine a body could desire.
So, there I am at Trader Joe's on the morning of September 11, 2001:
Everybody talking on their cell phones
Rushing down the aisles,
Gotta get those provisions:
Bags of pasta, cans of tuna fish, water by the crate –
And olives! We need olives!
And as I pass each cart-pushing, traumatized shopper
I realize MY face could have been the enemy
The way it was for my parents and grandparents.

And then I remember what an Arab American man said to me:
'They interned your people all at once,
they're interning us, one by one.'

Now, every time I walk into Trader Joe's
I realize: This time I am a precarious witness to a crisis
And somewhere secret within our US prisons
(*She places her fingers on the sides of her eyes and lifts them up.*)
our government has started another kind of internment camp
Where over 2000 people since September 11
were held with little or no evidence against them.
Many secretly deported, and others, citizens
Marked as 'Enemy Combatants'
stripped of their rights to a lawyer,
a phone call,
a reason.

And maybe there's one less customer in Trader Joe's today
One person who overnight was quietly 'disappeared'
and now maybe they're writing mental messages to us
(*she lets her eyes go*)
– Letters from camp.

Now, every time I walk into Trader Joe's
I wish there were something I could buy for this crisis
Something that could make millions of voices rise up and say:
'Not again, not again, this is an outrage!
And we will not shop quietly,
not while history repeats itself on somebody else.'

Hate Crime

In darkess, the voice of a newscaster on voice-over.

On October 21, 2001, a South Asian American man and his family were
assaulted by several East Asian American youths in Orange County.
Sundeep, a 27-year-old physical therapist who chose not to give his
last name was leaving a karaoke lounge with his family where they had
just celebrated his birthday, when he encountered six to seven youths
approximately 16–22 years in age, who were
Standing . . .

(*Video projector casts a bright white light over the screen, revealing
Denise, dressed in white. She slowly raises her hand above her head,
bringing it down to caress her cheek. She repeats this action several times.*)

. . . just outside the club. Two of the youths were female, the rest, male.

One of them asked, 'Hey, how are you doing? Did you have fun?'

Five of the youths began to assault Sundeep and his family, who tried to
defend themselves and not return blows.

Sundeep's wife screamed. 'What did we do to you? We never did
anything. Why are you hitting us?'

One of the girls said, 'They're going to get you mother-fucking Middle
Easterners.'

Sundeep suffered the worst injuries of the group. His body was bruised
and his jaw so severely broken and had to be wired shut for eight weeks.

Asian Pacific American organizations have gathered together to
denounce the crime and to draw composite sketches of the suspects.

(She runs her hand from her cheek down the front of her body, as if dissecting it, then, lowers her hands to her sides, palms out, and looks out at the audience.)

The FBI is investigating the attack as a hate crime.

(A gray animated clay figure projects over her. She moves inside and outside the image, sometimes attacking it, sometimes being the attacked. The clay man alternately hugs her and is torn apart by her.)

(chanting in loud whisper)
what does it take to hate a body? what does it hate to take a body? what does it take to hate a body? what does it hate to take a body? what does it take to hate a body? what does it hate to take a body? what does it take to hate a body? what does it hate to take a body?

Finally, she stands facing the screen, with both hands almost pressed against it, as if being arrested. The clay figure, now a demolished, amorphous lump, turns to look at her with hollow eyes. She looks at clay man as he fades to black.

Fourth of July

Centre stage.

Fourth of July, 2002. My sister and I sat at a picnic table, watching her children play.

I said, 'Remember that Fourth of July when we were little, when I burned my hand on a sparkler, and that fire raged in the apartment complex. And you found the ice cream bricks? Chocolate, strawberry, peach, vanilla, banana, pistachio, peppermint, lemon, orange, butterscotch, ice –'

And she said, '*You* didn't burn your hand on a sparkler. *I* did. That happened to *me*.'

(She walks to audience member who still holds her letter.)

Can I have that letter back now?

As she opens the letter, it is a song from Edina.

Edina's Song

She stands centre stage.

(*Sings as a ballad*)
When I have children I will sit them down
And tell them of this truly tragic time in history
when Muslims came under fire throughout the world.

But in that tragic time it was not a time for hopelessness
It was a test from God, to test our faith
Would we be mere words, or be people of action
Would we work for the justice we truly believed?

For in that tragic time, so many people stood up for us
That's something we should have done ourselves all along
But some among us were too afraid, some among us too insular
Yet many Muslims had been working for others for years.

(*She walks to stage right and sets up a super 8 projector as she sings.*)
And if anything I want my children to learn from this
to learn from all parts of life
and grow.

I will tell them
Being a good Muslim doesn't mean just working for our
community
But for all mankind
Work to eradicate things homelessness, domestic violence
That have peripheral things to do with Islam.

The Prophet Muhammad, peace be upon him,
Would say 'I love you for the sake of God.'

So in this tragic time
In this time
As in all times

Nothing is meaningless
No relationship is frivolous
And everyone who is placed in our path
Has a reason.

*Denise turns on a Super 8 film projector. The footage projects onto her
and spills over onto the screen behind her. They are images inside a
local mosque where Muslims are holding an event recognising various
organizations and individuals for coming forward to help them after
September 11th. Among the recognised are the Nikkei for Civil Rights
and Redress, a Japanese-American activist organization. Cut to image*

of a quilt sewn by Muslim American women bearing names of those who perished on September 11th. Cut to images of Muslim women, men and children, praying, and then to a giant American flag that is draped over the wall outside the mosque. She lets the projection images fall cross her body and the paper as she silently repeats movements from earlier scenes.

The same footage, transferred to video, begins to project on the large screen behind her, so that she stands in two light sources as she moves. The film ends as a video cross-fades to an image of pastel-coloured clay figures, standing side by side in an old-style salute to the flag. Each gracefully raises their arm toward the flag. The people are distant cousins to the clay man.

Pledge

Standing with the clay people, to one side.

There is a photograph that I have seen only once.
I cannot find it anymore so I have committed it to memory.
It is a photograph of young women and men,
standing in the perfect morning light,
reciting the pledge of allegiance.

There's something different about this photograph.
It's not because they are reciting the pledge while behind barbed
   wire while in camp:
we've seen those pictures before.
And it's not because they have right arm raised, palms upwards,
the position for the pledge in those days.

It's because everyone is standing perfectly still,
And yet they are not.

And in that moment
before they speak their first lines,
'I pledge allegiance to my flag',
I think each one lives an entire lifetime, an imagined one:
they walk to the front gate and wave to the sentry
who waves back,
they walk into the bright desert sunlight,
board a bus,
And then a train takes them back to the metropolis,

where they are greeted again with signs that say *welcome home*.
Thousands of yellow ribbons mark all the lampposts and stop
   signs,
and those who owned land or rented houses return to their homes,
and out of their fireplaces they pull their kimono
which have miraculously been recomposed from the ashes
where they had burned them before the evacuation,
and they play their Japanese music records that have glued
   themselves back together from the fragments on the floor.
Everyone can find their neighbours and friends again,
no one has died in battle or prison or in childbirth.

At that moment, I wonder if they think what I do,
Whenever I hear the pledge these days:

I must remember this time history:
'Knowledge will become my America. My voice will be my
pledge'.

(*she walks to the centre of the clay people*)
And I see my great uncle Masamori Kojima
Standing among them. He is composing a letter, to me,
And he sends it out into the morning breeze.
(*she walks forward, still in the projected image*)

It says:
'Once upon a time we came to this land.
We thought if we worked hard enough, people would accept us.
But along the way, something went wrong and
many turned against us, or even worse,
they just pretended they did not see.
But there were others who risked their reputations and lives for us,
and for the future of this land.'

(*Clay figures fade out and video projects the sky alone, light blue chalk
and pastel lines move across the sky.*)
And since that time I have not been the same.

(*Reaching up, palms up, toward the streaks of blue in the sky.*)

No, I didn't actually see it . . . but I remember it clearly:

Giant flames licking at a two-story building. Trucks, ladders, water.
Firemen pushing us back.

'Was it arson?'

'A stray firework! Maybe someone threw a streaming Roman Candle up
into the sky until it landed on the rooftop!'

'Dad says a man fell asleep in bed while smoking.'

'Ice Cream! Ice Cream! Chocolate Strawberry, Peach Vanilla, Banana,
pistachio, peppermint, lemon, orange, butterscotch ice cream!'

'Look what the fire made!
Look what the fire made!'

'Ice Cream mixed with fire.'

(*She lowers her left hand until right hand remains alone, palm facing
out, as in the beginning.*)

I was the one – the one of many –
who filmed the fire on the Fourth of July,
We with our small heads, made big
filled with voices from the past
and the voices of now.
It was a small, poor, imperfect thing that I did – to remember.
Maybe I even got the facts wrong,

(*Looks at hand*)

or did I?

(*Looks out at audience*)

What will we do, in the fire this time?

(*Looks left, then right, then back out*)

Lights fade to black.

Story, Silence, Song and Site: The Multiplicity of Testimony in *The Fence*: Alicia Talbot Interviewed by Caroline Wake

Established in 1981, Urban Theatre Projects has been producing work for more than 30 years.[1] For the past 11 of these, from 2001 to 2012, Alicia Talbot has been the artistic director, overseeing the company's overall output as well as directing a series of her own works including *The Cement Garage* (2000), *The Longest Night* (2002), *Back Home* (2006), *The Last Highway* (2008), *The Fence* (2010) and *Buried City* (2012).[2] These works are bound not only by their aesthetics, but also by the ethics of their development process. Like Rimini Protokoll and Quarantine, Talbot works with people who are 'everyday experts' – individuals who have a particular area of expertise because of their passion, profession or life experience. Unlike Rimini Protokoll or Quarantine, however, Talbot does not place these experts onstage but instead works with them backstage, casting them in the role of consultant or dramaturge. These consultants are not asked to disclose their personal stories, but rather invited to share their opinions and observations about the world as they see it. They attend rehearsals on a regular basis in order to provide critical and dramaturgical feedback. Importantly, the consultants are paid a fee for their contribution, which both acknowledges them as cultural workers and encourages a strong sense of ownership.

The Fence is the fifth major work to be created using this process and, according to Talbot, perhaps the most difficult because it was in consultation with people who had lived experiences of the Stolen Generations and the Forgotten Australians. The former refers to children of Aboriginal and Torres Strait Islander descent who were forcibly removed from their families and placed into the care of white families and institutions. The latter refers to children who, between 1930 and 1970, were forcibly removed from their families and placed in institutional care. Talbot's task, then, became to create a rehearsal environment and through that a theatrical work that could hold the stories of two traumas, which although similar in some ways, are profoundly different in others. Incredibly, she succeeded as evidenced by the overwhelming praise the production received.[3]

In order to arrive at *The Fence*, the audience had to traverse a few obstacles themselves. The site of the performance, a former institution, was not revealed to them. Instead they were directed to meet at a nearby theatre venue, where they were given a map which provided both a history of and directions to the performance site. On the 10-minute walk there, audiences passed between buildings boarded up for decades, alongside sandstone walls made by convicts and onto a disused tennis court surrounded by wire fencing. When they finally took their seats, they could see a small purpose-built house perched in front of the large and looming walls of the institution. Sitting in the background, these walls evoked a sense of past experiences, which were almost never mentioned during the piece. The overall effect was compelling: as if the back wall to the house had been removed and the audience had become witnesses to the events within. In what follows, we discuss Talbot's work in general and *The Fence* in particular.

Caroline   Testimonial theatre is a broad category, but even so, your work would seem to sit at its very edges. Having watched your work over the past 10 years, I would say that it both is and is not testimonial: it is, in the sense that it's based on real, often traumatic, events in real people's lives; yet it's not, in the sense that it doesn't disclose people's stories and it often doesn't even refer to particular events. Would you agree with this characterization of your work?

Alicia   Yes, absolutely and I think that tension is key to my work. On the one hand, I'm interested in producing testimony to the act that's happened and also in positioning the audiences as witnesses in Tim Etchells' sense of the word, when he says 'to witness an event is to be present at it in some fundamentally ethical way, to feel the weight of things and one's own place in them, even if that place is simply, for the moment, as an onlooker.'[4] On the other hand, I am not interested in soliciting testimony from consultants nor am I interested in seeing actors stand on stage and repeat those testimonies. When I think of witnessing in a broader sense, beyond the context of theatre, I would say that to testify is to declare that something has happened and that it is real. So if testifying is telling the truth and art is a way of grappling with how we might perceive the truth, then that's where my work becomes testimonial – it deals with a set of truths that are fictionalized but embedded in some kind of reality.

Caroline   That combination of fiction and reality certainly struck me when I saw *The Fence*, as I wrote in my review.[5] What also struck me was that while testimonial theatre typically privileges story, *The Fence* balances story against silence, song and site. *The Fence* deals with two stories, or sets of stories, which are told separately more often than they are told together: the Stolen Generations and the Forgotten Australians. Why did you decide to tell these stories together and how difficult was it to do so?

Figure 4 Courtesy of Urban Theatre Projects.

Alicia   When I was working on *The Longest Night* (2002), I was based at the Parks Community Centre in the western suburbs of Adelaide. One of the consultants told me about his experience of institutional care. He was removed from his home at the age of 6 and he said simply, 'all I saw for the next eleven years was a fence'. The phrase stayed with me. That same man was also a security guard at the nearby housing estate, where he was renowned among the young Indigenous and African residents for his tough tactics, even though in a way his experience of disadvantage was not dissimilar to theirs. I thought to myself, how could I bring their worlds together? How could we have a discussion?

This more immediate experience intersected with my longer-term interest in reconciliation and the possibility of Indigenous and non-Indigenous having an honest, not necessarily politically correct, conversation. That's why I was so keen on having a black-white marriage at the heart of the work, because I think that it is one of the few forums in which we can have an honest conversation – you can say things in a partnership that you can't say anywhere else. That robustness means that Mel and Joy's marriage becomes the basis on which everything else is built. *The Fence* is about them and their friends, who've all been touched by the experience of removal or institutional care in some way or another, remaking family without family.

Caroline   So for you these two stories couldn't be told separately, they had to be told together. Did your consultants feel the same way or did they want their stories disentangled?

Alicia   Some did and some didn't. It is always difficult to speak the words of others so here are a few responses to give you an idea of the range of feelings among consultants. One said, 'you took the time to seek us out, to authenticate stuff. To make it real. That's a major thing – it validates us and gives us recognition. That's unique for us.'[6] Someone else said, 'I felt overwhelmed by taking part in the project. I feel that deep down, there was a spiritual belonging place for me. It was a great honour hearing and seeing it from both sides of the story. Being Stolen Generation myself, I congratulate everyone who played a part and I dearly thank Urban Theatre Projects for putting it on.'[7]

In contrast, the responses of consultants who identified as Forgotten Australians tended to be more ambivalent. One organization declined to continue their involvement with the project after the creative development because the CEO felt that the work did not adequately represent the experience of non-Indigenous people who had grown up in care and welfare institutions and that it focused too much on the experience of Stolen Generations. Similarly, another consultant told us: 'I felt let down – not seen, misrepresented and very disappointed but I do believe that it was aptly named *The Fence* as that was where your producer [and] writer sat – "on the fence," so politically correct . . . I spoke to a few people after the play ended and asked them what they thought the play was about. The majority responded with "The Stolen Generations, of course" . . . So finishing up this experience for me has left a sour taste in my mouth. There is a story that has not been told yet!'[8]

Prior to the government apology to the Forgotten Australians, there was a degree of anger that the government had apologized to the Stolen Generations but not to Forgotten Australians. The apology actually happened while we were making the work, which not only brought publicity but also very painful memories.

Caroline   Some of the preview publicity also mentioned that one of the actors had some experience of the Stolen Generations. Was this a deliberate choice on your part, to cast an actor whose own life story overlapped with that of the character, and was it the case with all of the actors?

Alicia   Yes and no. I was not aware, when casting the piece, that the performer had direct experience of being part of the Stolen Generations. That said, I was not entirely surprised when it later emerged: in part because it seems that there are few Aboriginal families who were not touched by this practice; and in part because that sometimes happens with my work. Even when a performer's story does not overlap with that of their character, audiences will often make this assumption anyway.

Figure 5 Courtesy of Urban Theatre Projects.

Writer James Waites, for instance, was surprised that the actors hadn't been cast for their stories as he initially assumed that was the whole point. But this goes to a broader point about my practice, which is that for better and for worse I don't look for actors, but for performers who can carry the energy of testimony, who can be testimonies themselves.

Caroline   For all that we have been talking about stories, the specific stories of these characters remain somewhat elusive. How does silence inform your practice?

Alicia   Silence as a structure is key for both the consultants and for the personae (performers) in the work. For the consultants, I am very clear from the outset that they do not need to tell me their personal stories. They may emerge in part during the devising process, but people are never expected to provide those stories; they are there to give the artistic team their opinion of the world and of the work, not to rehearse or rehash testimony. Similarly, even as the fictional characters in the work speak I also like to give them the space not to speak, as the silences and the unsaid often conveys a stronger emotional impact, opening meaning rather than containing it.

Caroline   Is there ever any tension between these two silences? Do you ever find the consultants wanting your characters to be more voluble, for instance?

Alicia   Yes, sometimes. With *The Fence*, we finished its development and had a community showing in December, a short break and then began the final week's rehearsal for the January premiere. The consultants enjoyed the December showing, but I struggled with the overall work. Prior to the January rehearsal, I took at least half of the words away to get a work that had an emotional fabric and that wasn't just people talking or testifying for that matter. One of the things I edited out was the wife's story because, while it worked to a point, everything had become over-spoken. I tried to take out everything that was explanatory, because the work had become too obviously meaningful. That really upset some of the performers and some of the consultants because, actually, they wanted testimony. In retrospect, taking out the wife's story added to the disappointment of two of the consultants, who felt that the work did not represent the Forgotten Australians' experiences. I took out the words because I felt certain theatrical and testimonial forms are becoming too familiar to audiences, which means that they can't always hear anymore even when the stories are true, but it is a difficult conversation to have.

Once it had been edited, I think the piece worked better because it carried less historical weight. There was more space within and around the work, which left space for the audience to do some of their own work. I'm not sure whether this space survives in the printed script though. There's a lovely block of material that was reduced to one line – I've lost my earring – and then to none! In the meantime, Lucinda Williams is playing, Joy is drinking, Mel is crying, Connie is in the kitchen, Chris is on the couch. It's just one line in print, but it takes 10 minutes in performance.

Caroline   Yes, the Williams' song really does hold that scene together, which brings us to music more generally. How does music inform your practice?

Alicia   Within *The Fence* music operates in a few ways. In development, it functioned to facilitate and sustain the long-running improvisations the performers and I do in order to devise the work. In performance, it's about the characters singing to themselves as well as the actors singing to the spirits present. The didgeridoo was magical every night because Kelton was in conversation with the spirits and ghosts in the real institution that rose up behind the set. Similarly, for Richard, his song was about talking to that particular piece of land. Music was how protocol and business were housed within the show; and for an audience it's really great theatrical material. Beyond that, music is about affecting the audience and shifting the way they are listening. I worked with sound designer Liberty Kerr, who has an extraordinary way of manipulating the live sounds of the environment and combining them with pop songs, silence and original compositions to produce haunting soundscapes. Liberty's soundscapes in combination with pop culture music embeds the work in an emotional terrain, whereas dialogue and words can reduce our capacity to listen and when we listen to songs float out over the backyard, we're not being told; we're just witnessing an evening unfold.

Caroline   Of course, all of this unfolds outside in the night air. What is the relationship between testimony and site in your work?

Alicia   It's almost like the site, in particular with *The Fence*, the site *is* the testimony, the land *is* the testimony. The entire work, its silences and its images, is made in dialogue with the land. To borrow a phrase of Aboriginal protest about land rights: 'This land always was, and always will be, Aboriginal land.' Our nation is a black nation and we walk on black land, specifically Darug[9] land in the case of *The Fence*. For me *The Fence* was very much about the ancestors of the area being in the audience. Indeed, I always felt that it was crowded land and to be honest, I'm not sure that it was the right piece of land. I'm not sure that we were strong enough to be on it. But I think that was my problem. I probably should have checked more deeply with elders and knowledge holders before deciding on the site. I always ask and abide by protocol and for *The Fence* I went through about two years of asking, but perhaps I still didn't ask or more importantly, didn't listen enough.

Caroline   Beyond that land or atop it, there is the institution too, looming large in the background.

Alicia   Yes, that is very important. Here we are in front of an institution that housed children or to which they were committed. That's why, even though we are talking about it at last, that location – that institution – is in fact the first testimony for me. This is the area where Pemulwuy[10] fought, where convict women and children were held. This is where children were confined in the Roman Catholic Orphan School and then at Parramatta Girls' Home. In fact, one of our consultants was institutionalized in that very building. That's why the journey to the site is so important: it reminds the audience that this is not fantastical, this is real. The building is real, the air is real, the moon is real, the wind is real.

Caroline   So both the institution and its surrounds are real and yet, of course, the house is not.

Alicia   The house is obviously not real and this reinforces the duality or the theatricality of the situation. By the time you arrive at a seating bank, you know you're at the theatre, there's a real-looking house placed artificially. The next artificial level is that it's fourth-wall theatre, in the sense that there's no direct address. But at some point in the night the dramaturgical framework collapses, the trappings of theatre recede and the ritual of witnessing takes over. In this, the whole set up reveals itself as an elaborate, expensive, time and resource-intensive process to have a bare moment of testimony. But that's the whole point of the work, for the audience to witness a story, silence, song or site, as you put it, which opens our minds to the fact that life can be different.

Notes

1   For more information on Urban Theatre Projects, see the company website at: www.urbantheatre.com.au.
2   For more information on Talbot's time at Urban Theatre Projects, see Caroline Wake's Archive Highlight in *RealTime* arts magazine: www. realtimearts.net/feature/Archive_Highlights/9732 (accessed 1 July 2013). For an account of *The Longest Night* and *Back Home*, see Celina McEwen, 'An Empowering Practice?: Urban Theatre Projects' Recent Work in Residence, Community Cultural Development and International Arts Festivals', *Australasian Drama Studies* 50 (2007), pp. 123–37.
3   See for instance, Alex Lalak, 'Big Issues without Being Preachy', *Daily Telegraph*, 18 January 2010, p. 38; John McCallum, 'At Home with the Misfits', *The Australian*, 18 January 2010, p. 14; Lloyd Bradford Skye, '*The Fence*: Urban Theatre Projects', *Australian Stage Online*, 15 January 2010, www.australianstage.com.au/201001153111/reviews/sydney-festival/the-fence-%7C-urban-theatre-projects.html (accessed 26 August 2012).
4   Tim Etchells, *Certain Fragments: Contemporary Performance and Forced Entertainment* (London: Routledge, 1999), p. 17.
5   Caroline Wake, 'Home Is Where the Hurt Is: Urban Theatre Projects, *The Fence*, Sydney Festival', *RealTime* 95 (2010), p. 16. www.realtimearts.net/article/95/9741 (accessed 1 July 2013).
6   Urban Theatre Projects, *The Fence: Partners Report* (2010), unpublished.
7   Urban Theatre Projects, *The Fence: Community Consultant Interviews* (2009), unpublished.
8   Urban Theatre Projects, *The Fence: Partners Report* (2010), unpublished.
9   Darug signifies a people, a language and a country. Sometimes it is also spelled Dharug, which indicates that the speaker is from the same language group but a different clan. We use the former spelling here based on the advice of Lily Shearer and Aunty Edna Watson. For further information see the recently archived Darug Tribal Aboriginal Corporation's webpage: http://web.archive.org/web/20100303171654/http://www.darug.org.au/main.html (accessed 1 July 2013).
10   Pemulwuy (c.1750–1802) was an Aboriginal warrior, who led the resistance to the British occupation of the Sydney area. For more information see his entry in the Australian Dictionary of Biography: http://adb.anu.edu.au/biography/pemulwuy-13147 (accessed 1 July 2013).

The Fence

Urban Theatre Projects

Performance text of *The Fence* transcribed by Alicia Talbot, Raimondo Cortese and Lina Kastoumis in 2012 and 2013

Characters:

Mel:　43, Indigenous-Australian, husband of Joy, used to be a footy player but has padded out over the years. Hard-working man who is proud of his home and his shed. Works for the local council.

Joy:　46, Anglo Australian, wife of Mel, broad Australian accent, manages the bar at the local club. Joy still looks good for her age, she loves a post-work drink and a good time.

Chris:　42, Indigenous-Australian, Mel's best friend from work who is childlike, a bit of a drifter. He is having troubles at home with his own missus.

Lou:　44, Greek-Australian, Joy's best friend of 25 years. Full of energy, larger than life, though insecure of her looks, dwindling romantic prospects and ageing.

Connie:　45, Indigenous-Australian, Mel's estranged sister. Hypersensitive and cantankerous, Connie is not comfortable in a social setting.

Music: 'In the Colours' by Ben Harper & The Innocent Criminals plays as the audience arrives and settles into the outdoor site. It is early evening. Dinnertime, on a summer night in western Sydney.

Looking down from the raked seating, we see a structure that looks like the realistic back of a modest fibro suburban house. Dollhouse-like, with its entire back external wall removed, we see a furnished open-plan kitchen and dining area, a lounge room and a hallway that leads to the imagined bathroom and bedrooms. A set of steps connects the house to the backyard and represents the back door of the house. To the left, the audience sees an old timber garden bench sitting behind a rusty oil drum that contains a steadily burning log fire. To the right is a wooden outdoor table and plastic chairs. Set further back to the left of the house, sits a prefabricated steel garden shed with a stool near the doorway. A plastic banana-lounge chair lies in the foreground of the shed.

Joy, shoes off, though still in work clothes, is in the kitchen preparing dinner while half-watching the TV in the lounge. Mel is outside sanding down the garden bench, stopping only to stoke the fire in the oil drum. Joy moves to the steps and looks out to Mel.

Joy   Dinner's nearly ready luv.

Mel   Coming.

Joy   You wanna eat in or out?

(*Mel looks up at the sky, there are threatening clouds.*)

Mel   Inside.

(*Joy goes back into the house, grabs her plate and sits on the coach, watching TV and eating. We catch a glimpse of another woman, in a dressing robe, on a mobile phone and moving briefly between the doors of the hallway. Outside, Mel soon finishes working on the bench and comes into the house, going to the bathroom first to clean himself up, before collecting his dinner from the kitchen bench.*)

Mel   This one babe?

Joy   Yeah.

(*Mel prepares his food. Joy continues watching TV.*)

Joy   Oh look! This is what I want. One of those . . .

(*Mel joins her on the couch.*)

Joy   Hey guess who came into work today?

Mel   Who babe?

Joy   Vanessa and Collin.

Mel   Vanessa! Man . . . she's hot.

(*Joy gets up, goes to the hallway and calls out. Music fades.*)

Joy   Lou? Lou? Oh, she's on the phone again. (*She goes to the kitchen and potters about*) Vanessa said they went up to Noosa for their honeymoon.

She said they went at it like rabbits for two weeks . . . They loved it!

Mel   You know Collin? He's a dirty old prick. You know he's on Viagra, luv?

Joy   He's ninety-years-old, darl!

Mel   Hey I still wanna be doing it when I'm ninety, love.

Joy   Mel . . . you get a ring on this finger then you might be in with a shot, luv.

Mel   Yeah.

(*Lou enters crying.*)

Joy   Oh Lou what? What is it luv? What? What?

(*Joy hugs Lou.*)

Lou   I was talking to Ron, Joy . . . I miss him.

Joy   I know.

Lou   He told me I was too fat.

Joy   He is a dickhead. Mel, did you hear that?

Mel   What?

Joy   Ron said she was too fat.

Mel   So? She is.

Lou   (*Startles.*)

Joy   Oh Lou! . . . Lou . . . (*Lou exits tearfully*) Oh why would you say that?! (*Joy sits on the couch again and resumes eating*) She's just broken up with her fella and you say she's too fat. You don't say that.

Mel   Luv, we sit here and talk about her weight all the time.

Joy   How would you like it if someone said you were fat?

Mel   I'm not.

Joy   (*Pointing to Mel's stomach bulge*) Well, what is that?

Mel   My guts.

Joy   (*After a pause, playfully*) You have food in your beard.

Mel   Want some?

Joy   No, that's not what I want for desert . . . Nooo!

Mel   Go on.

Joy   Nooo! . . . No.

(*Chris crosses the front lawn and enters the house.*)

Chris   Hey, what's for dinner?

Mel   G'day.

Joy   Hi Chris. (*To Mel*) You're bad!

(*Chris throws his hat down, then puts a sixpack of beer in fridge. He pours orange juice into a mug and sits on the floor in front of the TV.*)

Joy   You right there for a drink mate?

Chris   I got one thanks Joy.

Mel   Lou! Lou can you come out here please?

Joy   You want a feed mate?

(*Joy gets up and gives Chris a gentle kick on the bottom as she walks past him towards the kitchen. Meanwhile, outside, Connie has arrived in the back yard and stands near the tables and chairs, in darkness.*)

Chris   Yes thanks, I'm starving.

Mel   Lou! I'm really sorry Lou . . . I am.

Joy   (*Offering food*) You want this Lou?

Lou shakes her head.

Joy   Here you are.

(*She gives a plate of food to Chris.*)

Chris   Oh thank you. (*Chris wolfs down the food*)

Lou   I don't know why I keep attracting the same men Joy? Do you think it's my vibes? Do you think it's the way I talk? The way I dress?

Joy   I think it's their loss.

Lou   Maybe I shouldn't sleep with them on the first night?

Joy   It's not a bad idea. You could try it.

Mel   Luv there's something wrong with this bloody remote. I'm gonna smash this thing in a minute.

(*Joy goes and checks it.*)

Joy   Oh Jesus, it's not even the remote.

Lou   You know I called him a jerk?

Joy   Good on you.

Lou   I don't know why he keeps putting me down like that. He's no oil painting.

Joy   Yeah, well you can say that again.

Lou   He's a great root though.

Joy   Was he? Better than Adam?

Lou   Way better than Adam!

Joy   Oh yes!

(*They laugh. Joy fixes the TV. Lou makes a call.*)

Joy   There.

Lou   (*On the phone*) Mum . . . Yeah, she's not allowed to do that. (*Lou exits via the hallway.*)

Joy   Leave it on channel one. Don't change it! I told you that many times.

Mel   Yeah yeah.

(*Joy gets a bottle of wine from the fridge. Connie is still outside in the dark.*)

(*After some time, she pulls out her mobile and makes a call. A phone rings inside the house.*)

Mel   Where's my phone darl?

Joy   Oh I don't know!

(*Mel searches around and pulls his phone out of the folds of the couch.*)

Mel   Yeah.

Connie   You took your time.

(*Mel, quietly stunned, sneaks a look across the room at Joy, who is oblivious.*)

Mel   Where are you?

Connie   Get off the couch and take a look in the backyard.

(*Mel gets up slowly, takes his plate to the kitchen bench and moves to the back step. He sees Connie, descends the steps and stops. Mel and Connie look at each other from a distance. After an awkward approach, they hug.*)

Mel   Jeez you're skinny girl.

Connie   Well you're not!

Mel   Your hair's grown. So where you been, sis?

Connie   (*After a pause*) Oh, I'm here now, eh? That's what counts.

Mel   Yeah. You want to come inside?

Connie   No no . . . I'm right here.

Mel   What about a drink? You want a beer?

Connie   Yeah . . .

(*Mel makes his way back up the steps into the house.*)

(*Mock threateningly*) None of that light shit, alright!

(*Mel goes to the fridge and grabs a beer, he doesn't look at Joy as he passes her on his way out.*)

Mel   Connie's here.

Joy   What?!

Mel   Connie . . . she's outside.

(*Joy, shocked at first, but now concerned as she goes to the doorstep to sneak a look at Connie. She sees Connie and exhales. Mel goes outside and gives Connie the beer.*)

Connie   Thanks. Where's yours?

(*Mel doesn't answer. Inside, Joy tidies herself up before she comes outside to the yard. Joy doesn't approach Connie, but stands at a distance, next to Mel.*)

Joy   Hello.

Connie   Oh G'day.

(*An awkward pause. There is an unease between Joy and Connie.*)

Connie   Oh I really like what you've done to the backyard.

Joy   Mel's done it.

Mel   Do you want a feed or something, sis?

Connie   Yeah, that would be nice thanks.

Joy   Alright I'll get it.

Connie   If it's not too much trouble.

Joy   (*Cutting in*) No! No.

(*Turns her back and is up the steps and back in the kitchen.*)

Connie   I don't want to put you out or anything.

Mel   No, you're right sis . . . plenty there. Go on.

(*Connie approaches the doorstep and enters the house. Mel stays outside.*)

Joy   Chris, this is Mel's sister, Connie. (*Chris looks up briefly then goes back to his footy match on TV.*) Chris! (*He startles*) Get up off the couch and let her sit down. Can you turn that off please?

(*Chris gets off the couch, turns off the TV and goes outside. Lou comes out from the hallway drinking a glass of wine. Connie sits on the couch.*)

Lou   Connie! Oh my god.

Connie   Hi Lou.

Lou   You look good.

(*Mel makes his way back into the house and stands silently at the kitchen bench as Joy takes Connie a plate of food. Lou joins Connie on the couch.*)

Connie   Thanks.

Lou   Where have you been?

Connie   Here and there. Up North mainly.

Joy   How far up North?

Connie   Far enough.

Mel   So where you staying sis?

Connie   Between places at the moment.

Mel   Have you got a boyfriend yet?

Connie   Wouldn't you like to know? (*She chuckles dismissively then turns to Lou.*)

So how old is Chloe?

Lou   She's fourteen. She's in year nine.

(*Mel goes outside to the fireplace where Chris is sitting.*)

(*The dialogue between Connie and Lou in the lounge overlaps with the dialogue between Mel and Chris out by the fire.*)

Chris   Is that your sister?

Mel   Yeah.

Connie   What do they do at that age?

Lou   They're very cheeky.

Mel   Haven't seen her in ages, eh?

Chris   Well, where she been?

Mel   Dunno.

Connie   Does she look like you?

Lou   No she looks like her father . . . arsehole!

*(*Joy goes outside to Mel and Chris.*)

Joy   What are you doing out here? Your sister has just arrived. Don't you think it's rude? Oh come on Mel! . . . I'm gonna go and get changed.

(*She goes back inside.*)

Chris   It's put Joy in a bit of a pickle, bud.

Mel   Yeah. Well Joy and Connie don't see eye to eye on a few things, do they?

Lou   So what are the men like up North?

Connie   Pretty much like men anywhere else I guess.

Lou   It's not what I've heard.

(*Mel goes to the side of the house. He returns with more firewood and tends to the fire.*)

Mel   Hey! You shoulda seen Ten-To-Two and Alfie go at it today. Ten-To-Two said something to Alfie . . . so Alfie picks up a bit of wood and threw it at him . . . and just missed his head, boy.

Chris   They're a pair of ratbags. They're gonna end up hurting each other one day.

Mel   Nah man, weak as piss, the pair of them.

(*Inside, Connie is looking at photos on the lounge room wall.*)

Connie   When was this one taken?

Lou   Years ago. Joy and I did a ceramics course at TAFE together (*Calling out*)

Hey, Joy! It was a ceramics course we did at TAFE together?

Connie   I hardly recognised you, you know.

Lou   Oh, I've lost a lot of weight since then.

Mel   Sis! Come out here.

Connie   Hang on! I'm just catching up with Lou.

Mel   Ah plenty of time for that.

Connie   I'm coming.

(*Connie goes to the doorstep and watches Mel briefly as he resumes work on the garden bench. She steps out onto the yard.*)

Connie   Ah it looks about ready for the tip, wouldn't you say? Ah, come on! It's rusted right through!

(*Chris passes her on his way back into the house. On route to the fridge.*)

Chris   It's rustic.

Connie   It couldn't support my weight let alone yours. Where'd you get it anyway?

(*Mel is tinkering away in the garden shed.*)

Mel   Found it at a rubbish chuck-out . . . on the side of the road.

Connie   Some things never change.

Mel   Eh?

Connie   I said . . . And I bet you that shed is full of shit as well!

Mel   Yep! My shit, sis. You stay out of here.

Connie   Oh, is that right?

(*Connie approaches Mel playfully and they begin a physical yet childlike tussle in front of the shed. Meanwhile Chris, at the kitchen bench, is grazing on leftovers and having a beer.*)

Lou   I'm worried about Chloe.

Chris   Who?

Lou   Chloe . . . she's my daughter.

Chris   Well what are you worried about?

Lou   You know she's fourteen . . . back chatting . . . picking up boys and partying.

Chris   Least she's fourteen. What were you thinking of when you were fourteen?

Lou   That's what I'm worried about!

Chris   You wanna do what we do. You wanna get one of them boys and mould them into what you need.

(*Chris takes the newspaper from the dining table and heads back outside.*)

Lou   You got kids?

Chris   I've got two daughters.

(*Chris sits on the steps with his beer and newspaper and lights a cigarette.*)

(*Mel and Connie have finished their tussle.*)

Mel   Here sis, make me another cup of tea, please?

Connie How do you take it?

Mel Like my woman . . . white and sweet.

(*Mel hands her his mug, Connie shakes her head and goes inside.*)

Connie Put a cuppa on, eh Lou?

(*Connie sits on the couch, Joy passes her as she carries a bowl of nuts outside and sits at the garden table.*)

Chris Looks like Brother Boy might have to fight the way it's going.

Mel What? The fight back on, bro?

Chris Yeah.

Mel I thought you said it was cancelled.

Chris Well it's been rescheduled, Mel.

Mel He had to lose three kilos didn't he?

Chris He's gonna fight at middle-weight.

Mel What about the title?

Chris He's gonna fight for that in Japan. If he can win them titles dropping in weight, he will be the first man in history to do it.

Mel Yeah?

Chris Affect his rankage, that fight.

Joy Mel, can you pass me a hammer, luv?

(*Inside, Connie is now at the dining table looking at photos with Lou.*)

Connie She does look like her father doesn't she?

Joy (*To Chris*) It's really nice to hear you talking about your family.

(*Mel comes back from the shed and gives Joy a hammer.*)

Joy I don't mean to butt in, but that's your sister in there.

Mel Yeah. She's talking to Lou babe.

(*Mel goes inside*)

Mel Where's my cuppa tea sis?

Connie Oh come on! The kettle's still boiling.

Joy You want a nut, Chris?

Chris   Nah.

Joy   Why are you here Chris? Why aren't you at home shagging your missus?

Chris   Listen, what's all this water under the bridge between you and Connie anyway?

Joy   I don't think that's really any of your business.

(*Lou comes outside with her wine and joins Joy and Chris at the table.*)

Lou   Am I interrupting anything?

Joy   No.

Chris   No.

Joy   (*To Lou*) I was just asking him why he's always here and not at home with his wife. (*To Chris*) Do you still find her attractive?

Chris   (*Laughs*) Yeah.

Lou   Are you sick of her?

Chris   No.

Lou   We're women Chris, we talk about these things.

Connie   (*Calling out from the dining table*) Not all women talk about those things, Lou!

Lou   You know what your problem is? You don't know women enough.

Chris   (*Chuckling*) No.

Connie   Your kind of woman.

Lou   (*Laughs*) And what kind of woman is that?

Connie   I'm just saying . . . not all women are the same.

Chris   Yeah look, good-looking women . . . Joy, why did you have to bring them two into it? Now the whole world is gonna know.

Joy   Oh the whole world! I'm just asking what attracted you to her in the first place. Maybe you just need to nurture it a bit.

Lou   Court her again!

Connie   You're badgering the man.

Lou   Date her again.

Joy   (*Laughing with Lou*) I can tell you a couple of things she might like.

Connie   If it's over, it's over . . . just cut the cord mate, one time.

(*Connie comes outside and stands on the step.*)

Joy   I don't think that's actually right Connie. I think he needs to work at it.

Lou   (*To Chris*) Oil! . . . massage . . . candle light.

Joy   (*To Connie*) I'm not sure you've had a whole lot of experience either, have you?

Connie   That's making a very wild assumption there, Joy.

Lou   We're just helping the man put some magic back into the relationship.

Chris   Tryna get me to work a bit harder.

Connie   I know just how it is mate. You just want some space . . . for a bit of peace, ya know? . . . some perspective.

(*Connie follows Chris as he gets up and heads towards the shed. Mel watches from the kitchen window.*)

Mel   Hey sis! . . . don't you go in my shed!

(*Joy and Lou are talking quietly but laughing loudly.*)

Chris   I'm guarding it!

Mel   Guarding it!

Connie   Like you can stop me.

Chris   Mel! Mel!

(*Connie looks in the shed. Joy and Lou laugh.*)

Connie   Now I know all your secrets, eh bub!

Mel   I told ya so.

Connie   What's with all them titty mags anyway?

Mel   Ah Joy won't let me have any in the bloody house!

Connie   I don't blame her.

(*Mel is at the stereo near the couch. He puts on a record. Music: We hear*

'The Joker' by The Steve Miller Band. Mel begins dancing and singing along to the music.)

Joy   (*Calling out to Mel*) Hey good choice babe! Hey, what was that guy's name? The one . . . you remember . . . the one that . . . you know that one?

(Joy and Lou are now tipsy, laughing and on their feet, dancing slowly to the music. Connie is on the garden bench moving jerkily to the music, in her own world.)

Lou   The guy I rooted in a tree!

Joy   Yeah what happened to him?

Lou   Yeah guys root anyone . . . anytime . . . anywhere, Joy.

Joy   Not my Mel.

Lou   You're lucky.

Joy   I'm-a-lucky!

Lou   I've got my eye on someone else though.

Joy   Do I know him?

Lou   Yeah.

Joy   Not the one with the frizzy hair? Oh my god, have you seen the size of his hands?

Lou   Have you seen the size of his . . .?

(Joy covers Lou's mouth to prevent her from speaking.)

Joy   No and neither have you, ya liar!!

Joy and Lou crack up laughing again. They continue dancing to the music. Connie gets up from the bench and goes back into the house continuing her dance as Mel launches into some seated 'air guitar' during the songs' lead break. Chris goes back inside to get another beer. Connie playfully spooks him at the fridge then moves across to dance with Mel in the lounge room. Chris goes back out to the yard, moving to the song as he drinks his beer near the fire. He sits on the bench, Lou dances seductively around him before she joins him. Mel and Joy are now slow-dancing in the kitchen together and Connie, who was dancing by herself in the lounge, pauses to stare at them as she goes out to the yard again. Joy has gone to her bedroom. Lou and Chris are on the bench falling about laughing at Connie dancing. Nonplussed, Connie goes and sits in front of the shed. Mel, singing the final strains of the song before it fades, comes outside and joins her.

Mel Hey sis.

Connie Yeah.

Mel You remember that place you took me to, that old shack?

Connie (*Annoyed*) What are you talking about?

(*Connie moves away from the shed and opens the banana-lounge chair to sit on it.*)

Mel I can remember things that happened twenty years ago. I don't remember things that happened five years ago!

Connie (*Connie smiles*) Age . . . You can still see the watermarks from the fifty-two floods. Famous ones I think . . . mostly dried up riverbeds now though.

Mel Who owns that place?

Connie Dunno. Ya'know . . . when I go overseas, I'm an alien . . . But when I come back here, it just feels different, ya'know?

Mel Yeah well, I belong here sis.

Connie Yeah, you probably do.

Mel I know I do. Why? Don't you feel that way?

Connie Who says I don't? Look if you belong here . . . then I belong here . . . but doesn't mean I have to stay here.

Mel Nup. If you did, you know I'd have to build on another bloody room! You know that, eh?

Connie (*Laughs*) I wouldn't be able to close my eyes for the fear that the bloody thing would cave in! Nah . . . it's best that I just come to visit . . . keeps it special.

Besides . . . you'd get sick of me.

Mel No I wouldn't.

Connie Yes you would (*Softly*) Yeah you would . . . (*After a pause*) You know I got some ochre in my bag . . . from country.

Mel Ochre?

Connie Not much . . . just a little bit. I take it with me wherever I go. Just enough to get through customs. You won't dob on me will ya?

Mel   No.

Connie   Good.

Mel   Can I have some sis?

Connie   Maybe.

(*During this dialogue Chris sits on the lounge room floor with a guitar and strums away softly. Mel goes back inside and sits on the couch.*)

Mel   Sing a song for me Chris.

(*Music: Chris strums and sings 'Do You Remember?' throughout the following dialogue. Lou is in the kitchen putting on make-up. Joy comes out from the bedroom and bends over the couch to plant a kiss on Mel before she starts dancing slowly for him. Connie sits at the dining table and watches Lou put on her makeup. After some time.*)

Lou   I'm gonna go out!

Joy   Are you? It's pretty late!

Lou   (*Shrugs. After a pause, Connie jumps up.*)

Connie   You know what? I'm gonna go out as well.

Lou   Great!

Connie   Oh come on – you only live once, eh?

Joy   You're kidding.

Connie   Do I look alright?

Lou   I've got just the dress! . . . it'll look great on you, Connie.

Connie   Oh I don't know Lou. No offence or anything . . .

Lou   Trust me! Come on . . . Come on!

(*Lou grabs Connie by the hand and drags her away to get ready, stopping to announce to Mel and Joy.*)

Lou   I'm gonna go find me a man!

Connie   I'm gonna watch her find a man!

Lou   *Chuckles as she leads Connie into the bedroom.*

Joy   Hey come out and show us what you're wearing!

(*Some time passes, Chris continues with his song as Mel and Joy sit, cuddling on the couch. Suddenly, Connie comes out wearing a baggy white dress with red flowers on it.)*

Connie   Don't say anything!

Joy   Hey it looks good! It looks really good.

Connie   You're bullshitting me . . . right?

Joy   No . . .

Mel   Nah! That looks deadly sis.

Connie   Oh! Did you pay him to say that?

Joy   Course not.

Mel   What?

Connie   *(To Mel)* Who asked you anyway? No, it's not up for discussion.

Joy   *(Disbelieving)* What?

Mel   Connie!?

(Connie leaves and goes back into the bedroom. Chris stops playing guitar.)

Joy   Nooo! Hey I'm gonna go out with them. No, no it'll be fun it'll be fun.

Mel   No, no what do you mean?

Joy   *(She laughs and gets up off the couch)* It'll be good. *(She goes to the bedroom calling out to Lou and Connie)* Hey I'm comin out!

Lou   *(Off)* Woo-hoo! Get some lipstick.

Joy   Yeah lipstick . . . lipstick.

Lou   *(Coming out from the bedroom in just trousers and a bra)* Joy, which one do you think – this one or this one?

(Lou holds up two dresses)

Joy   Oh Jesus Lou . . . put them away! . . . *(To Mel)* . . . the pervert here, god!

(Chris sits on the steps and lights a cigarette.)

Mel   *(Chuckling)* Are you going out too, Chris?

Chris   No way! Lou's insatiable!

Mel   Someone needs to look after these bloody women!

Chris   And who's gonna look after the men, Mel!

(*Mel joins Chris on the steps they smoke as some time passes.*)

Chris   You know I wanna get back into them hills and work tomorrow.

Mel   Stay away from there, Chris.

Chris   Why?

Mel   That place is poison, brother. Just stay away from there, OK?

(*Chris throws his beer bottle lid onto the lawn.*)

Mel   Eh! Pick that up please! And don't you go throwing it in the bloody fire either.

(*Chris gets off the steps to pick it up and grabs his foot in pain.*)

Mel   What was that?

Chris   Prickles!

Mel   What?

Chris   Prickles . . . they're everywhere.

Mel   Bullshit! Where the bloody hell did they come from?

Chris   Well they're not coming from the birds, Mel. You're gonna have to get Joy to clean your boots properly.

Mel   Do you want to say that louder so she can hear? Joy!

Chris   Eh, c'mon, eh!

Joy   (*Off*) What?

Chris   (*Pleading*) It's chicken casserole tomorrow night!

Mel   (*Reconsiders*) . . . I love this lawn nearly as much as I love you, luv!

(*Connie comes out dressed in a simple long maroon dress, deflated. Lou and Joy follow her out.*)

Connie   Nah I'm not going. I feel like mutton dressed as lamb.

Lou   Oh come on Connie!

Joy   You look good.

Lou   You look fantastic Connie.

Connie   You're deluded.

Joy   You're just out of practice. It's just like riding a horse luv, you just gotta get back on.

Connie   I don't think I was ever on the horse.

Joy   What was that guy's name? The one you used to . . .?

Lou   Tony Tucci!

Joy   Yeah Tony Tucci yeah . . .

Lou   I remember Tony Tucci.

Connie   He was so hairy we used to think he was the missing link. Oh he had a hairy crack and everything. It was disgusting.

Lou   I need a wax!

Joy   (*To Connie*) She has the whole lot . . . the Brazilian.

Lou   No, Sunset Strip.

Joy   Yeah, Sunset Strip

Mel   Keep it down in there!

Connie   Just thinking about it makes my eyes water.

Mel   Sis! Shame! The whole bloody block can hear you!

Connie   But it wasn't me. See!

Lou   So what are we doing girls? Where are we going?

Joy   I don't know, what do you reckon?

Connie   Oh the moment's past!

Joy   Oh come on Connie!

Lou   I'm dressed to kill!

Joy   Yeah . . .

Connie   I can't pretend to be something I'm not.

Lou   Come on Connie.

(*Connie heads towards the bedroom.*)

Joy   Where are you going?

Connie   I'm gonna take this clap-trap off. Sorry girls.

Lou   You party pooper! Where's your zest for life?

Connie   (*Off*) Sorry.

Lou   (*Combing her hair*) Come on Joy . . . Hurry up, it's you and me babe.

Joy   Oh . . . I don't know.

Lou   What?

Joy   (*Pours herself a glass of wine and sits at the dining table*) I don't know.

Lou   Come on Joy.

Joy   Look I might stay in I think. Yeah.

Lou   I'll never find a man.

(*Lou walks to the couch, takes off her scarf and lies on the couch with her glass of wine. Some time passes.*)

Lou   I wanna have a baby.

Joy   What?

Lou   I wanna have another baby. I love babies.

Joy   You're pissed, Lou.

Lou   (*Laughing*) Do I look pissed?

Joy   Yes, you do . . . and it's mission impossible baby anyway, because you're too old.

Lou   I'm not too old!

Joy   You're forty-five.

Lou   I'm forty-four.

Joy   Lou! You're forty-five in three weeks.

(*Lou gets up off the couch and heads towards the kitchen.*)

Lou   In my culture women have babies right up to their fifties. In fact I've got an auntie who had her last baby at fifty-three.

Joy   I bet there was something wrong with it.

Lou   No!. . . It was a perfectly happy . . . burping . . . farting . . . spewing little baby.

Joy   Oh oh yuk please . . . hey, yuk . . . jesus.

Lou   (*Chuckling*) I'm ovulating now.

(*Lou pours another glass of wine.*)

Joy   Ah Lou, it's too much information. Tell Connie.

(*Connie emerges from the bedroom, back in her own clothing, holding her shoes.*)

Connie   No! No! Keep me out of it!. . . (*She sits at the dining table, time passes*). Allright, go on then.

Lou   I wanna have a baby.

Connie   That's ridiculous. You can't even run around the house.

(*Joy laughs.*)

Lou   You don't have to be a marathon runner to have a baby, Connie.

Connie   Yeah but you gotta have some level of fitness.

Lou   We're women . . . we have a uterus and ovaries . . . we're meant to reproduce.

Joy   Oh Lou! You sound exactly like your mother.

Lou   I'm not like my mother.

Joy   You are.

Lou   (*Laughing*) I'm not like my mother – Thank you very much!

Joy   You are so, so old fashioned . . . that . . . have a uterus, have to have a baby stuff.

Connie   You're like a throw back to the fifties

(*Lou is laughing*). Pardon? No personally I'm all for zero population growth myself.

Joy   God, we agree on something! I reckon there's plenty of women who should never have had kids. My mother for starters . . . and most of the homies I grew up with . . . their parents . . . Jesus!

Connie   Oh come on, the parents weren't all that bad.

Joy   No some of them aren't.

Connie   Nobody has kids thinking they 're gonna give them up.

Joy   Well that's not what I'm saying.

Lou   You'd make a great mum, Joy.

(*Connie joins Joy on the couch.*)

Joy   Ah seriously Lou . . . you are pissed and you should go to bed.

Connie   Nah but she's got a point. Oh come on. We didn't turn out all that bad did we?

Joy   No I didn't actually . . . I turned out alright. You're pretty fucked up though!

(*They all break into laughter.*) No we did good . . . we did good . . . considering how fucked up our parents were . . . we did good.

Connie   What do you mean 'our parents'?

Joy   I mean, some women should not have babies.

(*Connie jumps up from the couch.*)

Connie   Nah! Nah! Speak for yourself! Don't speak about my mother. My mother loved me.

Joy   Oh I never said she didn't love you . . . but it was no bed of roses, was it?

Connie   What would you know about my family?

Joy   I know . . . I have lived with Mel for twenty years.

Connie   What would he know? He was too young . . . he romanticises everything.

Joy   He was there.

Connie   He was not.

Joy   What? Oh you're living in some kind of denial Connie.

Lou   Girls . . . calm down.

Connie   He's not stupid and neither am I.

Joy   I never said you were stupid.

Connie   After nine years in a home . . . 'Number 184' doesn't need a mouth piece, thanks!

Joy   I don't want to talk about it.

Lou   Calm down girls.

Connie   You know what . . .? You wanna learn to keep your mouth shut.

(*Connie goes out to the yard. Joy jumps up from the couch and shouts after her.*)

Joy   Don't you speak to me like that in my house!

Lou   Joy . . .

Joy   (*To Lou*) You have no idea.

Lou   Connie . . .

Lou joins Connie outside

Connie   No, that was your fault in there. Babies? What were you thinking? You know she is a loose cannon when it comes to things like that! I pegged you for a smart woman. If I didn't know any better, I would've sworn you engineered this. It took us so long to get this far. How can I go back inside now, eh?

Lou   Well come inside with me and we can talk about this together. Please.

Connie   No. You go back inside and fix it!

(*Lou is crying as she ascends the steps.*)

Lou   I'm sorry.

(*Connie won't look at Lou, she has her back turned. Lou goes into the bedroom after Joy. Mel comes out of the shed and approaches the side of the house and stands by the fire.*)

Mel   What's going on, Sis?

Connie   Joy and I had a blue. Oh it was like ten years had come and gone in one fell swoop. You gotta give me points for trying . . . It's like you and her, or you and me. I'm not the same person I was ten years ago. (*Mel sighs and goes back into the shed*) I just think you'll choose her.

(*A couple of beats later, Mel begins to play his didgeridoo in the shed.*)

Connie walks off to the right of the house. The lighting appears darker now, the night is no longer young. Lou is in the hallway and is drawn outside by the sound of the didgeridoo. She approaches the shed and watches Mel. Transfixed, Lou begins to dance a slow circular dance, raising her arms and moving in time with the didgeridoo as it becomes faster paced. While this is happening: Connie is in the darkened empty field on the right hand side of the audience, dancing her own dance. Chris walks to and fro in a line alongside the left-hand edge of house. Joy comes out from the bedroom, sits on the couch and watches a mute TV. Mel finishes playing. The live didgeridoo is replaced by an ambient soundscape. Lou sits on the bench outside the shed, Chris sits close-by, on the banana-lounge. Mel enters the house, walking past Joy as he goes to the bedroom. Connie comes back, walks up the steps, sees Joy on the couch and decides to not enter the house. She sits on the steps, wrapping her arms around her lowered head.

Lou   I loved what you were playing earlier.

Chris   Yeah, thanks Lou.

Lou   You got a really nice voice.

(*Lou is off the bench and crawling across the grass slowly towards Chris.*)

Chris   Ta.

Lou   Is it an original?

Chris   Yeah I know about a hundred songs but I can only play my own, eh.

Lou   Well I think you should get it published.

Chris   (*Chuckles*) Yeah right!. . . What. .? Minor third to the fifth to the major seventh . . . What . . .? Get Carlos Santana to play one of my songs? I wouldn't have to get off my arse for the rest of my life . . . Please!

Lou   You got a better voice though.

Chris   Yeah right. (*Some time passes*) You want a drink Lou?

(*Lou nods. Chris gets up and goes back into the house, opens the fridge, grabs a beer, pulls down a wine glass. He starts watching the TV, sitting on a kitchen stool as he opens his beer. Joy is still on the couch, also watching the TV.*)

Joy   Shouldn't you go home Chris?

Chris   You try living with three women Joy. I don't know how to live with a family. It doesn't matter what I say . . . she's not going to listen. I don't have a say in my own home.

Joy   Oh come on . . .

Chris   My own mother put us in a home, alright? Then right before
I turned fourteen she kicked me out. How am I meant to have skills to
raise kids . . .? Least of all daughters?

Joy   I know it does your head in doesn't it?. . . I know.

Chris   Totally. Everyday I wake up and think about it. Completely
dwells. I'm just stopping my insides from fraying. I'm a nervous wreck
from it. The other day I went to your fridge and smelt milk . . . next thing
you know, I'm waiting in line . . . for porridge! . . . I don't know how
many times I've nearly got my head stuck in your freezer.

Joy   (*Absently*) Yeah I know what you mean.

(*Joy gets up off the couch and goes into the kitchen*).

Chris   Yeah sorry for bringing it up. I don't mean to bring it up.

Joy   It's ok! (*Joy sighs*)

Chris   Are we ok? Am I all right? How do you know? I didn't know my
arsehole from my breakfast time. Got a lot of bad habits, Joy. They beat
the shit out of us. I didn't have time to catch my breath, let alone breathe.

Joy   Well I decided to put all that shit behind me. They got me. They
got my brother at six months. He can barely string two words together
but they aren't going to keep me down now.

Chris   Yeah, just gotta pull my socks up.

Joy   No! You need to go home to your family, Chris!

(*Chris quickly leaves the house and heads outside to join Lou.*)

Joy   (*Calling out loudly after him*) Go home!!

(*Mel appears in hallway*)

Lou   Hey, where's my drink?

Chris   Ah sorry . . . I forgot it.

Mel   (*To Joy*) Why you gotta talk to him like that for?

Joy   What?

Mel   Hm? Do I talk to your friends like that? Eh? Lou . . . do I talk to
you like that? You want me to start drinking again do ya? Then I'll be the
only one in this house.

(*Lou has made her way back into the house to get her own drink.*)

Lou   Hey! It's not Joy's fault that Chris is here . . .

Mel   (*Interrupting Lou*) Excuse me Lou! I'm talking to her, right?

Joy   How dare you come in here and speak to me like that! You're the one who's being rude. This is rude. This isn't about Chris. What's going on for you?

(*Mel goes outside to find Chris sitting in the shed.*)

Mel   Chris! Mate, I don't mind you coming over every now and then . . . but every night . . .

Joy   (*She yells out*) Tell him!

Mel   (*To Joy*) Will you shut up! I don't butt in when you're talking shit with your friends.

(*Music: We hear the song 'Hurt' by Johnny Cash, begin to play from inside the shed. Joy comes outside into the yard.*)

Joy   Is that what this is about? What . . .? There's three women in the house and you're not getting enough attention? I asked him a couple of questions. (*To Chris*) Hey Chris!. . . I said you should go home*!* (*To Mel*) What is wrong with you? Why can't you talk?

Mel   And you do?

Joy   Well why are you so angry?

Mel   (*Angrily*) How can't I be angry? You're always pissed. Lou's always in the room crying. You can't help but argue with Connie. And Chris is always here. I don't want to argue with you Joy.

(*Mel begins to walk away to the right hand side but stops by Joy and sits on the table instead.*)

Joy   You should be angry. You can be angry . . . but not with me. Not with the people who love you. I am not the enemy Mel. Well why did you choose me?

Mel   I thought we chose each other Joy.

Joy   Well we did but I don't want to be yelled at!

Mel   I never get to say the things I wanna say. I'm such a good boy.

Joy   Is this not what you want anymore?

Mel   It's all I want Joy. Don't you understand? When you get upset . . . it affects me! I didn't mean to take it out on you, OK?

Joy   Well I'm not perfect.

Mel   No one's perfect. No one's perfect.

(*We hear Chris, still in the shed, singing along to 'Hurt' by Johnny Cash. Connie is in the kitchen. Lou comes out of the bedroom to get a glass of water.*)

Lou   And you call us Greeks drama queens. I'm tired. I'm gonna go to bed.

Connie   Can you really imagine a baby being brought up here?

Lou   Maybe they're just too self indulgent to nurture a child Connie . . . to receive love . . . to receive love, Connie. No one in this household knows how to receive love.

Connie   No, we don't know how to do it. Does that make us indulgent?

Lou   Good night.

(*Lou goes back into the bedroom. Connie lies on the couch.*)

Connie   At least you can say I gave it a go.

(*Mel is sitting on the bench near the fire and Joy is at the outdoor table.*)

Joy   I am really trying here. You didn't tell me she was gonna to stay.

Mel   I didn't know she was coming, babe. She's my sister. What do you want me to do? Go tell her to sleep in the park?

Joy   Don't you remember what happened last time? . . . Well we've already started arguing. And I don't want it to happen again.

(*Joy goes back inside and sees Connie lying on the couch.*)

Joy   Can I get you anything?

Connie   No I'm right thanks. I have this theory . . . if I just keep perfectly still, we might all just relax.

(*Joy goes and gets a pillow from the bedroom and dumps it on the floor near Connie. Joy starts cleaning up the dishes, noisily.*)

Connie   You know what? I think I'll go.

Joy   What?

Connie   Oh don't worry about it . . . but I think I will go.

Joy   Oh God, I'm doing the dishes, Connie. I am tired and then I'm gonna go to bed.

Connie   That's not what I meant.

Joy   It'll take me five minutes. It's not like anyone else round here does 'em.

Connie   It's just that I can see you're upset and I don't want to make it any worse.

Joy   It's fine . . . I just can't put you in the spare room – I've got Lou in there. She's been in there for three days bawling her eyes out . . .

Connie   But it's not fine, is it?

Joy   Oh what do you want from me?

Connie   It's just that I see . . . I see I'm making you upset.

Joy   It's not like you got anywhere else to go, is it? No! So lie down. We're not going to put you out on the street, are we?

Connie   See? I knew it! I knew what you meant by the tone in your voice.

Joy   I don't want you to go . . . you're putting words in my mouth. You don't have anywhere else to go, do you? No. So lie down.

Connie   That was not a question.

Joy   What do you mean it's not a question? What does that exactly mean?

Connie   The tone in your voice . . .

Joy   It was not a question it was a statement!

Mel   (*Yells over to Joy and Connie*) Shut up!!

(*Joy stops arguing and goes outside to join Mel who is sitting on the bench. Joy bends over to hug him. Connie has come to the backstep and looks on, until she is noticed.*)

Joy   Connie . . . we have not seen or heard from you in ten years and you just show up.

Connie   You know what? You wanna open up the lines of communication with your man.

(*Connie comes down the steps.*)

Joy   Oh yeah . . . what does that mean?

Mel   Don't sis.

Connie   What . . .? So all of a sudden I'm the bad guy?

Joy   What does she mean? What?

Connie   Will you tell her? Or will I tell her?

Joy   Tell me what?

Mel   She loaned me some money, OK?. That's all. I just had to pay a debt off, babe. It's over . . . it's finished.

Joy   You're a liar.

Mel   No Joy.

(*Joy goes inside. Mel follows.*)

Mel   Come here babe. Come here.

Joy   You lied to me. You've been lying to me. You embarrass me.

Mel   Sorry.

Joy   What else have you been lying about?

Mel   Nothing.

Joy   What?!

Mel   Nothing.

Joy   Fuck she has been here for five minutes. I have been working at this for years.

Mel   Come on babe.

(*He tries to hold her. She becomes angrier and pushes him away.*)

Joy   You are fucking it Mel! Don't touch me!

Mel   Come on Joy.

Joy   You fucked it, Mel!

Mel   Come on babe.

Joy   You fucked it. Get out! Get out! Get out!

(*She throws a tea towel at him. Mel goes outside.*)

Mel   (*To Connie*) Are you happy now?!

Mel storms off towards the right and out of view. Lou comes out of the bedroom, picks up the tea towel and goes outside to find Mel. Chris has left the shed and sits behind the garden bench. Connie goes back inside the house.

Connie   (*Remorseful*) I am so sorry Joy. I didn't mean it to turn out like this.

Joy   I don't think you understand, Connie. He is all I have. He's the only family I have . . . He adores you. He idolises you Connie.

Outside, Chris starts playing clapping sticks and singing a powerful lament in Dharug language. In the distance, backlit by floodlights, Lou catches up with Mel, soothes him and brings him back into the yard. An agitated Mel sits at the table, watched over by Lou. Chris' song fades as an intense ambient soundtrack takes over. The lighting also seems dimmer as we enter deep night. Joy goes outside and joins Mel at the table. Lou leaves them alone. As Mel begins to talk, Chris gets up, goes back inside the house and lies on the couch, exhausted.

Mel   Joy, you keep taking the poison . . . wanting them to die. It's not your fault, babe. I feel your pain. You don't like to talk about it but I do understand. My mum was taken away. My nana was taken away. My nana's mum was locked up because she went looking for her. My sister . . . and you. I couldn't go through what you went through . . . I just couldn't.

Mel slowly reaches over for Joys' hand. Music: We hear 'Fruits of My Labour' sung by Lucinda Williams. Mel gently pulls Joy's arm across to him and kisses it. After a few beats, Joy retracts her arm playfully, Mel gets up and goes to the shed. Connie goes into the kitchen and is soon standing at the sink, moving to the music while patting out its' rhythm on her leg. Lou comes from the side of the house and goes inside. She starts looking for a lost earring and ends up on all fours, trying to retrieve it from under the couch. Chris is within reach and after watching her for a few moments, smacks her on the arse then gets up to lift the couch so that Lou can reach under it to get her earring. Chris puts the couch down then lies back down. Lou sits on the floor nearby. Chris's hand flops back to meet Lou's hand, he doesn't let go. Lou sits calmly and watches, as they hold hands. Mel is now sitting by the fire. Connie goes outside and sits with him. Mel has been crying.

Mel   I've never stopped talking about you Connie. Why did she give you away?

Connie   You act like mum didn't love me as much as she loved you. Mum loved me.

Mel   I know she did. Why couldn't I go with you? I was at home by myself.

Connie   You couldn't, bub. You needed mum.

Mel   You needed mum.

Connie   I can look after myself. I'm your big sister. I can survive on my own.

Mel   So much of your life was lost, sis.

Connie   No it wasn't. It wasn't easy. But it's OK, we know each other.

Mel   Do we? I haven't seen you for ten years.

Connie   It's better than not at all. I just didn't want to make waves. But you can't be telling Joy none of what happened. You don't know everything.

Mel   When you came here, I just asked you where you'd been. You wouldn't tell me anything. You went straight inside and told the girls, didn't ya? Yeah, well who the fuck am I?

Connie   Cause you don't see me. You think I'm a big success. I'm not a big success. It's like I'm Santa Claus. Well I'm not like Santa Claus. I had a job . . . I fucked up and I got fired, but it's not the end of the world for me.

Mel   I just wish you woulda called me.

Connie   You called me. Ah I'm glad you called me. (*Connie gets up and puts her arms around Mel*) Don't be sad. And don't get angry. None of that pillow talk, it's like World War Three in there . . . next thing, she'll know the colour of my underpants. I love you bub. You know that eh? (*She holds him tightly and they remain that way, in silence, for a few moments. Connie breaks out of the hug, shoving Mel gently, then calling out to the rest.*) Jesus you're a maudlin bunch! . . . There is a perfectly decent fire here getting wasted. Come on fellas.

(*Lou comes out to the doorstep.*)

Lou   I don't wanna grow old and lonely.

Connie   Oh Lou, that'll never happen to you. Some people can be in relationships and not say two words to each other . . . You wanna come up North with me?

(*Lou smiles. Joy, who has until now, been lying on the ground near the table, perks up.*)

Joy   Hey Lou! Lou!. . . You know . . . you have got three generations of girls living in one house. You've got Yiayia, you and Chloe.

(*Chris sits up, gets off the couch and heads towards the stereo to choose a record.*)

Chris   Three generations of woman under one roof? That would drive me mad! . . . Three generations under the one roof? I didn't even have one.

(*Connie sits on the garden bench. Joy comes over, wipes down a spot on the bench.*)

Connie   Jeez Joy, you must have the patience of a saint to put up with those two. Now me . . . I'm rather low maintenance by comparison, wouldn't you say. (*Lou chuckles*) . . . Easy going.

(*Meanwhile, Chris has chosen a record. Music: We hear Willie Nelson's version of 'Help Me Make it Through The Night' begin to play.*)

Joy   (*Laughing*) Oh get up!

Connie   Don't ask for much. Ah come on!

Joy   I might sit down.

(*She sits next to Connie.*)

Connie   Your job as a host though, comes into question.

(*Chris stumbles outside. The music continues to play, becoming louder. Chris clears his throat and extends his arm to Lou.*)

Chris   You wanna dance, old girl?

Lou smiles and gets up off the steps. Lou and Chris dance a slow waltz on the grass as Connie and Joy watch them, laughing. Mel comes over and tries to get Connie to dance with him. She jumps up and shoos him away. They briefly play cat and mouse around the garden table.

Connie   Nah! What are you doing? Dance with your woman. Get away! No, keep moving! You're a rotten kid . . . If my hands weren't full . . . I'd smash ya!

Mel laughs, gives up the chase and walks away from Connie to sit next to Joy on the bench. Connie sits on a chair at the far edge of the table. Lou and Chris stop dancing. Chris flops to the ground, singing along and gazing into the fire as Lou drags over a chair to sit in. Joy strokes Mel's face and beard, they kiss. Connie, out of view of the rest of the group, slowly takes out the piece of ochre from her bag, and puts it on the table before she leaves. A few moments later, as the song is winding down, Mel looks across the yard and registers that Connie has gone. He continues massaging Joys' shoulders. The lights go down and soon after, the song ends.

<The End>

Alecky Blythe Interviewed by Alison Forsyth

AF (AlisonForsyth)   Could you explain how you decide upon the subject matter for your plays?

AB (AleckyBlythe)   The subject matter needs two important factors, firstly characters who are open to being interviewed and secondly narrative potential. When I first go out to investigate a story that I might have read about in the paper or seen on the news, I might find one without the other. The only way of knowing whether it has both is by going and talking to people. Lots of things I hear about make me think, 'That could be an interesting verbatim piece' but if you can't get access to the necessary people to bring it alive, or they don't want to talk you are not going to get very far. Likewise I've met some wonderful, extraordinary people who will talk to me until my batteries run flat but if there is no story to journey on with them, the piece will lack a narrative drive.

I suppose I am driven more by a desire to find a 'way in', an opening to people's lives if there is any identifiable design to my work. Something like a siege or a talent show in Stoke on Trent is a 'way in', whereas just shoving a microphone under somebody's nose and saying tell me about your life would not produce the sort of material I am looking for, people would feel very exposed and uncomfortable. Also I am not so interested in people's life stories in an autobiographical way; I am more interested in seeing how we as humans react in certain situations. A situation such as a siege is the catalyst. It happened to be an extraordinary situation which became all the more interesting as it was ordinary people who were dealing with it, people who I could relate to. The siege provided an 'in'. This eventually provided me with a narrative arc whereby you can pin those relationships which you are forming with people and structure the individual interviews around the key event.

AF   Would you say your approach to verbatim testimony gathering is quite serendipitous and 'open'?

AB   Yes very much so. A given event might be a starting point which ultimately takes me down different routes or in another direction. You must always be open to other things. I could decide to set out to make a piece on, say, the evictions at Dale Farm, but then something or somebody you might meet – say, a particular person, takes you on a particular tangent and the interview evolves in another direction. I think I am probably very open to those changes, perhaps sometimes too open because I can go down lots of dead ends. There are hours of material which I never end up using in my work. But at the same time this open, inquisitive approach gives me a perspective on the material that is really good, what is really useful . . . It is a bit in my nature to be a bit 'OCD' about it, I know. I become quite obsessed when making something, saying to myself 'you never know, I'd better go and try and get that interview as that could be the bit of gold dust I'm looking for'. Of course I don't really know what I'm looking for until I've found it.

Also I should explain that the making of *Come Out Eli* is a brilliant example of being open to where the interviews lead you. Being my first play, I was following guidelines I'd learnt from Mark Wing-Davey's *Drama Without Paper* workshop at the Actors Centre which involves, choosing a good talking point and going to interview a wide variety of people on the subject. The end result would be more a collage of anecdotes and fascinating stories, rather than having any overarching narrative. I decided to create a piece on the subject of fear and this is what I initially asked people about at the Hackney siege. I figured the cordon of a siege might be a good setting for discussing such a subject and might generate some lively discussions. I didn't realize that what I was doing was documenting the unfolding siege. I just kept returning as I seemed to be getting good material which had an in-built spontaneity and freedom. Unlike more formally set up interviews, the conversations I was having on the cordon were overshadowed by the siege in the background so people were less self-conscious. This is a quality I really liked and something I have looked for ever since in my work, which links back to the first question. Some situations lend themselves to a spontaneity and present tense action which makes for rich material, others don't.

AF   I think it is fair to say that you are interested in the sound of the testimony just as much as its actual content. How far is observation, on your part, incorporated into the finished play?

AB   I try to observe as much as possible while I'm interviewing, as well as listen and make sure the person feels comfortable. I don't really write observational notes when I am interviewing, as I don't want to make people self-conscious by furiously scribbling away. This can make the process less fluid and natural. Instead, I want a genuine free flowing conversation. Afterwards if I am meeting a lot of people during the day I might jot things down like 'big gold hoops' if a detail like that struck me

Figure 6 Miranda Hart and Alecky Blythe. Courtesy of Ian Cole.

at the time. What happens is when I edit the interview, even when it is a little while afterwards, when you hear that voice, it sort of comes back. I just remember key moments or things like somebody playing with their hair, and even if I have not written anything down. It is amazing how the voice reminds you, and suggests what this person was doing.

AF   Does the process of transferring verbatim testimony to performance present any key challenges? How do actors engage with the taped interviews in your process?

AB   When actors first listen to an interview I do not tell them too much about the people behind the words, because they might subconsciously colour in and enhance things too much around a back story I have given them . . . it is better to just sort of start clean from the voice . . . I ask actors to just 'do it'. . . . That is the best way to let the character come through without too much invention on the part of the actor. First and foremost it is not about creating a character though; rather, I would say the actor responds to the sound of the voice and from that he or she 'finds' the character. It's often really impressive how quickly the actor 'finds' the character, if they are doing the technique faithfully, which actually requires not doing too much 'acting' but just listening and repeating, VERY precisely. The voice tells us so much about an individual that the actors have a very strong sense of the characters they are playing without ever having met them. Some bits of material are only included because of the delivery which is so revealing about the person they are, even if it has little to do with the forward driving narrative. Take Jean for example in *Eli*, the woman talking about how muggers 'steal your bag, no not steal it – cut it'. Something about how she said 'cut it' was so key to who she was as a person, at that particular moment in time, it's just gorgeous. So that's why it's so important for the actors not to embellish and just stick to copying what they hear.

Despite the supreme importance of audio, I do sometimes take photos of interviewees for the actors to work with, along with the recordings – although it is not always possible if it is a vox pop interview whereby you talk to someone for about 5 minutes in the street – but for an interview which stretches over a period of time, say over a year or so, the photographs become quite helpful for all different parts of the production team, not just the actors.

One of the challenges with some of the voices that are particularly characterful is for the actors to resist the temptation to make them caricatures. I find a good aid is to say to the actors 'imagine the person you are playing is watching tonight' and this usually helps to keep a lid on things.

AF After seeing *London Road* I was struck by the way you engage with laughter. You capture the laughter in testimony – often nervous, uneasy, artificial and even inappropriate laughter – and this in turn elicits genuine guffaws of delight from the audience. Could you maybe expand on this?

AB I think that laughter is quite present in my shows as I myself often laugh (encouragingly I hope, not mockingly) with the people I'm interviewing. The recordings are littered with my laughs that the actors just have to get used to. It is part of my interviewing technique if you like, but it is not something I do consciously, it is just me. Over the years, I realize that laughter certainly is a good way to help make people feel relaxed. I didn't realize when I started with *Eli* of course but I think I have some qualities that are well suited to collecting interviews.

As far as the audience then engaging with that laughter, I think that is because of the shift of context. When the interviewees speak to me so freely, sharing jokes and laughs, and then that interview is taken out of the intimate setting of the interview and put in front of a bigger audience, however maintaining the same intimacy and detail something extraordinary happens. People's words and behaviour seem to take on more power, ironically because of the delicacy of their delivery. In this new context, the lines often become funnier and more touching.

Figure 7 Philip Marshall. Courtesy of Ian Cole.

AF   The events of *Come Out Eli* occur just after Christmas and
similarly just before Christmas with *London Road*. Both plays appear to
juxtapose ritual festivity and tradition with the unexpectedly horrifying
and sensational, and although this was just how things happened
in reality, would you like to comment on how these unanticipated
contradictions help to shape the final plays?

AB   Not consciously . . . as you say, it just happened that way. Of course
when these events happen at a time like Christmas they are all the more
painful and difficult to comprehend for those involved and in my shaping I
tried to reflect this. *Come Out Eli* is similar to *London Road* in other ways
too – structurally – *Eli* and *London Road* are both created from interviews
collected at the very time of events unfolding and in the aftermath.

AF   As you have said some interviews make it into the plays, others do
not. Could you discuss how far a sense of ethical responsibility might
determine your decision about which material makes it to the final script?

AB   Ethically I do feel a big responsibility . . . you cannot have
somebody saying 'Those are my words and you are using them to make
a show but I didn't say you could.' You just have to be careful about how
you go about things. It's often the case that the play is produced a long
time after the interview was recorded so people may well have forgotten
what they have said. In the cases where there is something that might be
particularly controversial I have gone back to the interviewee to check

Figure 8 Alecky Blythe. Courtesy of Ian Cole.

they are ok with it being included. Of course there is a danger that they will retract their statement but I have to look after the interviewees as I would hate for their lives to be negatively affected as a result of the play. It's really not worth it for the sake of a good scene. A lot of what I do is about building trust and the best way to do that is to keep interviewees informed of what you're up to all the way along. It is a relationship I have with my interviewees and the best relationships are built on trust, this is no different.

AF   Class and inequality are themes raised in *Come Out Eli* and to me these themes extend far beyond the specific event of the Hackney siege. How far does your particular approach to the theatre of testimony start with a desire to foreground socio-political ideas, maybe by focusing on the voices of the hitherto unheard, alienated or marginalized?

AB   To be perfectly honest with you, on the whole, the interviews which are used in my plays are first and foremost those interviews I have had with people I am drawn to, people whom I respond to and who respond to me. Socio-political ideas are not things I'm very conscious of during the making. One character in *Come Out Eli* says well 'that wouldn't happen in Kensington' and one could say that here a socio-political observation is made. Yes, I know it ultimately provides a wider social context, but when I first heard it . . . well I found it funny! I had

Figure 9 Don Gilet and Miranda Hart. Courtesy of Ian Cole.

an emotional response to it! I have to have an emotional response to a person and something they say, and I think that outweighs any particular socio-political comment as a driving force behind my work. So although weighty political themes can be gleaned from *Eli*, that is not the reason for making the work in the first place. Engagement with me and the audience is more what it's about.

AF   Would you say there is a musicality to *Come Out Eli*? I am thinking about the range of dialects, accents and idioms present in the play?

AB   Yes, absolutely because I came to this sort of work as an actor first and foremost. To begin with I wrote plays so I could cherry pick parts for myself! As an actor I was drawn to characters and their speech and yes this included tone, texture, accents and whatever, of course, but actually most of the time it is about a response to people, and the need to want to perform and be other people. In Hackney there was a real range, and from an actor's perspective this was great! I'm sure my background as an actor still comes into my decisions about what interviews to include in the plays.

I suppose since *London Road* – which on a creative level was a huge development – I have reflected on my earlier plays, particularly *Come Out Eli*. As the work has become more talked about, and people like

Figure 10 Alecky Blythe and Don Gilet. Courtesy of Ian Cole.

yourself and critics see certain things in the plays, there is a danger
one can become self-conscious in the making of them which is very
debilitating creatively. It's been wonderful to come back to *Eli* and
remind myself that I had good instincts and hopefully they are still there.
It's easy for them to become deadened by critical acclaim, especially
the sort that *London Road* received . . . . You can become too theorized
and affected by what critics think or 'read into' plays. I have to get on
with the job of following my instincts again and to take myself back into
the head space that was open and daring to make *Come Out Eli* and see
where that takes me.

Introduction

Alecky Blythe

I never intended to make verbatim plays for a living. I only ever wanted to act. However, the opportunities to appear in exciting new work, or even unexciting new work, were scarce so I decided to create my own. I was inspired by having taken part in a workshop at the Actors Centre run by Mark Wing-Davey called *Drama Without Paper* which passed on the verbatim technique of Anna Deavere Smith.

The technique involves recording interviews from real life and editing them into a desired structure. The edited recordings are played live to the actors through earphones during the rehearsal process, and on stage in performance (this was Mark's choice, Anna learnt the lines verbatim). The actors listen to the audio and repeat what they hear. They copy not just the words but exactly the way in which they were first spoken. Every cough, stutter and hesitation is reproduced. The actors do not learn the lines at any point. By listening to the audio during performances the actors remain accurate to the original recordings, rather than slipping into their own patterns of speech.

I chose fear as subject to explore with my microphone and then looked for situations where this topic might be ripe for discussion. A siege that was taking place up the road from my home seemed like it could lend itself to some fruitful material. I investigated other avenues on the same subject, for example an anthrax scare in Wood Green, however the siege that I was lucky enough to capture from near its beginning, gave way to the most lively conversations. Unwittingly I had walked into a narrative unfolding around me. Instead of just collecting interviews about a particular theme which thus far was all I had learnt to do with the technique, I had the potential to tell a story, beginning, middle and end.

The play is created from a combination of interviews collected at the time of the siege at the police cordon with onlookers and then in the aftermath with residents and shopkeepers who were affected. The interview with the hostage was the last interview I did in an attempt to balance out the more light-hearted material with some pathos which it did indeed accomplish in places. However my encounter with him was so unexpected, it also provided some of the funniest material in the whole show.

A special thank you to all those who contributed their stories.

Come Out Eli

Alecky Blythe

COME OUT ELI was developed at the Actors' Centre. It premiered at the Arcola in 2003 where it won the Time Out Award for Best Performance on the Fringe and transferred to BAC as part of the Time Out Critics Choice Season.

Original Cast and Creatives

Alecky Blythe
Don Gilet
Miranda Hart
Philip Marshall
Sarah Quist
Director   Sara Powell
Designer   Atlanta Duffy

A note on the text lay-out:

A forward slash indicates the point at which a character is interrupted by another. The line that interrupts it is preceded with a forward slash.

For example, **Jean** *A lady just died a few weeks ago long 'ere/. She was mugged.*

Mary*/Over there, she died.*

1. Request

At home on the phone.

Alecky – Blonde, middle class, thirty. Shocked and amused but tries to remain polite and business-like.

Alecky   Oh hello Mr Okere? (*Beat*) Hi, it's Alecky Blythe here (*Beat.*) Hi (*Beat*) a – are you ok to talk? Ok great. Um yeh (*Beat*) I've um -I've had a think about your (*Beat*) erm (*Beat*) Your sorry? (*Beat*) Your requests yes, yes huh, erm but I'm afraid my answer is -is still no. Erm you, you are very obviously a special case which is why I'm so keen to talk to you but erm we don't have any money and like I said yesterday, I'm not, I'm not wi – willing to (*Beat*) NO! That, it's a no, I just don't – I'm not gonna, you know I'm desperate to get an interview with you but I am not that desperate (*Beat*) Heh, heh, heh, heh (*Pause*) Well if you're so good then you should be getting it elsewhere shouldn't you? (*Beat*) If you're so good, why haven't you got a girlfriend? (*Pause*) No I know, I know, well you know, it'll get better, you know it's (*Beat*) you know (*Pause*) Well it's a very -I can't- it's a very big deal having sex with a complete stranger (*Beat*) tcah (*Beat*) I mean I just don't, that's not the way I kind of erm, you know I lead my life (*Pause*) Ha -I -yeah I am a modern woman but you know I've kind of got morals and erm (*Pause*) Well like I said I will treat you to a very nice lunch. (*Pause*) Well I know lunch is a bit different to sex but erm . . . if you've got, if you have got a busy -a busy calendar (*Beat*) You know (*Beat*) erm I can wait. (*Pause*) N -no –no, there's not going to be any sex!

2. Nasty

At the siege cordon.

Research Criminologist – A tall man in his twenties wearing a parker and glasses. He looms down the street past the cordon shouting.

Research Criminologist   It's the vagrant research criminologist, Middlesex University. Longest siege you're gonna capture on film and I can tell you that I think with the sharp shooters on the roof, you're gonna see something nasty.

3. Sharp Shooters

At the siege cordon. Very cold and raining.

Good Cop – Kind faced, thirties. Speaks quickly and matter of factly, much of this is a well-practised speech. Happy to oblige.

Good Cop   I wanted to come to Hackney because I knew it was a busy ground, I knew I'd be dealing with a lot of different things, very early on in my service, and I wanted to gain the experience of jumping in at the deep end. There's the officer obviously covering the line of fire there (*Pointing behind him*) er (*Beat*) at the Land Rover and up on the roof, there's er, if you step this way, you can see the tent area up there, there's er (*Beat*) sharp shooters up there -snipers. Erm he's in a flat . . . in a little street, down -down to the right yeah. (*SM19 Officer walks past*) He'll be one of the (*Beat*) er armed officers and SM19's, Specialist fire arms officers, they'll be very busy, they'll be on standby, in case anything's happening, erm and rushing round feeding each other, erm and they're not known as the greatest er greatest talkers as well. No it's five days now. The first contact they had with him was when he was shooting at our officers, erm I believe he's been involved in several other incidents across London where he shot at police officers. It was a friend of mine actually spotted his car on routine patrol, then went to seize the car for forensic evidence, at which point he started shooting at the officers, armed officers turned up, there was an exchange of fire with them and since then he's been held up, (*Beat*) and he's actually got a hostage in there as well, which is why there's the big stand-off.

4. Parked

Mr Henry's Barber Shop, Graham Road.

Barber – A thin man with a wrinkled face and white hair. Sixties. Speaks with a slight lisp and stammer. Deep voice, North London accent.

Barber   He's parked the car in the middle of the road –left it in the middle of the road. So people, want to get out -out their cars -couldn't get out (*Beat*) get their cars out. So someone's phoned the police, an the police come down to sort it out. Cause they recognised the car they said the car they'd bin looking for, because apparently . . . he shot somebody last year -in the West End -shot a policeman. And plus ya know a couple of armed -armed robberies he's s'pose to 'ave done. An like the police phoned back to the station to check on the car and they c-come back wiv er (*Beat*) 'Oh don't touch it, we're send the forensic people down to pick it up to take it back to the police station for f -forensic,' and they didn't know 'e actually lived there. Cos they all they want was to get 'is car, obv -obviously fort it bin dumped. Cause when the -when the police come -come to pick it up to tow it away (*Beat*) 'e opened the winda an started shootin at 'em . . . That's how it all started. But if he kept his m – if he kept 'is -kept quiet – 'e could ha' walked out that flat a free man. He, he must be high on drugs or I don't know.

5. Answer the Question

At the siege cordon.

Rasta – Tall, skinny and stoned. London accent. Toffee Woman – West Indian grandma who continually chews toffees. Small but has a big voice. Boy – about sixteen, scruffy. London accent.

Rasta   The man ain't got no way out 'as he? It's either the cemetery 'ospital o' prison, innit, so, let people go back in their 'ouse innit, and jus just end it, innit. Stupidness, Madness.

Boy   That person should be in jail.

Rasta   He will be won't 'e when he comes out.

Boy   Yeah, when he comes out he should be in jail. What do'y -what d'you fink of what's happened here?

Toffee Woman   It don't frighten me that much because I know it comin up to the end of time. This ting will 'appen. The government not doing any better is he?

Boy   But what do'you fink the government could help?

Toffee Woman   The government, where the government need to help, they need to preach more re, more erm -Christianity, more repentance -and life -people life will be change. Coz when Tony Blair right now, Tony Blair leave from here right now 'I'm going down Saddam Hussein country', ain't no different from this.

Boy   Do'you -do'you know -do'you know if erm (*Beat*) if the Prime Minister would say that he is out of order . . . Would you say that?

Toffee Woman   You see most people look on the Prime Minister they look at God you know, but, they realise the Prime Minister -the Prime Minister ain't no different from 'im. I' – what I'm trying to say, he ain't no different. Reason what I'm sayin this. Him leavin, 'I'm going to Saddam Hussein country' (*Beat*) eh? and I'm gonna make war down there – so the people -'em not paying not'ing for the example for the people down ere is he? Is he setting any example? Answer the question.

Boy   Wh . . .

Toffee Woman   Answer the question, is he setting any example?

Boy   What d'you, what d'you expect?

(*Beat*)

Toffee Woman   Answer the question!

Boy   What d'you expect, what d'you expect?

(*Beat*)

Toffee Woman   Answer the question! Answer me the question. You asking the question, let me ask you is he setting any example?

Boy   He is exa-

Toffee Woman   Answer!

Boy   Yeah.

Toffee Woman   Is he setting any example? How would you like if you live into this country, right now and somebody?

(*Beat*)

Boy   I do live in this country.

Toffee Woman   Yes yeah. You live here, me live as well. Somebody Saddam Hussein come from this country and come we gonna check out in England here say, 'Who have weapon an who don't 'ave weapon and have weapon?' You tink the government would allow them?

Boy   No.

Toffee Woman   Ahh . . .

Boy   But what d'you?. . .

Toffee Woman   INJUSTICE!

Boy   But what d'you, what d'you, what d'you fink that's gonna happen if that guy comes out, an the police start pointin fire arms on him and trying to arrest him. What d'you expect for him, t' to the police to say, to say, excuse me, I need a word wiv you, cum ear. What d'you expect to do?

Toffee Woman   Tell me what -tell me what the reason why 'im doing it? What is the reason?

Boy   But what d'you expect to do?

Toffee Woman   What do you tink is the reason why 'im doing it, answer ya question!

6. I'm a Professional!

Still on the phone. More serious. Now twenty minutes into the call.

Alecky   I know he could have killed you. Yeah (*Beat*) so maybe you've got a different attitude to life but you know that's not gonna make me come round to sleeping with you. All I require is to get your story, record it, and that's what the actors work from in the show, they hear it playing through earphones and they copy you exactly, s' sex does not come into it (*Pause*) Yeah well it's not just -you know it's not -I'm a, I'm a professional, so you know I'm doing a job. It completely- Listen I'm not going to – listen I'm really not, can we please stop talking about it?

7. Western

A Vegetarian Café in Hackney.

Reporter – Female late twenties. All in black with trendy specs. Unimpressed by the siege in general, speaks with pace and confidence. Northern roots can slightly be heard behind London influence on accent.

Reporter   You know they kept talking about the siege, an the gun fire an all this, an it sounded like summing out of a Western but actually (*Beat*) was just standing there, it was pissing with rain and you couldn't see anything an it was jus a house that apparently someone was in, apparently with a gun. There was all this commotion going on outside but it jus it wasn't ever that apparent what was going on.

8. Sore Throat

At the siege cordon.

Mary – Little, chatty, friendly and excited. Slight lisp, London accent. Jean – Serious and gives impression of being uninterested. The larger of the two. Suffolk accent, slower speech and movements than Mary. Both holding shopping bags.

Mary   We've been here, 'aven't we since boxing day, 'aven't we looking at that, ya know.

Jean   Yeah, we've bin down nearly every night- havin a look. Mostly evenin's, not in the day.

Mary   That's how I got my sore throat ya know, standing here.

Jean   Ha, ha.

Mary   Oh a lot of people.

Jean   Yeah there's quite a crowd of people come to 'ave a look every night. You see we're not gonna see nothing, even in the end if he comes out, we won't see 'im, he'll be covered.

9. Confusion

A Vegetarian Café in Hackney.

Reporter   The -the first confusion was actually trying to establish who was a reporter, who was ya know -who was a resident, you know who -who was just sort of there to sort of like stand an stare you, ya know? It was quite confusing at first it was like, 'Who are all these bloody people, where have they all come from?' you know, 'Why 'aven't -why an't they got jobs, why aren't they at work?' ya know.

10. I Saw Gun Shots

A Newsagents on Graham Road

Son – Late teens, chubby, shell suit, London 'street' accent. Quite quick delivery. Dad – Grey, large and tired looking. Strong Pakistani accent, slow speech. Dad sat behind counter and Son leaning by door.

Son   I saw gun shots, coz I was round my mates there, could see everyfing. I saw ther -I saw 'im shoot, because they tried to break into his door and -and as 'e lives on top and the doors like below im -and the -and his windows right here (*Beat*) that's the only window 'es got I think -and he- he shot four times. So luckily my mate pulled me in like I was gonna get shot.

Dad   We are open not that day, and ah suddenly police car came and we look there, policemen say, 'Go back is gun man.' Then after ten minutes they close everything.

11. Starve Him

At the siege cordon.

Jean   I think they're doin the wrong thing by feeding 'im anyway, he'll never, he'll never come out while 'is being fed will he?'

Mary   If you don't feed 'im he'll die won't he?

Jean   No -no, he'll come out. He'll come out. I can guarantee he'll come out.

Mary   You can't starve people can you love? Can't starve 'em.

Jean   No but he wouldn't starve he'd come out (*Beat*) Oh I get, I've 'ad my bag taken on a number of occasions, er cut -they always cut it, and they take your money out . . . But now I don't carry the money in the bag. They can take the bag there's nothing in it -not that -there is something in it, but not money, you understand?

Mary   No we're always out love, we're always out . . .

Jean   We go out, it doesn't stop /us going out. You can't stop livin because of some 'ooligans running around.

Mary   /We go out.

Mary   Yeh we do go out, we go out.

12. Fireworks

Vietnamese Takeaway Restaurant on Graham Road.

Hong – Meek, softly spoken Vietnamese woman in her early forties. She stutters as a result of her struggle with the English and also the emotions that come back as she talks.

Hong   It's about 2.30, we heard shooting, boom, boom, boom, an I said, 'Oh that's a firework.' Must be because it New Year, so maybe Boxing Day they- (*Beat*) But we heard shouting as well, I said, 'What happened? Why it's er some shot -shooting and it's shouting' and when we look outside and we came (*Beat*) because we- our room is upstairs but we look to the back road as well (*Beat*) so we look outside, oh no some armed police and I say, 'Oh no what happened? Why is armed police around here.' So we came down here, we see armed police there as well -they hiding behind like (*Points to car in street*) -that white car they parked the car parked there, two police hide- when the -the gun point at here. We say 'Oh my God what happened here? It Boxing Day, why police at the back and police at the front? Oh no!'

13. Safer

The sitting room of a pretty Victorian cottage near Graham Road.

Mr Field – Early sixties. Ex-Naval Officer and retired solicitor. Slow and carefully chosen words. Well spoken, distinguished voice. Sits confidently in his arm chair. Mrs Field – Early sixties. Delicate frame and softly spoken but not easily outdone by her husband. Avid reader, researcher and archivist.

Mr Field   We had absolutely no problem at all. We had twenty four hour police presence outside our house for fifteen days (*Beat*) And we felt safer- than we've felt -in a long, long time.

Mrs Field   We only heard the sirens go once.

14. Duty

At the siege cordon.

Good Cop   We've actually been sending food into him I think. Mmm, because of course we have a duty to protect everyone's life, even his -even though he's shot at our colleagues, we still have a duty to try and save his life (*Beat*) an have a peaceful resolution to the incident.

15. Old Fashioned

The kitchen of a quirky Victorian flat near Graham Road.

Charlie – Traces of Welsh roots drift into his more measured middle-class educated voice. Mid thirties. A set designer by profession, part of Hackney's artistic community.

Charlie   It's a sort of weird, sort of sometimes it feels like a synthetic sense of uhm (*Beat*) a code of conduct being observed by the police uhm (*Beat*) a sort of gentle, quite business-like slightly old-fashioned sort of way they have of talking to you. It sort of – it's -it is weird because it suddenly feels like -you know? There were -you know – there's never any- as it were -bobbies on the beat around here, we don't -police men generally do not walk around Hackney.

16. Bullet Screen

A Vietnamese Takeaway Restaurant on Graham Road.

Hong   Cos my daughter's car parked there, it just . . . that day, she have nowhere to park she have to park at the end of the road there. The bullet -his bullet go -went through her windscreen. Yes. And now every time I see her I'm scared to drive that car . . . but she like the car, (*Holding back tears*) but I feel nervous (*Beat*) I don't like. But the car we jus bought it for her only two years because she go to uni so she need the car to drive but we can't afford. Cos in the three weeks we lost the income and the takings and the rent rate we have to pay. So I don't know- we want to change the car for her but -may be have to take time.

17. Hungerford

At the siege cordon.

Jean   A lady just died a few weeks ago long 'ere/. She was mugged.

Mary   /Over there, she died.

Jean   Mugged.

Mary   Yeah mugged and she hit her head and she died./ Just over there.

Jean   /An old lady in her seventies died a few days after bein knocked to the ground on her own door step, jus puttin the key in the door an they got her. You have to look behind you when you're walking around here – or where I live. Same thing, so it's bad (*Beat*) but it's bad everywhere now. I mean my daughter lives in a little country place an it's bad there (*Beat*) but more or less you know who was done it to you in them small places, unless strangers come in from outside (*Beat*) Yeah. We 'ad a big siege there a few years ago, a very big one he killed 'is mother and he killed er, -ss about fifteen people he shot dead in the village where I come from (*Beat*) Hungerford, do you remember- the Hungerford massacre? Hungerford, -he . . . a boy went mad, he killed his mother first, he had a (*Beat*) a brainstorm or something like that -an then he started to kill. My daughter, I kept ringing her up, 'Don't let the kids out till they catch him' / ya know because he was dangerous. But with him he killed hiself -killed hiself in the end cos (*Beat*) well he thought was the best thing to do, he killed so many people -people that. A woman who was in the woods with her children havin a picnic . . . he killed her, he left the kids -he didn't touch the children, he killed the mother . . . It's a very famous thing. That man I was talking to a while ago, he was there that one, (*Pointing to photographer at cordon*) he was there, yeah, he went to the siege. He said he was there.

Mary / (coughs)

Mary   Ask 'im go on. Yeah we've 'ad enough now.

18. Street Bobby

At the siege cordon.

PC Emma – Pretty, and cheerful, early thirties. First day on the job. Middlesbrough accent.

PC Emma   (*Directing* Mary *and* Jean) You're gonna have to walk up Amhurst or go that way, up- the other way, alright? PC Kennedy or Emma (*Laughs coyly*). I was a fitness instructor- personal trainer, so I've moved from Middlesbrough to London to become a police officer. It's a good job, good career, pension at the end of it, so (*Beat*) things like that. At the moment I'm stood on a cordon where there's a gun siege ok going on. Uhm basically we're stopping the public from walking up this road cos there's armed officers up there. I'm just a basic street bobby.

19. Bonhomie

A studio in a fashionable block in Hackney.

Anthony – Middle-aged, short grey hair, specs. A theatre designer. Well spoken, with carefully thought-through speech. Juliet – Pretty French assistant, twenties.

Anthony   To begin with it was, it seemed you know quite ahm . . . well light-hearted is the wrong word but there was a kind uhm (*Beat*) er (*Beat*) bonhomie among the policemen -it was all like, 'Well we're on incredible overtime', you know, 'So we', you know, 'We don't really mind how long it's gonna go on.' Then it snowed, then it was very cold, then they got very bored, and then -they -they made a snow man at this gate. That was phenomenal -took a photograph of it.

20. Pen-guins

A children's dress shop on Graham Road.

Connie – Attractive Ghanaian owner. Forties. Well presented. A strong faith. Ghanaian accent which is colourful, lively and loud.

Connie   I was coming in here an giving the police cup of teas an even though they say no I say 'No don't worry, I'm -I'm paying for it', you know, 'if not open my shop let me go in, I'll be the tea lady then.' Just for a joke but we laughed about, they were – they were cold the policemen, they were freezin', ha, ha. It wasn't a nice weather at all, it was so cold I mean you literally see them shivering. You know? Let's -let's face they are not (*Beat*) pen-guins to be on the snow an cold area. They are human beings. An I thought it was not fair on them but at the end of the day they were making money so it was alright.

21. Rabid Dogs

A textile designer's studio next door to Anthony and Juliet.

Bernie – Stocky with a Yorkshire accent. Penny – RP accent, softly spoken, mild mannered. Both mid-forties.

Penny   The police were wandering around fully armed you know with their helmets and their machine, (*Coughs*) their machine guns and er

Bernie   Yeah, like, slightly unsettling, you know/ all that sort of

Penny   /Yeah

Bernie   Er, military hardware around you know (*Beat*) type thing . . .

Penny   With the dog handlers.

Bernie   I mean they had fantastic uniforms and you know the big guns, that sort of er/ tough kind of air about them.

Penny   /Yeah they were, the poli, the dog handlers were particularly uhm . . . unapproachable, they were rather horrible I thought.

Bernie   Who?

Penny   The dog handlers.

Bernie   Yeah, the ones with the dogs looked a bit rough -they -they -those in particular were a bit – mean-looking. You know? Whether they actually were or not I mean, they looked it. They had guns and dogs ha ha, kind of thing ya know?

Penny   And . . .

Bernie   Just guns was ok-

Penny   (*Laughs lightly*)

Bernie   – but big horrible rabid looking dogs as well as guns, ya know what I mean? That/ image was a bit much.

Penny   /Well the dogs were getting bored because they'd let them out and run round the garden -our garden, I might say and erm (*Beat*) and then of course the inevitable happened and they started (*Beat*) shitting everywhere.

22. Kensington

A studio in a fashionable block in Hackney.

As the interview progresses Anthony's frustration with the siege comes flooding back, making his speech more fractured.

Anthony   Caroline, she saw a policeman urinating in the garden, that was like the beginning of, kind of, like, you know -it -this isn't maybe such a great idea. And then the police handlers with the dogs, used to use the -the garden as a kind of dog toilet. So they used to come to top of the steps there, just let the dogs loose -and there was still snow on the ground at this point, an and er you know the dogs -so then -then a battle began of whoever was like looking out of their window seeing this -screaming at the policeman to clean up their crap, you know? If ya -if ya -dogs gonna -kind o' do – if ya dogs gonna crap, then you normally have a plastic bag or something, ya know, ready to do it but they didn't . . . They must have had a bag? As erm (*Beat*) er Caroline from upstairs said you know, 'If this had been Kensington, they certainly wouldn't have been bringing their dogs in to crap in the garden.'

23. Clear-up

Children's Christmas Party, Hackney.

Chief Superintendent Derek Benson – Mid-fifties. Slight tinge of London accent. Carefully chosen words, very diplomatic. Genial and matter of fact. Well practised in answering questions.

Chief Superintendent Derek Benson   I was aware of er one local resident who had a police dog, wasn't peeing in his garden. But we- as soon as we were told about it, we had people go round there and then clean it up.

24. Fox Droppings

A studio in a fashionable block in Hackney.

Amuses himself as well as the listener with this story.

Anthony   They kept on saying that they were getting uhm . . . professional cleaners to come in, come in (*Laughs*) it was so funny, to come in and you know, well professional cleaners aren't gonna want to clear up the dog shit from the police dogs ya know and uhm so- er on the Saturday morning he hadn't uhm (*Beat*) and Penny also tal -talked to a local policeman about it and nothing had happened so- I said well I'm gonna ring this number. So I rang the number I said look no-ones -I'd left a message that -ya know -that we were unhappy that no-one had cleared this up. In fifteen minutes, that guy that I'd met the day before was round here Ya know Inspector whatever it -with his flat cap, an he said 'Have you got a plastic bag and I'll clear it up myself.' So uhm Penny took him on a guided tour of the dog turds . . . uhm, and of which there were about twelve . . . ya know little . . . piles and er . . . he . . . cleared them up. Erm . . . but -but when he got to number twelve, he said I'll clear this up -but I think you should know this is fox . . . ha / fox droppings!

Juliet   Because er /I remember . . .

Anthony   /Yeah no we had a fox but we think the fox was displaced by the siege!

Juliet   Yeah.

25. Not in Command

Children's Christmas Party, Hackney.

Chief Superintendent Derek Benson   My day-to-day role is as the Borough Commander for Hackney I -I'm responsible for the policing of Hackney. With regard to the siege my role was round coordinating how we would respond to the needs of the local people. Working in liaison with the local authority, so in terms of actual command of the incident we were part of that command but not in command. Officers were brought in from outside, obviously we do not have borough-based fire arms officers so the -the specialist fire arms officers were brought in

. . . er obviously other emergency services, there were -the London fire brigade -that wasn't simply resourced with fire officers from Hackney they were coming in from all different parts of London. The London Ambulance service similarly had to have their staff brought in from all over London -it became a London-wide response.

26. Sneeze

The sitting room of a pretty Victorian cottage near Graham Road.

Mrs Field   Sort of Romford, Hillingdon,/ Edmunton,

Mr Field   /Uxbridge.

Mrs Field   Lewisham, Brixton.

Mr Field   Just about every buther, every borough other than Westminster and Kensington, an Chelsea and Brent. We had them from Camden, from (*Beat*) Lewisham from Peckham, from Uxbridge, Hillingdon, Ealing, (*Beat*) Camden, Ching/ford.

Mrs Field   /Said that. Walthamstow.

Mr Field   (*straight in*) Walthamstow. You name it we had it. Ha, ha, ha, ha and so all these characters- (Alecky *sneezes*)

Mrs Field   And they didn't know the area of /course.

Mr Field   /Don't, don't ever hold in a sneeze . . . Don't . . . because you'll ruin your back. Mmm, if you're going to sneeze, sneeze. Don't ever, ever hold it in.

27. Ten Officers

A trendy flat in Hackney.

Louise – Early thirties. Direct. Party/rave organiser. Sheffield accent.

Louise   We had ten -ten officers a day out there, none of them from Hackney, some of them being quite rude about, 'You must be used to this, this is Hackney, this is what's like, isn't it?' So you're like, 'Well no actually, no it's not, it's not like that, this is where we live.'

28. Two?

The sitting room of a pretty Victorian cottage near Graham Road.

Mrs Field   Apparently the catering was fantastic they said-

Mr Field   Oh the food was fantastic. I mean I saw it I didn't eat it, but I -but I saw it because I went over there and the food that they were producing was fantastic.

Mrs Field   I believe they took their own catering stuff upstairs.

Mr Field   They took it in.

Mrs Field   They took over some part of the Town Hall. I think so . . . whether they actually put in their own cookers and things I don't know. (*To* David) You went up how many stairs?. . . How many floors?. . . One floor, two?

Mr Field   Two.

Both   (*Gently but with assurance*) Mmmm.

29. Fantastic

Children's Christmas Party, Hackney.

Chief Derek Benson   The people of Hackney and in particular the Graham Road area were fantastic. They were very, very accommodating, they were very understanding -they had many, many questions, which we tried to answer as best we could. Sometimes we didn't answer them as quick as they wanted them answered, sometimes we couldn't meet their needs.

30. Arrest You

A trendy flat in Hackney.

Louise   It was raining it was New Year's Day and they said 'No you're not, you're absolutely not coming in,' and erm at that point I didn't know if I'd be locked out indefinitely, I knew that they didn't have a right to do it and then I got really upset and so I said 'I'm gonna come through', and they said 'Erm I'm telling you're not', . . . and I said 'Well what you gonna do if I come through?' . . . and they said 'Well I'll arrest you.'

31. Shoulder of Mutton

The sitting room of a pretty Victorian cottage near Graham Road.

Mrs Field   And because they had nothing to do and al'- quite a lot of them had been asking about the area and the pathway we put information in the windows about it and so uhm . . . you know they could just stand and read that at -in the middle of the night you know when they were really bored or looked -look at the pictures. (*Smiles at her own eccentricity.*)

Mr Field   But it is a very old pathway it goes way, way back to sixteen hundred or even earlier.

Mrs Field   It was called the footway and it was the footway between Hackney . . . church which was in those days . . . St John but prior to that St Augustine and . . . uhm erm . . . oh dear I've forgotten/ mutton and, sheep of mutton fields. No.

Mr Field   /Spitalfields.

Mr Field   Cattle mutton.

Mrs Field   Cattle, no not cattle mutton, I can't think what it's called . . .

Mr Field   Shoulder of mutton.

Mrs Field   No. I'll think of it in a minute, anyway they, they're some fields just before the Broadway Market and they had an old name so that's what it was called, in the footway between those two points.

32. Woolies

A Vegetarian Café in Hackney.

Reporter   The status of the cordon kept changing so it wasn't simply I'm out or I'm in, for some people it was just a nightmare and they ended up having to pack stuff every time they just went to the shops, you know- pop up to Woolies they'd have like a little emergency kit, like, you know? Stuff on them in case they got kicked out again . . . yeah.

33. Onions

The kitchen of a quirky Victorian flat near Graham Road.

Charlie   I went out of the er cordon and was and I'd said 'Look, I just need to go and get some onions', and they said 'Well, you can go and get them but we can't let you back in.' So there was a rather bizarre thing on the way back when I came back having bought these (*Beat*) things, ha, and I went into er the pub because they said well you know 'You have to go and wait in there', because – it was at least somewhere warm and you know? And the pub was real spirit of the blitz, it went really spirit of the blitz and very friendly. I actually had a uhm, my only hot toddy of the whole of Christmas on the house in there because they took pity on me sitting there with my onions.

34. Tesco Bread

A Newsagents on Graham Road.

Dad   When I want to -I want to call police to take out – bring me.

Son   They 'ad to get us food sometimes like we run out o' food an tha'. From Tesco's like groceries an that, yer, we can't get yerr. Like milk, bread, fruit/ butter.

Dad   Tesco bread/ tesco bread. Ha, ha. ha. You like, if I give it to you free you like? If you answer then like you answer innit? Hm mm. We are not beggars, begging er, beg you four people one pint milk, is enough? One potato bag.

Son   /Yeah.

Son   If you do order it- it might come after a couple of days. But it's jus stupid innit? You ask for food and they give you, I mean what? 19p loaf o' bread an tha'. We ne'- I never had that in my life.

35. Falklands

At the siege cordon.

Same as Sc 5 joined by Dad – Black, greying, Nigerian accent. Mid-fifties. Very frustrated by the situation. Rasta has to work hard in his stoned state to make sense of the discussion.

Toffee Woman   Tony Blair need to set an example./ Margaret Thatcher goin to Falkl -

Rasta   /Yufe of today's getting worsa./ Innit?

Toffee Woman   /Mmm?

Rasta   Innit?

Toffee Woman   Mmm? Black people were placed into slavery because of the same ting. We ain't telling the truth. The Bible said on the end time there gonna be war or rumours of war, an ya know why? Man, every man want power. Tony Blair want power, Margaret Thatcher want power. If me go up there I'm gonna need the power to make everybody vote for me, make a hell of a lot of money and die quick.

Dad   Two weeks, two bloody good weeks now.

Toffee Woman   But I never realised it was so near me, I never realised . . . It's five days.

Dad   Five days? Your joking.

Toffee Woman   Day six.

Dad   But why? Why a single man?

Toffee Woman   Mmm?

Dad   One man. Ah, ah, it shouldn't take so long.

Toffee Woman   (*Laughs*)

Rasta   Yeah but there's somebody else in there that they can't shoot, a hostage situation.

Dad   Eh?

Rasta   It's the next person that's in there wiv -wiv that man, supposed to be a hostage.

Dad   Whatever happens, let me tell you what happens. There is what is called bullet proof for these police men, they can wear it at least twenty four of them . . . wait a minute.

Rasta   Yeah but . . .

Dad   Wait a minute – twelve or twenty-four policemen in there with their guns/ and –

Rasta   (*Nods*) /Mmm -whoever you know – comes out with the gun . . . they will shoot his legs.

Toffee Woman   /(*Laughs, continues to do so during next speech.*)

Dad   /Yes!

Rasta   Yeah but what abou' -what abou' if you was in there with a man and you not done nofin wrong and then they storm the place an there's shots firin.

Dad   No, no, no. They are not mad the policemen. They should use their assets. If I'm – let's say you are the one wanted and I'm there with you, they know whoever/ you know?

Rasta   /Yeah but hang on a second, anova fing for you right? Now if that's you, say it's your son of your daughter in there, yeah?

Dad   Mmm . . .

Rasta   Aan you hear that the man's sayin 'Well if the police do anything snide I'm gonna shoot that person', an they storm the place an that man shoots your daughter dead.

Dad   They shoot the leg- no no no not my -you know what I mean, they are -they are looking for a man.

Rasta   Now your talking a man.

Dad   Wait a minute. They are looking for a man . . . they are looking for a man. They are looking for a man now. /They, they . . .

Rasta   /Yeah but the man's got a hostage.

Dad   Well I know! You see, my idea is this . . . We are looking for somebody- we bombard that house at least twenty four of us, that whoever has the gun in his hand is the criminal and that is the one they have to target.

Rasta   No but, him who's got the gun in his hand, he's sayin if they come there/ he's gonna -

Toffee Woman/   (*Laughs raucously*)

Rasta   -shoot the person that he's got/ So what do you do shoot that person?

Dad   /Let 'im.

Dad   You mean the one that is held hostage?

(*Short pause*)

Rasta   Sorry?

Dad   Goin to shoot who?

Rasta   The hostage yeah.

Dad   Ok. Ok. That is . . .

Rasta   The hostage could get shot by the gunman.

Dad   That is the – that is the point.

36. Basic

Children's Christmas Party, Hackney.

Chief Superintendent Derek Benson   There were people who were moved into accommodation, we went to visit them at the emergency accommodation, and we thought it wasn't up to scratch so we immediately arranged for them to be moved into hotels. Well in the first instance the Council (*Beat*) err provided emergency accommodation which was . . . was basic.

37. Yes Way

At the siege cordon.

Mary as in Sc 8, and Cat Owner – A black woman in her thirties standing with a suit case. Attempting to smile through her anger but being interviewed is making things worse.

Mary   Look at this girl 'ere she seems nice.

Cat Owner   I live in there, in among it all. My home and my car have been held to hostage basically, ha ha that's all I can say, ha, ha, ha. (*Beat*) Yes way. Yeah I mean I'm actually not that excited about it, I'm actually really quite peeved now cos I just wanna be able to get in an out at my leisure, at my choice . . . an the same with my car. I'm now hanging around streets waiting on bus's an everything else which I don't do, ha, ha, ha. If it wasn't for this now I'd be in my house now, I'd be celebrating the New Year in by/ myself.

Mary   /Yeah, it's sad is't it?

Cat Owner   I do like my anonymity. I really do. Well really and truthfully I just wanna feed my cat, really.

Mary   Ahh . . .

Cat Owner   That's why I'm here, /other than that I wouldn't be.

Mary   /Poor pussy cat.

Cat Owner   Obviously they're worried about my security an everything else so you know (*Beat*) doin there job.

Mary   Sad isn't it. Poor pussy cat eh?

Cat Owner   I know, poor little Wang.

Mary   Can't let her go in, can't let her go in. It's dangerous innit? She might get shot innit?

Cat Owner   (*Laughs*) Well they're ere to look after us.

Mary   The pigs'll fly eh?

38. Slippers

Mary   Come on let's go up there now. Got a bit from 'er – bit of information. There's my friend Jean, look. (*To* Jean) I just taken 'er all over, just getting a little of bit of talking like. D'you get the slippers?

Jean   No I got trainers got over there £2.99./ Lovely ones.

Mary   / £2.99, trainers. That's cheap. D'you get a pair Jean?

Jean   Yeah.

Mary   Let's see them. (*To* Alecky) She won't even let, let me see them. She's a nice black girl isn't she? (*To* Jean) See that young black girl -she not let a go home, she wants to feed her cat. (*To* Alecky) Her cat 'as been in, how long four days? (*To* Jean) That black girl, she can't go in, an the ca . . .

Jean   They let her in, they take 'er . . .

Mary   No because she might get shot innit?

Jean   They go with 'er.

Mary   They won't even go with 'er Jean. Oh the poor cat eh?

Jean   He'll catch a mouse.

Mary   Ah, wicked though innit?

39. Evacuated

Children's Christmas Party.

Doctor Maria – Attractive mum in her late thirties with a toddler in a push chair that she attends to. Often has an upward inflection at the end of her sentences. RP accent.

Doctor Maria   Well we were evacuated like very late at night, I think it was about two o'clock in the morning and everybody had to come out through my flat, I'm ground floor so all of the upstairs people had to come down and gather in my sitting room. (*Beat*) And we had to get out the back (*Beat*) And the firefighters came in and had to- erm knock down the garden fence so they could build us a kind of bridge- and a tunnel to get onto Hackney central station. And they actually started breaking fences in the wrong direction -and then realised and then came back and started breaking them in the other direction.

40. Venture Out

A Vietnamese Takeaway Restaurant on Graham Road.

Hong   I don't want to venture out in case I can't come back in but now I feel if I know it last fifteen days I would have gone out. I don't care

wherever I live because I don't want to be still (*Beat*) You know. You got
fed up with this siege like this. You feel now you- I been through that and
I feel really value my freedom (*Beat*) You know- you can move around
and -but when that time it's lucky thank god only fifteen days in between
the four walls and you can do nothing. You even can't walk a lot you
can't- after you eat something, you want to move around so you can feel
(*Beat*) indigestion and digest and exercise -but you feel so frustrating, so
angry -you wish him dead. And say 'Oh why don't they come in and jus
kill him?'

41. Catford

At the siege cordon.

*Mum and teenage son both overweight with East London accents. In his
eagerness to get his point across, he stumbles over his words.*

Teenager   An at the end of the day, like New -Hackney's turning into
New York. An before you know it like -London's startin to get a place
you can't even live now. Look people are getting shot all over the place,
what's this all about, people getting shot all over the /place?

Mum   /He's not, he's not even from Hackney, he's from Souf
Lon – don.

Teenager   Why don't 'e go back to 'is own bloody/ patch an do it?

Mum   /'es from Souf London. Seriously that's where 'es from. /I don't
know,

Teenager   /Why don't?

Mum   (*To rest of gathered crowd.*) Have any of you read the Standard?
(*Beat*) Well I fink was in yesterday's Standard?

Teenager   Yeah.

Mum   It said that 'es from Souf London.

Teenager   Do know what they should do? Get a helicopter, let 'im hold
onto it and just send 'im over to Catford, somewhere like that, send 'im
over to Souf London plonk 'im on a hous and say, 'Right, you, you 'old
the hostage there.' Like eh the police even let 'im get cannibis in. Right
how stupid is that? Of course his friends, his friends are 'ardly just gonna
bring 'im a KFC are they?

42. One Sun Newspaper

KFC on Mare Street.

KFC Manager – Smiles throughout. Amused by story in papers. Early thirties. Combination of Pakistani accent and well-spoken RP.

KFC Manager   Because we, we are not going to put cannabis in because it's expensive. We sell one piece chicken £1, I think with cannabis it would cost £10. So how can I sell £10 things in £1? (*Beat*) Actually my area manager err phoned me, he was err just joking with me, 'So you started to sell cannabis as well?' Ha, ha, ha. So I said, 'What do you, what do you mean?' He said err, 'Buy one Sun newspaper and read it.' So I read it, that night, and some customers was asking as well. Ha, ha.

43. Secret Blend

The sitting room of a pretty Victorian cottage near Graham Road.

Mrs Field   I've -I've got the cuttings next door on the table but erm (*Pointing to Max the dachshund on sofa*) – don't let him come down. (*Goes out*)

Mr Field   No don't get down Max, you stay where you are. Then they had a, at one time, they had a high pitched screech on the -which they blasted on the tannoy at him you know? Really to try and keep him awake, it was a sort- I suppose it was a sort of erm, torture into, either keeping him awake or trying to wear him down and . . . we got the benefit of this- if you see what I mean. (*Smiling*)

Mrs Field   (*Re-entering with newspaper cuttings in hand.*) Well uhm, I think this is the Sun and the Guardian . . . Let's see, what does it say? (*Reading*) Colonel Saunders original recipe may contain a secret blend of eleven herbs and spices but until now (*Stifling a laugh*) the popular recreational drug was not thought to be one of them. Erm . . .(*Looking for more to read out.*)

Mr Field   (*Laughs and claps his hands twice.*)

Mrs Field   (*Continues to read*) Junior Skerrett err, attempted to sneak, dum-de-duddle-dum, it is claimed that Mr Skerrett unemployed from Brixton brought a portion of fried chicken up to the cordon last Sunday. Aleg – this was allegedly found to have cannabis stuffed underneath its deep fried skin.

44. Mr Henry's

Mr Henry's Barber Shop, Graham Road.

Barber   This is a man's barber shop, Mr Henry's -that's not my name it's what I -I call it. Obviously the time it was like over the New Year, was our main busy time, well most shops ya know and er 'course we close down completely. We're tryin to get compensation but I doubt we get it because (*Beat*) the police a' sayin they close roads down every day of the week like gas leaks, demonstrations things like that. But our argument is, yeah, you do that only for two or three days not sixteen days, that's our argument. We 'ave got a good case but I don't know if we'll get anyfing at all, I don't know. We're fighting, I mean we got an association going now, we gotta try from there, ya know. It'll be a long road I reckon but we gotta try for it, ya know?

45. Flower Shop

At the siege cordon.

French girl – Little and scruffy in an artistic kind of way. Mid-twenties. Her agitation and preoccupation with getting to the flower shop makes her speak very quickly and pay little attention to the overweight teenager from sc 42.

French Girl   I need to go -to -you know to the flower shop -to get some flowers because it's my favourite shop . . . and I'm going mad because it's the only flower shop I use -and it's been closed now for about two weeks now and you can't go round can ya?

Teenager   Well vat's the uva fing. The business's are loosin money. That's, that's erh . . .

French Girl   But I need to go to the flower shop -cos it's my favourite one, I need to get some plants -it's my favourite plant shop. It's nice an cheerful/. . . it needs

Teenager   /But at the end of the day the, right the police should use the news, the police should use the news . . .

French Girl   Don't you think that, to shoot everyone, I don't know, ha, ha! No I love plants you know cos they died and some of them got nicked. Oh I'm going mad, you think I'm mad?

Teenager   It's comin up to half a million/ it was-

French Girl   /So stupid.

Teenager   -quarter of a million two days ago.

French Girl   For real?

Teenager   See cos don't forget, that's how much it's costing them to patrol it all that, at the end of the day, after that I reckon the costs are gonna saw, if it carries on for much longer / the costs . . .

French Girl   /It's gonna go on for ever. Surely they can just get the army or I don't know or just shoot the whole fucking bastard, they should just shoot everyone, I don't know I would anyway. Bye-bye. (*Hurries off*)

46. Rent

A children's dress shop on Graham Road.

Sadness and depression now showing through. She has lost her high spirits of Sc 20.

Connie   A friend of mine she closed down three days after we came because don't getting any customers coming by and the landlords they don't really care about the rent whether or not we have money we -you know? It's like they demanding their money we have to pay. I mean as I'm talking maybe by Monday I may get a bailiff here or something because I haven't got a money and no money's coming in and I have to survive with four kids and I'm a single mother.

47. Mick the Stripper

The kitchen of a quirky Victorian flat near Graham Road.

Charlie   There's a guy who strips doors, Mick the Stripper, as we call him, who, whose business was right next to it, so . . . it was- obviously he was- quietened.

48. Beckett!

Outside his workshop.

Mick – Bearded, very warm smile. Late sixties. Dressed in plus fours and bow tie, somewhat shabby repair, complete with crumpled hat. Soft Southern Irish lilt. Slow speech.

Mick   I was doin nothing, it's cold, it was very cold. You couldn't claim for nothing, you couldn't claim for nothing because I wasn't there . . .

too cold. Oh I come past it and seen it yeah, (*Beat*) seen the siege (*Beat*) but I don't know much about it. No I do odds for the hospice -Saint Joseph's hospice, I do all the charity do's for Saint Joseph's hospice in between -in between mi work. John Wayne, yeah, yeah. John Wayne, I go as Beckett, I dress up as Beckham -Beckett, the footballer (*Beat*) the footballer!

49. Good Claim

A textile designer's studio next door to Anthony and Juliet.

Bernie   The Indian chap who has the grocers, the little er well-tobacconist and Newsagent. We're on sort of noddin' terms ya know? He seems more friendly and err jovial actually after it. Whether he's had a good claim from the insurance company or not, I don't know which had cheered 'im up, I don't know.

50. Not a Penny

A Newsagents on Graham Road.

Newsagent   Yeah he's my son.

Son   We lost out on quite a bit of business, a lot of business, that's the busiest period of the year, New Years and Christmas, especially New Years, we haven't made a penny. (*Kisses his teeth*) (*Beat*) and the government don't wanna give out no money now (*Beat*) full stop.

Newsagent   (*To son*) You want to go bank?

51. Dig Deeply

Children's Christmas party.

Mayoress – Short and stocky. High-pitched voice shouting over the party game music playing in the background. Wears her chains of office.

Mayoress   My name's councillor Sharon Patrick and I'm the speaker for the London Borough of Hackney so basically -I'm the mayor but wiv anuva name. They had to find a new name for the civic mayor, which is me (*Beat*) so they call me the speaker after Betty Boofroyd -who was a very popular speaker of the House of Commons. I go round representing the Borough uhm (*Beat*) when the borough needs -a presence, when they need a formal presence -someone to represent the Borough, so I go uhm (*Beat*) I'm here today to represent the Borough, I go round -I open fings -I go -I do whatever I'm asked to do. I had a very minor role wivin the siege, the only really role I had was at the end of the siege where I had a collection at the Council meeting . . . just asked people to uhm dig deeply (*Beat*) Uhm, ya now I suppose yeah they dug deeply (*Beat*) We raised uhm a 100 pound which (*Beat*) -was ya know (*Beat*) -it wasn't bad. Well I believe the compensation had to come from the police as far as I understand the legislation; the council has no powers to give them compensation, it was a police uhm (*Beat*) matter. Councillors can only -Councillors operate wivin laws that tell us what we can do -and you can only do soming if there's a law to say that you can do it.

52. Fascinating

At home on the phone.

Thirty minutes into the third phone call. She speaks very firmly.

Alecky   Listen I'm not interested and it's none of my business who you want to have sex with or whatever ok? That's not part of the interview, ya know? As fascinating as it may be, (*Beat*) erm I kind of want to talk to you about what happened to you in that flat ok? And your love life and your sex life is a separate issue. Ya know? If you want to tell me about it fine but please don't try and involve me in it.

53. Temperament

At siege by the refreshments catering van for police officers.

SM19 Armed Officer – Large build, very relaxed wearing a bullet-proof vest and helmet with a large gun over his shoulder. Late forties. Yorkshire accent.

SM19 Armed Officer   Yeah I mean err (*Beat*) – they pick ya because of er ya temperament really, they don't want anyone who's too hot headed sort o' carryin' fire arms around London do they? So I mean the majority of people in the firearms department have got a lot of basic police experience, been in the force for more than five years. It's no good bein a good shot but bein sort very err (*Beat*) ya know, easily sort of wound up, so you have to be sort of like good at both things. (*Pause*) Alright?

54. On the Roof

A textile designer's studio next door to Anthony and Juliet.

Penny   We went on the roof which was so stupid because, / we didn't -

Bernie   /Oh I thought it was fun.

Penny   It was fun but you know we could see all, we could see all the marksmen on the different rooftops and what was a . . .

Bernie   Yeah we spotted all them before they spotted us / and

Penny   /Yeah

Bernie   That's a dead cert / well we think so.

Penny   /That's what I think's a bit worrying and I said.

Bernie   We think so.

Penny   My worry slightly was that the police maybe were so bored and frustrated themselves because after nearly two weeks and they'd been on duty in all that freezing weather. I mean they had these little blue polythene sort of tents on various roof tops around and I thought, God they're gonna be so bored and jumpy and they might suddenly see us an you know? I think probably it was a really stupid thing to do.

Bernie   But, but they changed them very, ya know on a regular basis -that's why there's so many of them.

Penny   They're on forty minute shifts apparently.

Bernie   Forty minute shifts those marksmen. Yeah.

Penny   An then they go and get warm and someone else takes over.

Bernie   They go off for a bit of target practice. (*Smiles*)

55. Record Book

A Vietnamese Takeaway Restaurant on Graham Road.

Hong   Ya know nobody will fink the siege last that long. This it go into record -later we learn that it go into record book because it . . . no siege last that long. We were finking he's coming out. We no -we never fort he that mad.

Leroy

A textile designer's studio next door to Anthony and Juliet.

Penny   The auntie visited him I think to try and get him out earlier. We don't really know anything / actually.

Bernie   /Pass me that biscuit barrel pet please.

Penny   This one?

Bernie   Yeah. It's got fig roles in that one. I'd rather have one of those. Would you like one?

Penny   Would you like one of these? (*Offering a packet of custard creams.*)

Bernie   I limit myself to just fig roles because I read somewhere they're good for you. He's psychologically imbalanced he must be, ya know there'a definitely ya know he's probably had a shit upbringing an he's got 'imself in such f- such a mess. And erm er we heard them saying 'Leroy come out we are worried about you Leroy' / please come out with out -

Penny   /Eli

Bernie   -Your, oh Eli, (*Laughs*) 'Eli, Eli we are worried about you, er come an throw your weapon out first ya know we're really worried about you.' An ehm / you thought

Penny   /And you thought . . .

Bernie   Hello this is -they're doin, it sounded just like a public relations exercise.

56. So Many Eli's

A spotless kitchen in Hackney.

Hetty – Tall and imposing, with an arthritic hand that was permanently in a claw shape. Booming voice with gentrified Jamaican accent.

Hetty   We, we're developing a new breed of criminals because when kids are excluded there's no-where for them to go. There're so many Eli's in this world and that's why I do what I do -so we won't have too many of those Eli's takin hostages and doin this sort of thing to other people. And may the children of the siege learn through the trauma's that had been caused through err (*Beat*) Eli.

IRA

At the siege cordon.

Irish – Bearded in his sixties with a strong Belfast accent. Drunk. His flippancy and humour turns threatening. Little Man – Short and frail, in his seventies. Speaks with a formality and has a lisp. PC – Early thirties. Polite, slight London accent.

Irish   Yeh well I think they should just shoot 'im. I think so, yuh, what do you think? (*Spotting* Alecky's *microphone.*) What the fuckin hell's this shoot now? Come 'ere come 'ere. (*Laughs*) Put the IRA in there they'll fuckin take 'im out in one hit. (*Laughing*) No problem, no problem at all baby, no problem. We'll take 'im out one hit. You wanee mess wi' us- we'll fuckin mess wi' you boy . . . kill ya. (*Beat*) (*More serious*) What's gonna happen then? Somebody's gonna hurt here ya know? (*To PC on cordon*) What are you gonna do about it then? What are you gonna do about it then?

PC   That's not our decision.

Irish   It's not your decision? You, you are the ground troops, you boys. When somebody -if they do their business, you lads had to do it wouldn't you?

PC   Yes but it's the people abuv us that make them decisions I'm afraid.

Little Man   (*To* Alecky) Is this the news? I was looking, in actual -actually I was looking for a certain police PC, whose home beat officer where I live. PC Mark Cavanagh, you know him? I need to see him. Yes!. . . I just moved into the area in April. Thanks for your concerns.

Irish   (*Still to PC*) Yeah well you should go in there and fuckin sort it out. I tell ya.

Little Man   Shh, shh. Your language, there's a lady here. (*Referring to* Alecky.)

Irish   Listen mate, come 'ere. I don't give a shite. (*Aggressively to PC*) GO IN THERE AND SORT IT OUT!

PC   Leave it to the boys with guns I'm afraid.

Irish   (*Politely retreats*) Alright thanks son.

Little Man   I can't st -I can't stand filthy language. I can't stand the filthy language.

57. Know What I Mean?

At the siege cordon.

Cyclist – On his bike. Thirties. Strong Newcastle accent. Talks quickly but pauses between thoughts as he thinks of something even more impressive to say.

Cyclist   It just sums up society really dunnit? Know what I mean? Man with a gun Christmas, it's what it's all about innit? You know what I mean? Ya know? All the crap the police bringin out, all their, all their stuff, ya know, sayin 'Oh look we got guns, ah?' Not impressed. Nah *(Beat)* People shouldn't allow -allow anyone to 'ave guns in this country, ya know what I mean? What's it got like America where we all got guns? Be half us dead in the street by then ya know what I mean? It's just shit man, guns, weapons, we don't need'em, ya know what I mean? Us or the police . . . Ah? *(Beat)* It's just a sad reflection of the way society's goin, ya know what I mean? Ya know there's a geezer up there he's obviously schizophrenic, come out of hospital,. . . why the fuck 'as he got a gun?. . . Ya know what I mean? *(Spots SM19 officers walking past.)* Look at this, ya know what I mean? Geezer's looking like German soldiers, ha, ha, ha, they do, look at their -look at their helmets man, ya know what I mean? It's the storm troopers *(Beat)* If they got any balls they'd just go in there and blow his fuckin head off. Know what I mean? Job done!

58. Wounded

Mr Henry's Barber Shop, Graham Road.

Barber   Obviously he set fire to the house apparently himself -he was burnin fur, -his own furniture to keep warm -coz they cut his er electric off. An I fink that the police wounded him, I dunno where, in the 'ead somewhere. An it finished up he shot himself. An he got burnt then he got burnt as well. And err, he shot himself up -up in the chin.

59. Fire

The kitchen of a quirky Victorian flat near Graham Road.

Charlie   So the fire gradually got worse an worse and it sort of flared up and it got really out of control at one point and they were -ya know -the fireman couldn't put it out properly because *(Beat)* Oh yeah this was right outside my door.

60. Nail Varnish

The sitting room of a pretty Victorian cottage near Graham Road.

Mr Field   Because he had petrol up there, er which is how he set fire to . . .

Mrs Field   Yes but didn't they say that he'd, that that was untrue in the end?

Mr Field   I don't know. I didn't see -I didn't see the end / of it.

Mrs Field   /You didn't see that big report? I don't think, I'm not sure that he did.

Mr Field   But how did he set fire to the building so effectively?

Mrs Field   Well it wasn't effective. That morning, it was just white smoke, it was more like uhm . . . steam from a / bath but it was billowing.

Mr Field   /Yeah but then it. But then it really blowed, billowed out.

Mrs Field   Yes but not till the afternoon / by-

Mr Field   /No

Mrs Field   – which time it had been going on for three or four hours . . .

Mr Field   Yeah but without some . . . assistance that couldn't possibly have happened, I mean he had to have had some kind of . . .

Mrs Field   Yes but we've all got something / I mean nail varnish remover- I mean heaps of things you can find that are flammable.

Mr Field   /Ok it might not have been petrol but whatever it was . . . he set fire to the place.

61. Three Shots

A Vietnamese Takeaway Restaurant on Graham Road.

Hong   So it -the last day suddenly we heard shooting, three shot and one shot different and we heard err the police say, 'It's a fire we can see smoke inside you better come out.' They call his name, and said 'better come out.' So we just pray come on get out, you know the police keep like begging him. I feel sorry for police as well. It's just like you -they can show their, they feel sorry for the gun man, 'Please come out, I don't want you to get hurt in there, it's -you have to think about your family.'

62. Nice to Meet You

Wetherspoons pub on Mare Street.

Hostage – Strong Nigerian accent. Not sexually threatening at all in the flesh. Enjoys the chance to talk to someone. Stutters throughout (more than can be put onto paper) trying to find the right English.

Hostage   (*Chuckles nervously*)

Alecky   So anyway nice to meet you.

Hostage   Ok it's ok.

Alecky   (*Giggles nervously*)

Hostage   We had a very long . . . you know long conversation -you know on the phone.

Alecky   (*Still laughing*) Yeah, ha.

Hostage   All the days.

Alecky   Yeah so I kind of -you know hope you understand, it's just a sort of job you know.

Hostage   Mmm

Alecky   I've got £50 for you,/ ya know-

Hostage   /Mmm, yeah.

Alecky   – so that's cool / and I'm sorry it's not more.

Hostage   /Ok, it's because of the way -you know you said you are a struggling actor.

Alecky   Yes.

Hostage   So I decided to ya know / be a-

Alecky   /Yeah.

Hostage   -little bit merciful

Alecky   Yes, yeah, yeah.

Hostage   That's cool.

Alecky   (*Beat*) Ok, ok so uhm -how did you know Eli? You know, was it because you lived in the flats or how did you know him?

Hostage   I mean he's not my friend, I think I moved in there, I moved there to live -I think on –2001- November 11. You know he's just a normal person and we don't get on very well and- he's not my friend, we just 'good morning hi'.

Alecky   Right. (*Beat*)

Hostage   On that first day, there were three other people you know that lived there with us, that used to live there, I think they -they went to work to, I dunno, to their relative for Christmas or something like that so . . . by then, you know what I mean. He broke into their rooms -he didn't sleep in his own room any more he went and then sleep on the last floor. There was a cleaning lady that lived there, then he occupied the place, that place -I asked him why he was doing that and he told me that -that place he could have a bird's eye view -to shoot at the police . . . you know . . . so he was -at that place yeah . . . Yeah he told me to come in there to stay with him in the room -if I'm feelin a bit lonely or something like that. They-

Alecky   Did you not want to leave, did you want to leave?

Hostage   Er, I wasn't . . . from that second day third day it was all good, good, good, the situation was good, yeah, you know -he hasn't been getting stressed by them you know -it was just as, business as usual, normal, we were,/ aha

Alecky   (*Giggles imagining them hanging out.*)

Hostage   (*Laughs*) It was just . . . (*more laughing*)

Alecky   So for the first couple of days you were kind of just hanging out?

Hostage   Yeah, yeah.

Alecky   Not – thinking it would pass / and

Hostage   /Yeah.

Alecky   Maybe they would, maybe Eli would give himself up?

Hostage   Yeah, yeah.

Alecky   That's what you were thinking?

Hostage   Yeah. One -I think one of the reasons why I didn't bother coming out because I said to myself, you know previously, you know, he's not like my enemy.

Alecky   (*chewing*) In the newspaper article it says that he asked to have, he said he'd come out if he got to sleep with one of the police women. Is that right?

Hostage   Yeah that's right. Mmm hmm, Heather. The negotiators they were doing a shift person . . . ya know they were maybe sort of shift person (*Beat*) hmm. I think Heather came, it was Heather's turn that day. Heather was talking to . . . you know to him . . . Heather asked him ya know . . . what- what, how can they presume, what can they do to get him out of that place and he told Heather, if Heather can be able to take him -to his house and have a shower -and then have sex with Heather -and then he would then give himself up, so.

Alecky   (*Beat*) Mmm. What did Heather say?

Hostage   Mmm. What was, what was Heather's response? I think Hea – Heath-Heather was uhm- Heather wasn't, it wasn't agreeing with Heather. I told him that ya know that he should agree for the sex yeah then . . . (*burps and keeps eating*)

Alecky   Did you tell Heather that?

Hostage   Mmm hmm. Of course I did yeah. I told Heather that this what-this is what -this -this -I told Heather that the ball is- is in her court- in her court. (*Laughs*) He's ya know, he quite a nice, quite a nice, quite a nice-quite a nice-nice person, he's quite ya know good, intelligent as well yeah.

63. Undercover

Builder walks into the conversation. Mid-fifties. He's tall, skinny and scruffy wearing a pink crochet hat that catches Alecky's attention. London accent, silly laugh. Been drinking for a while.

Builder   Hello/. Alwite?

Alecky   (*unsure but amused*)/ Hello.

Hostage   Hello sir.

Builder   How are you?

Hostage   I'm fine thanks yeah. Please to- see you.

Builder   Eh? You? (*to Alecky*)

Alecky   (*amused by him*) Hello. Alright./

Builder   /Ha, hah.

Alecky   Ha. (*laughing at and with him*)

Builder   You're worried about my 'at. Aren't you?

Alecky   I like your hat. It's very smart./ Yeah? (*holding back a laugh*)

Builder   /Yeah? But everybody keeps coming up to me and asking me why, they think I'm doin it under protest or anything but that is- that is me- that is me. D'you like it?

Hostage   I like it, yes I like it. I don't have any problem with it.

Builder   Eh?

Hostage   (*slight laugh*) I don't have any problem with it, it's ok.

All   (*Laugh*)

Builder   I wear -I got black, white an everything ya know what I mean? It's just, just the mood -I'm in -I'm in a pink mood so, ha, ha, ha, so that's it. (*Laughs loudly*)

Alecky   Lovely. (*Laughing*) OK. (*Builder turns as if to go*)

Hostage   Nice one pal. (*Returns to conversation with* Alecky.) And ya know . . . back to the story, also while . . .

Builder   Just gonna say. Sorry, just gonna say I'm a silly old builder and I do anything. You alwite?

Alecky   I'm doing a play about the siege that happened, just after Christmas, were you around then, were you affected by it at all?

Builder   Well . . .(*over to friends across the bar*) You off? See you later.

Alecky   Were you affected by the siege or you weren't near it?

Builder   I was, I-I-I-was not but the point is I fink it could'a bin over wivin two days. On my life, believe or not, I could ha' dunnit./

Hostage   /You?

Builder   I could ha' got 'im out. I could'ha dunnit/ in two days.

Hostage/   No, no, no, no.

Builder   You seen the size o' the windas?

Hostage   Aha.

Builder   Ya know, it . . . it -it wasn't . . . well let me-I don't-I don't mince mi words, a load of shit, a load of waste of money.

Hostage   The man was armed, he was armed though.

Builder   I don't –no. It doesn't make no difference, it was a load shit/ (*Hostage bursts out laughing, Alecky giggles*) and everything. Ya know what I mean? It was very easy/.

Hostage   (*quietly*) /It wasn't.

Builder   Unless the hostage (*Beat*) was a policeman and that is the (*Beat*) the thing that people sayin.

Alecky   (*hiding disbelief*) Oh really?

Builder   Yeah. That's what I heard.

Hostage   So -so -sorry. Say again – say that . . .

Builder   That the hostage was a policeman.

Alecky   Right.

Hostage   Ok, ok (*Beat*) No.

Builder   That's wot we/ heard.

Hostage   (*amazed*) /Ha, ha.

Alecky   Is it?

Builder   (*nodding his head confidently for a moment*) Mmm.

(*Pause*)

Builder   Anyway . . . (*walks off as easily as he walked over*)

Hostage   So. So erm, wh-wh-where am I again? / I just lost it.

Both   /(*laugh*)

Hostage   He tell me that he want to shoot one of the police in the face, he meant it yeah. He wanted to shoot me in the face as well . . . yeah . . . I told him not to. He told me that if I- ya know, that if I stay in there, that it's ok but if he happened to see me leavin -you know if he happened to see me leavin -that he would -you know, that I might end up in a wheel chair, you know and he meant it. That's how, ya know . . .

Alecky   So how did you uhm, how did you make your move then?

Hostage   Ok yeah. On that day, after pointing, after pointing the gun at me, and I told the negotiators that ya know I could be coming out -I wanted it to be that day. That was why I started the cookin in the first place yeah, so that while cookin he would say, ok he's cookin and he would carry on with whatever he is doin. The door leading to that building where the police could have come in from . . . he has barricaded it with heavy objects -heavy big stuff. As soon as I see him goin -then I, ya know, I started removing those things -quickly but casually as well. Then I jumped, then I started coming down the stairs, I didn't even look back. When I came out, when I saw the daylight like this it was just like bein in a different -different place on my eyes, yeah. Because in there is all darkness . . . yeah, we are seeing a very little light because he blocked the whole place. I just breathe in and breathe and say, I'm ok now. I'm ok now (*Pause*) He . . . he died an untimely death -I mean -I think, he committed suicide. That's what I think, yeah. Because he was pointing his gun, ya know, while we were in there . . . on his head yeah, like this (*Beat*) Yeah. I felt uhm sort of . . . guilt like my brother. I felt, ya know? (*Pause*) It affected me . . . yeah badly (*Pause*) but I'm ok now. (*Pause*) A bit.

(Long *pause*)

64. Scraped

A studio in a fashionable block in Hackney.

Anthony   They didn't go in to find his body / before Friday. They didn't take the body until Saturday.

Juliet   /Before Sunday. After on Friday we were . . .

Anthony   The whole atmosphere totally changed-

Juliet   Yeah.

Anthony   – it was a kind of strange, strange day and I don't really know what happened at the end of it.

Juliet   I think we didn't know anything, I remember / I was walking

Anthony   /Was that when I scraped my car? I can't remember . . .

Juliet   Yes it was.

Anthony   And I was really pissed off then (*Beat*) Pissed off. What I hadn't realised was that suddenly the fact that we were in this situation

with people running past with machine guns has actually got to me . . .
finally. Why couldn't they have done something else?

65. Disturbing

Children's Christmas Party.

Doctor Maria   Reporters were outside and erm . . . police and they
were saying they couldn't take his body out because the building was
structurally unsound -and it became really sort of disturbing that I could
look out my window and I could see this window where I knew there
was a dead body inside. And you've obviously seen where his window
was and there was that er Moet and Chandon poster light? And it was
such a contrast -and as I would look out my window there was this
real -ya know, brightly lit, ya know, photograph of champagne and this
beautiful woman and it was all going on in that little dark window and
I found that really disturbing. It was very very -there was something
very sort of sad about the whole thing in the end. And I think I passed
by, -was it the following morning when the cordon was gone -and there
just one tiny little bunch of flowers, like ya know the kind you get on a
motorway when there's been an accident?

66. Postcard

The kitchen of a quirky Victorian flat near Graham Road.

Charlie   It was a sort of weird sort of . . . postcard -it's going to be next
year's post card I think for me because I took -I actually did take some
pictures of this whole debacle at the end of it. Erm, it's a beautiful early
January morning with ya know, beautifully clear snow, it's totally been
uninterrupted -because the police weren't moving around that much and er
(*Beat*) beautiful golden light washing across it. It's sort idyllic. You know
and in the middle of all this there are police vans -there are sort of little tents
with gun man -police gunmen in them -and all these things- all dotted around
very tastefully in the snow . . . It's like sort of -ya know -it's like Bethlehem.

67. Demolish

A Vietnamese Takeaway Restaurant on Graham Road.

Hong   Every time, I don't really want to go past that road. I just
imagine him, lying there dead. I just . . . I really hate it to go there.

68. Enormous Fun

The sitting room of a pretty Victorian cottage near Graham Road.

Mrs Field   You didn't get to sleep.

Mr Field   You just didn't go to sleep.

Mrs Field   We hardly slept for five – two weeks in fact I hardly slept for a month because I couldn't sleep after that / Yes!

Mr Field   /Yuh.

Mrs Field   You keep thinking you can rush to the window and see all the lights and see everything going on and this suddenly this theatre has stopped. It wasn't a crime incident at all (*Beat*) No it was the most enormous fun, drama until it was over when we kind of . . . overcome with sadness which was extraordinary since we'd been enjoying it really. (*Smiles wistfully*)

Mr Field   But it was, it was an exciting time I mean in -in a funny kind of way -in a perverse kind of way we enjoyed it. Because you know, there was a buzz that was going about and it was (*Beat*) uhm (*Beat*) scary -in that-

Mrs Field   What was scary about it?

Mr Field   Well scary in that one didn't know when there was going to be a fatal shot, if there was indeed a fatal shot . . . err we did hear gun fire from time to time. In the first night- on the Thursday night we heard seven shots?

Mrs Field   No that was boxing day.

Mr Field   Yes that's right.

Mrs Field   Right -but it was in the afternoon wasn't it?

Mr Field   No it was seven o'clock at night–

Mrs Field   Oh was it? Forgotten now.

Mr Field   – it was seven o'clock at night. There were about seven shots and then shortly afterwards -I can't remember how long after about twenty minutes or something there was a single (*makes gunshot sound and makes gun shape with hand*)- one shot- and then a little bit later another single shot. And then we didn't hear very much for a long time until we got (*Beat*) I can't remember which night it was but there were -a night or two after that when out came the tannoy 'ELI, ELI COME OUT, COME OUT', and I thought 'Elo-eh, Elo-eh, la'ma sabach-tha'ni', erm you know 'Oh God, oh God, why has thus forsaken me?'

69. That Was It

Children's Christmas Party.

Doctor Maria   Because he'd become such a totally huge ever-present figure for everybody in the road and suddenly he was dead and there was nothing said about it (*Beat*) That was it. It was a death and it had happened just there. And it sounded like -for whatever reason a really sad -violent death – no -we'd been speaking about nothing else for fourteen days and suddenly that was it.

70. Other Job

The building site where the siege flat once was.

Brickie – Skinny with Romanian accent, not confident with his English.

Brickie   I think here before have er one home but I think it's -it have a fire you know? Yeah. After my err company everything demolition, everything inside outside the building the -all everything down. After, I don't know what happened after, maybe construction other (*Beat*) maybe I don't know. I finished the job just clean here and after -after with err . . . my boss with the lorry -get a bricks -put a fings, it's finished job here in this area. Tomorrow morning get other job.

71. Tannoy

A Vietnamese Takeaway Restaurant on Graham Road.

Hong   The police keep telling him, please ehm, we won't harm you Ali Holme . . . his name? (*Beat*) Eli Hall, Eli you see I don't want to hear that name (*getting upset*). I hate to hear that name cos it remind me of that. Because our room at the back so that's why the tannoy from the back (*Beat*) and I hate to hear that name because it remind me of that time. (*Crying*) And uhm . . . why didn't he come out so it's -it would be better for everyone?

72. The Sex Thing

Wetherspoon's pub on Mare Street.

Alecky   So thank you so much (*Beat*) thank you – for (*Beat*) chatting to me/

Hostage   /Mmm.

Alecky   -for all the agreed -you know . . . whatever.

Hostage   Mmm. I'm quite cool about it. Ya know. But we stayed more than- more than -more than we – but anyway it's quite ok. So you know what I mean about the stuff that I talked on the phone?

Alecky   About what?

Hostage   About the – the – the – the. You know what I mean. You don't, no need to be still, asking me back 'about what about what?' (*Quietly but seriously after a short pause*) Think about it.

Alecky.   What about what I wasn't?

(*Beat*)

Hostage   You know what I mean. I don't know.

Alecky   Sort of. I'm still-

Hostage   You're still?

Alecky   – just doing the job and I've just given you the money and that's all I'm wanting to do. And I hope that's ok because we did agree didn't we?

Hostage   We did -we did agree yeah. Can –can -can't I -I have -have more than that then? Can -can't I get it. Yeah.

(*Short pause*)

Alecky   What more money?

Hostage   No -no, the -the -the still the sex thing or money if you want -if you want.

Alecky   No I can't ya know . . . like I said I haven't got any more money. I can see you want a girlfriend.

Hostage   (*chuckles*)

Alecky   You just want a bit of action -ya know?

Hostage   No -no -no. I'm not . . . sometimes I do, you know I mean. It's a, like we said, your's- it's a different case. I said we had a lot –lot -lots of conversation and I say to myself . . . what ya know what you are going to look like ya know . . . you're not uhm . . . you're quite good to my taste anyway I don't have any problem with you. I wouldn't mind ya know (*Beat*) having it or something. But I – I – I know you are a little bit hesitant -hesitant.

Alecky   Hesitant? I'm more than hesitant. (*Firm but can't help smiling at his persistance*) I'm not gonna do it with you!

The End

A Principle Rather Than an Accident: Some Notes on Forced Entertainment's *The Travels*

Tim Etchells

Based in Sheffield, United Kingdom, Forced Entertainment comprises an artistic core (Richard Lowdon, Cathy Naden, Claire Marshall, Terry O'Connor, Robin Arthur and myself as Artist Director) who, with a rolling cast of guests and colleagues, have collaborated since 1984. From *Jessica in the Room of Lights* in 1984, through *Speak Bitterness* (1994) and *Bloody Mess* (2004) to *Tomorrow's Parties* (2011) and *The Coming Storm* (2012) the group's projects are sometimes exuberant collisions of influence taking in theatre, cinema, stand-up, choreography, bad television, music culture, cabaret and conceptual art, at other times assuming more minimal and intimate form, figured largely through text and dedicated to the exploration of a single rule or proposition. Created in a process of improvisation, discussion, scripting and rehearsal, each project, in different ways, critiques, questions and extends the conventions, expectations and limits of theatrical form, while celebrating performance as a playful space of fiction and invention.

The group's output over nearly 30 years can be loosely grouped in four strands, from a ground in touring theatre projects, to durational task-based performances (often presented in galleries or non-theatre spaces), to occasional site-specific and installation works and finally, to a series of lecture, documentary or essay performances. Through this diversity of approaches are a set of concerns which the group have returned to over the years, with ideas from one project very often influencing the make-up and direction of subsequent works. Coming at the same thematics from different angles, the group has examined the problematic and fecund question of the role and construction of the theatrical performer (as persona, as character, as version of him or herself) and at the same time explored an equally fraught and foundational set of questions about theatre's relation to and construction of audience.

Even the earliest, overtly fictional works of the group signalled questions about the relation between theatre, truth and fiction, and from the outset there was a certain spotlight on (and suspicion of) the business of acting – framed very often as pretence. Indeed the group often preferred to approach theatre through concepts of anti-illusion, authenticity and supposed reality, drawing on or nodding to pre-dramatic forms of play and ritual as well as to concepts drawn from performance art as outlined, for example, in Ken McMullen and Stuart Brisley's 1984 documentary film *Being & Doing*. Nodding to Brecht perhaps, and to art performance, we were also interested in the notional reality of the performer beneath role or character, in the revelation or construction of the performer as an actual presence – someone making decisions, making choices, making fun, making performance in fact – in the real space and time of the theatre. If there was undoubtedly an aspect of mis en abyme in all this, there was just certainly a committed, rolling investigation of what it means to be a performer in front of others, with each project drawing and redrawing the lines of triangulation between performer and audience, between versions of truth and versions of fiction, between the transformed other space of narrative and theatrical fiction and the raw present space of performance, encounter with audience and task. The binary haunted us; we worried at it, and over years, learned to live with it. The shows were full of ruptures, glimpses, puncturings and revelations, sombre readings that opened to theatre, preposterous spectacles that collapsed to the failure and fragility of the here and now, apparently real things that became or were revealed as fake, fake things that took on, with time, a kind of reality.

Elizabeth LeCompte (Wooster Group), also channelling Brecht perhaps, once spoke of their performance *Fish Story* (based on Chekhov's *Three Sisters*) as having two stories – that of *Three Sisters* and that of the performers making their way through *Three Sisters*. It was an observation that spoke to us, naming a sense we'd long had, of the parallel journeys at work in the theatre – the actual and the fictional, the one braided through the other. And as time went on we learned to articulate and explore this dynamic mixture in different ways, building very often from the sense of the performers being present, here, now, simply doing something in space, in front of others. This workaday understanding of what theatre might be established was a point of departure (and occasional return) for even the strangest theatrical journeys we created, and provided the ground for our interest in documentary and projects like *The Travels*.

More concretely, *The Travels* has its origins in a number of works we made starting in 1994, 10 years after the company began its collective practice. We decided to make, that year, a kind of reflexive, autobiographical performance looking at the history of the group and at the 10-year period in and through which we'd worked. This performance – *A Decade of Forced Entertainment* – was a first for us in many ways. For it, the theatrical costumes and fragmentary fictions of our previous shows were abandoned and we took to the stage for the first time in our own clothes, answering to our own names. From positions seated at tables, facing the audience, with a projection screen behind us, we told versions of our own story – of the move we made to Sheffield in 1984 and of the start of our group practice, of 10 years making work during Thatcherism's defining period of economic decline and Conservative retrenchment. We talked about the work, and about the reality it had been made in and through.

In many ways, with its reliance on direct address and its easy-going speculation linked with autobiographical narrative, *Decade* prefigured *The Travels* and was the first to break the mould of our practice – there we were after all, in 1994, in real space and time, apparently without illusionistic cover of any kind, speaking of (and as) ourselves. Creating *Decade* though, gave us a direct encounter with the problematics of such a simplistic understanding of performer identity. Writing texts for the performance, arranging them in sequence, building arcs of revelation and thematic we understood quickly (if we did not know it already) that we were not dealing with 'ourselves' but rather with versions of ourselves. We were telling stories, making dramaturgies. The mode of truthful recounting of events (we jokingly, and with some scepticism, called it 'good, honest and true') was soon joined by elements of outright fiction, and by sections of the performance in which the collective 'we' of the group's self-description mutated to 'they'. Here it was as if we were describing another group, another city, another country, another time. It was us, but not us, a mirror, a shadow, a distortion, a doubling and a mutating. There was a liberation in this move (a small step sideways from the tyranny of the real), and a productive tension in the layers it began to produce; the inchoate fictionality of some parts of the performance throwing a generative question to the rest of the material. And in a strange way of course, at least as we understood it, the layered, semi-fictive version of our story that *Decade* produced was more accurate than any other.

A related approach informed another very different project – *Nights in This City* – made the year after *Decade* and in its own way very much a precursor to elements of *The Travels*. Taking the form of a disorientating guided coach tour of Sheffield, *Nights* was about as far from a lecture performance as one could get. Instead, the project took audiences on a commentated journey through the centre of the city, careering off into industrial wastelands, housing estates and suburban sprawls before returning to the centre for the conclusion of the work – an installation in the city's massive former central bus depot on Leadmill Road. Taking its initial cue from the subtle fictional refraction of our own narrative at work in *Decade*, the principle of the guided tour in *Nights in This City* was more playful and much more misleading in respect of its subject. Indeed, *Nights* contained no useful or accurate information about Sheffield whatsoever and audiences began the night in the care of a guide who seemed at once drunk, lost and incompetent – claiming variously that the city outside the bus windows was Rome, Berlin or Paris, or that 'the streets . . . [were]. . . named after famous football hooligans from history', before reporting on a series of improbable personal connections to the landscape beyond 'That park we just passed, that was named after my dad, because he used to take me there as a kid.' The second half of the project – returning to the city via dual-carriageway as night began to fall – featured a second guide, this one calmer, whose more poetic and reflective text focused on the audience themselves and their role in seeing and narrativizing the lives and landscape which lay outside the windows of the moving coach.

For *Nights in this City*, Sheffield was both subject and actor – the city and its inhabitants caught in the tangle of its voice/gaze and at the same time, with vigour, resisting the narratives we overlaid, proposing its own, affirming its own identity in spite of, or through the fog of, our intervention. The project also acknowledged that extraordinary amounts of space in the work belonged to individual spectators – such that any experience of the project was quite inevitably a mix of the city itself, the work we did in miss-narrating it, and the work that audiences did in bringing their own memories, stories and imaginings about the place to bear on what they saw. What *Nights* shared with the later work, *The Travels*, was a conception that the landscape might be a repository not just for actual history but also for imagining. It also shared what we began to think of as a process of giving in to the city and the landscape – we had no way of knowing what the city or its inhabitants would bring to the performance on any particular night after all, and the performance had to be ready for bad traffic and rain, drunks in the street, random bonfires on waste grounds and the endless coincidence – incidents of passers-by who would appear at any point on its route, going about their business, spinning the flavour, texture or the detail of the work in unexpected directions. In this sense, the piece was forged through an unsteady contract with the city; the bus windows were a frame, but what happened in that frame was beyond our control.

In some ways of course, this dance with unpredictability is a common feature of the company's more typical studio-based devising processes which, with their emphasis on collaging independent contributions from all group members, and on open-ended improvisation as an investigative tool, are designed to court the juxtaposition of otherwise disconnected material. Not knowing where we are going is a principle rather than an accident. But 'usually' in these studio works the filter of what comes into the room and how, is provided by the group itself.

The final work which prefigured *The Travels*, and which played a significant part in suggesting its process, was my 2000/2001 solo *Instructions for Forgetting*. That piece, conceived as a work made from donated video fragments and narratives, with me in the role of Narrator and conduit for material given to me by other people, prefigured *The Travels* in its use of a simple generative structure designed to let material emerge unchecked by authorial drift or intention. The process for *Instructions* began with a set of emails sent to friends, colleagues and acquaintances requesting that they let me have 5 minutes of video tape – any moving-image sequence which they felt (for whatever reason) was worthy of salvage from whatever tangles of home-shot video they'd accrued previously in the era (before digital) of more-or-less ubiquitous video-tape. As the video materials began to arrive (the sun reflected on the sea, a soldier stood on guard in a particular place, a home-video shot at a fairground, an amateur striptease) I wrote further emails to an overlapping group of friends and asked them to send me true stories, whatever true meant to them, and waited as the texts that would eventually form the performance arrived one by one. There were stories about childhood, about murder, about ways of earning money, about death, about love, about war and about silence. There was a kind of generous, if foolhardy, trust at the heart of *Instructions* – a belief that something worthwhile would come from my correspondents and from the collision and interplay of the stories and images they sent me. It was, of necessity, a blind trust, a gamble, because I had no way of knowing in advance what (if anything) would arrive. From the outset though I committed myself and collaborators Richard Lowdon and Hugo Glendinning, to working with whatever came, and to developing a dramaturgy, a line of argument and enquiry that came from the material itself, as it emerged, framed and guided by its offers, its opportunities and its limits.

I was staged in *Instructions*, in part by what I wrote or said in linking or introducing material from others and in part by stories that I wrote for the project myself. But I was also staged in it, more profoundly perhaps, by the negotiation I did with the donated material. I was trapped in the structure of donated stories and video, both constrained by the choices others had made and in a strange way produced by them and it was something akin to this structure that *The Travels* nodded to when we began work on it some years later. Indeed pretty much at the outset we conceived of the project and formulated a simple set of rules governing the process which would, for good or for ill, get us to the material of the performance. In the beginning we studied street maps and A-Z street indexes, selecting literally or symbolically named streets in England, Scotland and Wales – places like Hope Street and Love Lane, Achilles Way or Deadman's Lane. We made choices about which of the six performers would visit which of these locations, they made their plans and then set off. The task in each place was impossibly simple and simply impossible – to look, to see, to wait, to find, to observe, to listen, to hear, to ask, to venture. In each place something happened or did not happen. In each place things were seen, missed, heard and not heard. Observations were made, conversations were had or not had, notes were taken, stories written or not written or forgotten or misremembered. Returning to base from time to time through the weeks of the process, the performers shared material and we began to get a sense of what was interesting and what was problematic about the delirious human geography or landscape temperature mapping we had begun.

Approaching the project as it developed, trying to make sense and shape, we had two possible angles of attack. In the first we adjusted the task itself in certain ways – encouraging interaction with other people for example, or pursuing an interest in longer, more complex journeys and self-defined tasks on location developed by individual performers. As participants in the project out in the world, John Rowley, Terry O'Connor, Cathy Naden, Claire Marshall, Richard Lowdon and Jerry Killick functioned as performative researchers, interacting with people and situations in ways that were already out-of-the-ordinary, behaving according to logics quite different to those of strangers they encountered. As with all observers they were both watching the world and changing it, seeing things and causing things to happen. Each performer made his or her own choices on how to play it and each journey or encounter was at heart a fishing expedition, a search for an unknown object and a task undertaken in full knowledge that a second task (of relaying/narrating the experience in a performance) was looming. In the end, events in the research were inevitably shadowed constantly by the idea of how, if at all, they might be reframed and made again as performance account – creating a kind of double presence for the performers as they went about the research. They were performing researchers, acting already in anticipation of a future as-yet-unwritten performance whose possibilities, to some significant extent, would be bound up with their actions in the present.

The small adjustments or additions we made to the task itself made a difference to the raw material we were able to gather for the project – creating the possibility for different encounters and narratives. Even so, for *The Travels* (as in a different way for *Nights in This City* or *Instructions*) we were reliant to a significant extent on the world outside the studio – specifically here though the locations and the people that the performers chanced upon in them. Indeed, there was a foolhardy bottom-line to the work, unsurprising in a structure that encouraged people to travel 200 miles

Figure 11 Courtesy of Forced Entertainment.

or more to see a street chosen on the basis of its name alone, very often (of course) finding nothing too remarkable on arrival. This in-built absurdity defined one edge of the project – its comical trust in the world to deliver something, through (because or in spite of) the misguided method.

The other adjustment we could make of course was to how the material was presented as theatre and from the earliest parts of the travelling research process we began, in parallel, to explore different ways of presenting the work as reportage and narrative in the rehearsal room. Shifting the voice of the performers as they recounted places and events was one of the key ways of doing this – loose conversational accounts were tidied up, edited, strengthened and then sometimes loosened again as we searched for a tone we could work with and through. At other points we experimented with more radical edits. Whole visits to particular cities were reduced to single pieces of information – staccato, poetic, formalized. In the context of the piece we began to weigh and understand something of the relation between telling and imagining, between story and image, especially as different approaches to the telling of the material made different demands and invitations to the audience.

We also explored the possibilities of cross-cutting information – jumping mid-narrative from one performer to another and then back again, interweaving different story-tracks. The social dynamic of the presentation in performance – a playful, mildly competitive, easy-going 'team' of people recounting their involvement in a task that lasted several

Figure 12 Courtesy of Hugo Glendinning.

months – is at once a part-accurate reflection of the group, its experience and relations and, of course, a dramatic theatrical construct. As in any performance, film or written narrative the edit changes everything – material is privileged and foregrounded, while other material is discarded or side-lined. Transitions and temporal juxtapositions create linkages and connections so that longer arcs emerge. Arbitrary or pragmatic juxtapositions of stories and fragments, for example, creating relations between performers that were not there in the real unfolding of events as people undertook research trips alone.

As in any project undertaken by the group we understood the presentation of the material in *The Travels* as a new situation – a space of encounter in which material is shared and in which relations between performers and with the audience are inevitably formed. One limit on this in a project like *The Travels* is 'what happened' – in the material already gathered – but through the performance-making and rehearsal process, as in any other, we explored and stretched those limits as best we could – searching out the different edges, temperatures and dynamics for the work that were permitted by the task and the material it had uncovered.

The approach in all this to authenticity, and to the idea of testimony is of course pretty challenging. *The Travels* consists of reports and observations arising from a series of situations that were at once banal (day trips or expeditions to unremarkable places using public transport) and highly artificial (days on end spent in action determined playfully, without obvious utility or concrete purpose). The project was, in this sense, always at root, a collision and confusion of performativities – the daily quotidian performativity that is the condition in and through which human life exists, colliding with a heightened performativity generated through the rules of a project, focused, from the outset, on making a performance. Whatever natural or true was in it, was always already in an explicit dialogue with quite other impulses towards fiction or narrativization.

As a project it also stressed again and again the problematic (not to mention impossible) relation of lived experience to representation in language. What would it have meant to describe fully or tell the whole story of England Road in Bilton? How many words, how much time in performance, how much knowledge or what kinds of investigation would be necessary for such a task? Clearly there's a comical redundancy to the condensation of a location into a tiny linguistic fragment using only the words 'Black cat and dead chicken'. But as we know from W. G. Sebald, language fails anyway, it fails regardless. It edits and omits, forgets and invents. It makes versions. It tells stories, rather than truth.

The constructed identities of the performers in *The Travels* are, in the end, as layered and complex as the real and false landscape summoned in language by the work itself. The form shifts from time to time – from structured autobiographical anecdote to condensed poeticized list perhaps – such formal shifts as we were able to wring from the piece, allowing a small break from its otherwise rather tyrannous web of subjectivity. The performers' texts are based largely on their own direct experiences, actions and observations – with people for the most part (as in other works by the company) holding on to material that they've generated in improvisation. The texts are their own, though often heavily rewritten by me or by others. They're performing, reading/re-telling a telling/writing of their own actions in a previous time; a time during which they performed in the world, making journeys and encountering strangers as part of a research to make a performance, a research that was also, in any case, already a kind of performance, improvised within rules. They re-tell themselves from the page, invent themselves in the telling and reinvent the telling in the live moment of performance.

There is, we might imagine, somewhere, a kind of truth in it, but to be frank the whole thing is made on the assumption that to get the bottom of an experience, to get really close to a place, a moment in time, a landscape, a country or a person, you might very well need something more than truth – you might need something like fiction, or mischief, or blankness, or the plausible implausible, or accident, or the generative friction of all these things mixed. That's what, perhaps, we were trying to make with *The Travels*.

The Travels

Forced Entertainment

The Travels was first produced by the company in 2002.

Conceived and devised by the company

Performers:	Jerry Killick, Richard Lowdon, Claire Marshall, Cathy Naden, Terry O'Connor, John Rowley
Direction:	Tim Etchells
Text:	Tim Etchells and the company
Design:	Richard Lowdon
Lighting design:	Andy Clarke

Commissioned by Kunstlerhaus Mousonturm (Frankfurt)

JE I'm standing on the corner of a fairly nondescript residential road in North London called Achilles Road, and I'm feeling like I haven't really come properly prepared, because I don't really know anything about Achilles. I know he had a weak point that he was famous for, his heel, but I don't know which one, and I don't know what he did. So I think, alright, I'll walk the length of the road and see what happens. So I walk to the other end of the road, and of course nothing does happen, but by the time I have got there I've decided that what I should do is sit down and think about and also write down some of my own weaknesses.

First of all: 'Shyness'. That's particularly unhelpful in situations like this. 'Selfishness'. I wrote that down, but I don't know, now I'm thinking maybe that's not a weakness at all. 'My inability to think of the right thing to say until it's too late.' Again, that can be a problem. I've also got written here 'useless about the house'. I think actually I was being a bit hard on myself on that one, because I'm alright – it's basically DIY projects that I'm talking about being useless at – with things like cooking and cleaning I'm OK. 'Knowing the right thing to do and not doing it', and that's linked to this next one which is 'saying I'll do one thing and doing another' 'My eagerness to be led astray by anyone who's got any drugs'. And this last one, I've written, 'my violent temper'. When I was there on Achilles Road, I very nearly didn't write that one down – of all of them it's the one I'm most ashamed of. It's not even some kind of impressive fury, it's just pathetic. And it's a temper that's usually directed at inanimate objects that defy me. Like doors that don't shut properly, things that need fixing, machines that don't work, or anything that involves a screwdriver usually ends in shrieking. In fact I'm worried actually, that I might one day smash up my computer, because it's the most expensive thing that I own, and I'm also worried that one day I might lose my temper in this kind of violent way with a person, but it hasn't happened so far, so fingers crossed for tonight.

CA While Jerry's on Achilles Road, I'm about 180 miles north, on Hope Street. There's a boarded-up pub at one end of it and at the other end there's a boarded-up church. I'm standing there looking at the church and I'm thinking some people find hope in religion and spiritual matters but not on this Hope Street. And I look back to the pub and I think some people find hope in the bottom of a glass, but not on this Hope Street. And I decide to set myself the task of walking from one end of Hope Street to the other, from the church to the pub, and I'll look for any other signs of hope.

And I walk the whole length of the street, and I don't find a single sign of hope on Hope Street.

TE   I'm standing in the countryside and ahead of me there are two roads, one running to the left, and the other one running very slightly to the right. And I know that one of these two roads is the one that I'm looking for. It's called Rape Lane but neither of them is signed. It's quite hard to tell these two roads apart, I'm looking from one to the other and I'm wondering which one is Rape Lane and what crime or terrible ordeal the other one is named after. After a while I decide that Rape Lane is probably the one on the right, the one that by chance is the prettier of the two lanes and I decide to walk down it. Rape Lane is beautiful, and the sky's pink, and the sun's setting and as I walk I start to wonder if I'm going to meet somebody, maybe someone driving a car or somebody walking a dog. It takes half an hour to walk the length of Rape Lane and in all that time I don't meet another person, at all.

RI   I'm in Blackpool, and I've just turned into a road that's called England Avenue. England Avenue's pretty much a residential street, there isn't that much else apart from houses. I find myself drawn to one particular house, and it's a house that's got a big English flag in the window, and just underneath the flag it's got this little sign which says 'come on England' and this is pretty much just after England have been knocked out of the World Cup, and I'm outside this house and I'm trying to think of words, single words, to describe England. And I look at the house and I notice that it's number 5 England Avenue, so I think I'll just think of 5 words to describe England. And so I think Football, Defeated, Roast Beef (that's really two words but I let that go), American, and then finally, Semi-Detached.

CL   I've managed to find myself on Bacchus Road in Birmingham and I'm pleased about that, Bacchus being the god of merriment and excess and debauchery of all kinds. And I'm thinking this road is perfect for Bacchus because it's got a betting shop for gambling, there's Kumar's Food & Wine Store, for, food and wine, and at the top end there's a butcher's shop which I think could stand in for pleasures of the flesh. I go into Kumar's Food & Wine and I buy one of those little bottles of wine and I drink that as a toast to the old days, to the cult of the vine, and then I leave the bottle where other people have left offerings of empty beer cans and crisp packets. And I'm standing there on Bacchus Road and I'm thinking am I Bacchanalian? Am I? Am I Bacchanalian? I've never been a gambler, I was invited to an orgy once but I didn't go, I was busy, but I've done a fair bit of drinking in my time, so standing there on Bacchus Road I think about all the different kinds of drunk that I've been. I wrote them down. I've been a happy drunk, I've been a bossy drunk, and I've been an argumentative drunk. I've been a dancing drunk.

I've been a not quite as good a dancer as you think you are drunk. I've been a tearful drunk. I've been a sexually predatory drunk – not quite as much these days. I've been a cruel drunk. I've been a stupid drunk. I've been a very stupid drunk, I've nearly got us killed a couple of times. I've been a competitive drunk. If you're stuck at a table in a bar with me and I want to give you some advice about your life, you're not going to get away that easily.

JO   While Claire is drinking wine on Bacchus Road I'm 100 miles away standing in the doorway of a doctor's surgery on Universal Road in Cardiff. And I'm on the inside of the door trying to keep it closed and the young drunk guy who's been trying to mug me is standing on the outside trying to open the door. And somehow he manages to get his arm through the gap in the door and grabs hold of my face, but I think he realises he's not going to get the door open, I'm pushing it too hard, and in a gesture of ending our little interaction he manages to pull my face round to his and gobs on it really close up. His girlfriend with the spacey eyes is going 'don't wind him up' and I'm not really sure if she's talking about him or me, but anyway, they suddenly go off and I'm left there. I see them trailing around the side of the social club on Clay Road and I look around in the waiting room with the spit all over my face and nobody in there will actually make eye contact with me at all, they're all pretending to read newspapers or looking for interesting detail on the end of their shoes, or in the carpet, so I go and sit down on one of the benches and wipe the spit off my face and I decide to think of words that go with universal, and I write down universal suffrage, universal copyright, universal declaration of human rights, universal soldier, and then finally Universal Studios.

CL   It starts with a list of street names. A list concocted from United Kingdom *A-Z*s and from internet map sites. These are streets with literal names. Streets that seem directly or indirectly to promise adventure, or at least metaphor and allegory. Achilles Road, Hope Street, England Avenue, Rape Lane, Bacchus Road, Universal Street. The list goes on and on forever. Real places. Twisted names.

TE   12.06.02. Picking slips of paper from a box, each of 200 slips bearing the name of a street somewhere in the United Kingdom. A lucky dip to determine who will go where – which places, journeys, destinations and streets.

CA   I pick first. The first five – Paradise Street, Agamemnon Drive, Narcissus Way, Memory Lane, Luck Street. A journey that takes me from Sheffield to Birmingham to Dorset, Manchester and Glasgow.

JE   I pick second. My first five – Riches Street, System Street, Fortune Street, Valiant Road, Ulysses Road. A long journey from Cardiff to London to Cornwall to East Anglia and then a long trek to Cardiff again.

CL   I pick third. My first five – Dead Lane, Dead Lane, Neptune Street, Dagger Lane and Dead Lane again.

RI   I pick fourth. The picking goes on and on. 30 streets each. It takes half the afternoon, at least once you've allowed time for the complaining about who got the long distances and the moaning about who got all the Dead Lanes.

JO   I pick fifth. I'm writing down street names, locations and I'm planning routes. From city to town to middle of nowhere. Mostly places I've never even heard of.

TE   I'm last to pick and when the last destination is chosen *The Travels* can begin.

CL   I'm in Scotland, on Harmony Street, Bonnyrigg. Harmony Street is so new it's barely finished. You can still see the seams in the strips of grass that have been lain outside the houses. Not so long ago all this was fields and mud, now it's a new beginning, a stage set all ready and waiting for the future.

Fast forward one week. I'm at the top of Hell Lane in Dorset. It's a steep country lane that leads down – to Hell Farm. It doesn't look good at the bottom – there are two crashed cars and a green abandoned caravan sat next to the rusted gates of Hell. I really wonder who's in the caravan.

Fast forward. 11.07.02 I'm on Lucky Lane, Bristol. I head for the church which has an old, very vandalised, graveyard. I think this is not a good sign on Lucky Lane. On one defaced tombstone it says – Jaine Braine 86 Ears. Not lucky at all. Other stones have been vandalised with apparently random numbers sprayed on in red paint. I think this might be what's Lucky here – Lucky Numbers for the Lottery maybe and I stand to read from the gravestones – the numbers are 32 and 63 and 22 and 1 and 8 from the farthest gravestone – 59 the bonus number.

TE   Fast forward. Gun Street, Manchester, broken windows. Fast forward. Dagger Lane, Hertfordshire, Bio-products lab. Fast forward. Invincible Road, Leeds. A sign says land for sale.

Fast forward. 22. 07.02. I'm sat in the car on Love Lane, Wakefield. Who would have thought that of the nine Love Lanes's in the country's A-Zs that one of them would be a private road that cuts through a prison? My plan was to walk the length of the road but instead I'm just sitting in the car and turning the facts over in my head – Love Lane that cuts through a prison. A prison on Love Lane. Love Lane that cuts through a prison. A prison on Love Lane.

When I look up a police vehicle is coming towards me. He winds his window down. I do the same. He asks if I'm lost. When I say that I am here to look at Love Lane he laughs and shakes his head but he doesn't ask why. What kind of prison is it? I ask and he nods, 'High Security – which is why I'm asking you to leave.' I think I've got maybe one more question: Do you ever think about Love while you're working here? He doesn't believe I just asked that. He doesn't know if I'm flirting or not. He's smiling and I'm smiling back at him. 'No,' he says, No. I'd have to say No.

JO   Fast forward two weeks. I'm on Memory Lane, Gatehouse. A narrow path that leads to a graveyard. Fast forward 3 days. I'm on Defiant Way, London. A little road on an estate with a grass-covered mound and a big defiant tree. It must have been there before this whole thing was built. A bloke with dyed hair and a knee support is jogging. Four kids lean over a railing on one of the walkways and spit. Fast forward.

Who would have guessed that of the nine Cut Throat Alleys listed in the country's *A-Z*s one of them ran directly through a zoo-come-safari park? This one seemed like a must-see, promising a mayhem of exotic-cum-institutional animal violence.

09.08.02. I'm at the entrance paying out a full 11-pound day ticket just to go and stand in there. What I get for my money is Cut Throat Alley – a wide tarmac strip with a 10 mile an hour speed limit that cuts through the North African section. On one side are zebras and scimitar horned oryx, on the other ostriches and a very lonely looking hippopotamus. I see an ice cream kiosk built like a log cabin and a bench shaped like a crocodile. In the shade of a tree some rat-like animals the size of small dogs stare vacantly at visitors.

It is not the bloodbath anyone dreamed of but the name haunts the thing. I head for the ice cream kiosk. Ahead of me in the queue there's an unsettled atmosphere. A kid asking for an ice cream is told to say 'The Magic Words' and he pauses before answering not PLEASE, not ABRACADABRA or even OPEN SESAME but OPEN MUMMY.

TE   One week later. I'm on Love Lane (Essex) hundreds of miles away. It's a narrow country track with only one house. What happens next is pretty well the usual routine. Two blokes on horseback stop and ask me if I'm lost. I say I'm here to look at Love Lane. They laugh. Then there's a silence. 'Don't steal the Love Lane sign' says one of them, 'People always steal the sign.' I leave and don't look back.

JE 10.08.02. I'm walking on Folly Lane, Chingford. It's a no-through road running round the edge of a reservoir – the kind of half abandoned road where cars come to die. On the other side of the road is a travellers' site and a Muslim cemetery. The travellers' site is organised with what look like little garages with sloping roofs and a caravan in front of each one. At the end of Folly Lane lots of huge articulated lorries from Holland and Romania are parked up, the contents of their containers un-guessable, their drivers asleep in their cabs.

When I get to the Muslim Cemetery there's a bare-chested man in shorts putting stuff on a bonfire. He makes me a cup of tea ('that'll bring you luck') and tells me some stuff about Folly Lane. He says that the first policeman in England to be shot in the line of duty died here. Just after the First World War a bunch of Russians tried to start a revolution in Tottenham. They were chased over the River Lea by some policeman and a load of kids, along for the excitement. On Folly Lane they made their last stand killing a policeman and one of the children.

While we are talking some men arrive to visit graves, bringing flowers and bottles of water. One of them's obviously a regular and he stops by for a bit of a chat before walking in among the headstones. The bloke I'm talking to's mate turns up and when he learns that I'm an actor he keeps asking me if I've done any porn. I tell him that I haven't and he seems disappointed. He goes quiet for a bit and then tells me a joke, it's a dirty joke so it seems clear he's got sex on the brain. He says that an Australian man wants to teach his son about sex so he takes him to a brothel. The man's son goes into a room with a prostitute and immediately starts clearing the room of all the furniture. The prostitute asks him what he's doing (the bloke telling the joke actually does lots of really good voices but I'm not going to) and the Australian guy's son says, well if it's anything like it was with the kangaroo then we're going to need a lot of space.

After the joke is finished there's some laughter and some of the mourners look up from the graves, disturbed by the sound but these guys that I'm standing with don't seem too bothered. Stood at the bonfire drinking the tea I feel as though I have stepped, very quietly, into another world.

CA Fast forward. 21.08.02. It's after dark on Eclipse Road, Cardiff. I'm standing by a rusting abandoned van whose headlamps have been removed.

Fast forward. I'm just round the corner in Cardiff at the first house on Comet Road. A garden chair stands alone in the centre of a room stripped for decorating. The chair facing the un-curtained window as if set up simply to watch the skies in this impromptu observatory, the whole scene lit by street lamp spill and moonlight.

Fast forward. I'm round the corner again, this time on Planet Street, Cardiff, again after midnight. It's a street of 50 brick-terraced houses. I count them. In one window there's a selection of ornamental dolphins, some crystal, others ceramic, all modelled in a leaping fashion, frozen in mid-air. In another window there's a model of a ship made from wood, exceptional in its intricate detail. Next to it, on the same windowsill, there's a sculpture made from shells, preserved under a glass dome.

Fast forward. Dusk. Cutthroat Alley leads to Melancholy Walk although neither is signed. 22.07.02. This is parkland surrounding a stately home in Richmond. Melancholy Walk is a long, straight avenue leading up to ornate iron gates at the front of the house. As if melancholy were connected only to coming home, or to journeys that run in straight and pre-planned lines. There's birdsong and the buzzing of insects.

RI   02.09.02. I'm on Head Street, Liverpool. The graffiti ranges from the predictable FUCK YOU to the slightly more inventive FUCK YOUR MUM and beyond that the incomparable SAUSAGE. I walk down the street to the place where a kid has stuck his right hand in a pot of white paint and slapped its outline all over a metal door. I'm thinking that Head Street is a bit of a road and a bit of a dump, probably great for kids up to mischief at night. I'm thinking if this place is a head then it is the jumbled inside of one. Inside the head of some disorganised person – probably me.

Paradise Street, Bury. Incomprehensible. A winding hill of uneven cobbles intersected by a wide gravel path called Killer Street. At the top Paradise and Killer open onto a waste ground signed clearly MEMORIES CAR PARK.

Medusa Road, Lewisham. Incomprehensible. An Asian girl in a red dress scoots up and down on a micro scooter. She won't let her sister have a go.

Pandora Road, London. Incomprehensible. Net curtains everywhere. Only one bit of graffiti – in large high letters – a single word that is posed as a question – 'WHITE??'

Scar Lane, Barnsley. Perfect. A cinder track cutting across the side of a hill. A scar on the landscape.

JE   Luck Lane, Huddersfield. Perfect. Men swap stories of broken ribs.

JE   Neptune Road, Bristol. Incomprehensible. Blokes having races on fork-lift trucks.

RI   Folly Lane, Penistone. Perfect. The middle of nowhere.

TE   Paradise Street, Birmingham. The centre of the city.

CA   Hope Road, Leeds. Back of the station.

JO   Fortune Street, Liverpool. Impoverished.

CL   System Street, Bristol. No Parking.

JO   England Lane, Pontefract. Quick route to the dump.

RI   England Road, Bilton. Black cat and dead chicken.

TE   Empire Road, Bristol. Perfect. Cut price long distance phone calls.

CA   Fortune Street, Bolton. Stroke Association.

JO   Star Street, Cardiff. Crypton Tuning.

JE   Luck Lane, Huddersfield. Gigantic Co-op.

CL   Friendship Way, Glasgow. 2 kids fighting with sticks.

JO   Lump Lane, Sheffield. Pub at the top.

RI   Folly Lane, Bristol. Blue plaque and toy.

JO   Harmony Road, London. Over a hill.

CL   Limb Lane, Sheffield. Good place to dump a body.

CA   Head Street, London. Split in two.

JE   Atlas Street, Sheffield. Wasteland.

JO   Orpheus Road, London. One way.

RI   Luck Lane, Huddersfield. Wealthy.

TE   Meteor Way, London. Almost off the edge of the map, at the bottom of a page and hard to see precisely where it ends.

CL   So often the feeling that yesterday, even 5 minutes ago might have been a better time to arrive. That maybe yesterday there were lovers on Love Street in Birmingham where it cuts through the Science Park, but that for now there are only gardeners. What to make of gardeners on Love Street? How to interpret? Is it nothing? Are they nurturing love? Or is 'Gardeners on Love Street' also drawing a kind of blank?

05.09.02. An awareness of the contingency of everything. The flux of time and events in which you're caught. Five minutes later and the gardeners would've been on their tea break. Ten minutes before and a man might have walked the length of the street calling a lover on the phone. Ten minutes ago. Ten minutes from now. Next week. Yesterday. Tomorrow and now.

JE   I'm standing on the South Bank of the River Thames way out east near the flood barrier, and according to the map this section of the path going along the bank is called Nagasaki Walk, and a bit further along the bank it becomes Hiroshima Promenade and I'm trying to find the place where I guess one joins into the other. And I'm standing there, and because there's no sign anywhere saying what this place is called, I'm thinking that I must be the only person who actually knows. In fact there aren't many people around, apart from me; just a couple of women who go past on bikes. And I sit down on the bench overlooking the river and eventually this guy turns up and walks in front of the bench where I am, and he's one of these guys who doesn't look like he's got a neck, and just at the point where he's right in front of me he sort of trips over, stumbles over a loose paving stone. And then he makes this big show of coming back in inspecting, wobbling this loose paving stone. And I'm sat there, and I'm thinking would he have done all that if I hadn't been there. I don't know. But he goes on eventually, and leaves me alone, on Hiroshima Promenade. And I look out over the river, and it's bright sunshine, it's a sunny day, and the river at this point is wide and all around me there are low-rise industrial buildings. And I look up at the sun, it's bright, and I can't look at it for more than maybe a second without it hurting my eyes, and I look out over the river again and I try and imagine what it would be like if the sun was one hundred times as bright.

RI   While Jerry is arriving at Nagasaki Walk I'm on Endymion Road in Hatfield, and I'm glad that on the way there I did my homework by reading in a book of mythology about who Endymion was – I'd never heard of him before. According to the book he was one of Zeus's sons who fell into a dreamless sleep when his lover kissed him on the eyes. I think about this on Endymion road trying to figure out what a dreamless sleep might feel like. And wondering also (after my earlier trip to England Avenue in Blackpool) if England is in such a sleep. It's a street of double-glazing, shut curtains and blinds. It's very quiet. And the quiet feels like it is very deliberate – as if this is a sleep that's being defended. And I think: England – Dreamless Sleep. And I think Endymion. And I wonder if this dreamless sleep is like the sleep that babies have or if it's

like the state people are in when they are in a coma. And then an image
comes into my mind for no reason – an image of Elvis. And at first I
don't know why. And then I remember a story a friend of mine told me –
that when Elvis was in his fatter more sentimental years he was also
still doing lots and lots of uppers and when he wanted to rest he'd get a
doctor to inject him with a powerful sedative that would let him sleep
without waking for several days. And stood on the corner of Endymion
Street I can't get this image of Elvis out of my mind – lain on his bed in
a white suit with rhinestones, in mirror shades and snoring.

JO   I'm on Scar Lane in Barnsley, and like Richard I'm getting a very
strong image, well more like a sensation, that everything here is very
very familiar, a horrible déjà vu, I can see the cinder track and some
allotments and a grassy hill, and there's a playground at the end of the
track. And I know I haven't been here before, and I'm thinking why do
I know this place, and then it suddenly sinks in; Richard has actually
shown me a photo of this place a week before, he'd actually been there
before, he'd beaten me to it. And I'm sitting there in my car thinking
that's great, that's really great, this is my job for the day, Scar Lane,
I'm thinking what am I going to do now. And then I remember Richard
telling me in the description of the place that there's a pub at the top of
the hill. So I think, I'm not going to waste any time, I'm going to get
to the pub and have a few drinks. So I'm in the pub, called The Drop,
and I suddenly start thinking about my own scars, the scars on my
body. There's quite a few of them. But the one that's most obvious as
I'm sitting there is the one on the hand I'm holding my pint in, which
is a small one, it's a thin white line about an inch long, it's quite tidy
really. It's what I call my performance-related scar and it came from a
performance I was in about 8 or 9 years ago. I'm in the back of a white
transit van, as you often are at the beginning of shows, and I'm wearing
a second-hand suit, like a dead man's suit, and at a certain point the van
stops and I smash the doors open and there's the audience all waiting
and anticipating – they're all standing there in a factory unit. My job is
to jump out of the van, and I take the knife, a Stanley knife out of my
pocket and I have to cut my suit off completely to reveal my naked body
underneath. And all the audience are looking at me now, I'm the focus
of attention. And, as is often the case with these theatre things, you've
not had any rehearsal time for this, and so I'm standing there, naked
underneath, with my knife, and I'm thinking, oh well, here we go. So I
stick the knife in, and it's alright so far, it moves about an inch, and then
it jams on the lining and everyone's still looking at me, and then I force it
again and it goes up to the cuff and it jams again, and I'm trying to force

it further and I look up out of the corner of my eye and I see that my colleagues are moving on to the next part of the show, the book-burning section, so anyway, one last mighty push, and the knife goes through, but it also goes through my hand, and a small arterial spray of blood goes into the air in slow motion. Well, I'm thinking what am I going to do now, it's the beginning of the show and normally I guess I'd go to the St John Ambulance and get it seen to, but there's no time for that now because I'm standing there naked with the words of William Blake emblazoned on my chest in six-inch letters, and everyone's looking, and somebody's going to put some books into my hands and set them on fire. So I just carry on, through the show, and it's about 10 minutes, quarter of an hour later, somebody taps me on the arm, and I say what is it, I'm in a performance, I can't talk now, and they point to my hand and the blood's kind of congealed, it's all over my hand, and dripping off my finger, and they say here, take this, and they give me a paper handkerchief to wrap around it, and for the rest of the performance, about another hour, I hold onto it, like this.

I've got another scar, a little one, about an inch long, just behind my ear, but I've never seen it because it's in such an awkward place. I know it's there because of the story that's attached to it. I must have been about 8 years old, around 1974. Christmas Eve, in my house, my family house, and I'm fighting on the floor with my brother, he's two years older than me. And it's pretty violent, he's punching me in the face, and he's got his knee, and he's putting it into my groin, and it's painful, and we're rolling around, and it's all about what bloody TV programme to watch and stuff, and I kind of think it's over and he backs off, and then suddenly he picks me up and throws me over the sofa onto the edge of the radiator, and it bloody hurts, it cuts the edge of the skin quite easily, and I start crying and I'm going 'Mum! Mum! Mum!', and my brother's laughing at me as he does, and my mum comes in and she's normally pretty mild mannered really, but she looks at us and she goes 'what the bloody hell do you think you're doing? I hope you realise you've ruined Christmas!' And me and my brother sit there quite shame-faced, with our tails between our legs so to speak. And well, we never really spoke for the whole of Christmas, really miserable.

Part Two: Just Girls / The Futures

CA 09.09.02. It's the middle of the afternoon and I want to know the future. To find it I'm headed to Salford, near Manchester, and in particular I'm on my way to Oracle Court and Delphi Avenue. On the train I don't know what I am going to do when I get there but I read up about the Oracles. I read about the five shrines at Delphi and all the different methods of prediction using birdsong, or dice throwing or even the rustling of leaves.

The best Oracle I find is where the person that wants to know the future – that's me – has to perform some tasks. They have to bathe in a sacred river to get purified and drink from a spring called the water of Memory. This is supposed to help them forget the past and to remember the future which is going to be revealed to them. They have to go down and sit in a dark cave and wait for an invisible voice to speak to them.

I think that getting all this to happen in Salford is going to be hard but I am determined to find out about the future and when I arrive I am pleased to see that there is a public bath just around the corner from Oracle Court. I think that that will do for the Sacred River. Unfortunately I don't have a swimsuit. They don't hire them but the attendant kindly offers to look in lost property, in case there's one someone has left behind. I'm disappointed when he comes back empty-handed but I don't give up on being cleansed in the sacred water. Instead of swimming in the pool I decide that I'll wash my hands in the changing rooms.

Delphi Avenue and Oracle Court turn out to be part of a big 1970s housing estate. I go and sit on the steps that lead down into Oracle Court and I drink from a bottle of Mineral Water that will have to stand in for the water of memory. This is supposed to help me forget the past and to remember the future which is going to be revealed to me. Then I close my eyes to make it dark and I wait for the invisible voice. It speaks. It says, 'WHAT ARE YOU DOING?'

It's a little girl, about 8 years old, on a bike. We get talking and soon I'm surrounded by kids. It's like word is spreading on the estate that there's a curious stranger sitting with her eyes closed on the steps at Oracle Court. I can't get my predictions done. The girl on the bike comes back with her two little brothers. She tells me she wants to be a fire-fighter when she grows up and when her brother grows up he doesn't want to die. I think these will have to do for the predictions I get today.

When I get up to leave the girl sees the camera in my bag. She wants me to take a picture of her and her brothers. There's a couple of shots left, so I do. Then I leave.

At the station a car pulls up behind me. A woman winds down the window and calls me over. She cuts straight to the chase. Our kids say you've been on our estate taking photographs, our kids say you've been on our estate taking photographs of them. I turn cold. I look and I see that the kids in the back are the girl and her two little brothers. They won't look at me. There's a bloke at the driving wheel, he's staring straight ahead and he doesn't say a thing. The woman says again. You were on our estate taking photographs; you were on our estate taking photographs of our kids.

I try to explain. Something about street names and journeys. It sounds crazy to me so I don't know what they make of it. But in the end they leave. I'm alone and kind of shaken.

While I am waiting for the train I decide to use the events at Oracle Court to make my own prediction about the future.

The future will be paranoid. The future will be suspicious. The future will be recorded on the tape of surveillance cameras. The future, more than anything, will be scared.

CL   I'm not the sort of person who scares easily but after we've drawn our destinations at the start of the project I'm a bit anxious. There were five DEAD LANES on the list of streets and I got three of them, as well as a more than fair share of Hell Lanes, Hades Lanes and Dagger Lanes. Most of these places are in deep countryside, middle of nowhere's – as if hell and death were best kept as far as possible from where people congregate.

Like Cathy I decide that I'm interested in the future – only I'm much more focused than she is – I decide to use these DEAD LANES to make predictions for my death.

I put them off for ages, going to other places, finding excuses. In the end I grit my teeth and I decide to do them all in one week. Dead Lane. Dead Lane. Dead Lane. Just the Dead Lanes. Other people are having fun. I'm setting off for Dead Lane.

My first death is hard to find. Dead Lane, Baignton is a country narrow lane whose entrance is obscured by overgrown hedges. Nearby there's a closed pub with a single bunch of flowers leaned outside – it's one of those shrines that people leave after road accidents, only here there's only one bunch. When I find it the end of the lane is a clearing of mud with a caravan encircled by trees. Beside the caravan there are a bunch of rotweiller dogs in cages barking and going crazy and out front on the mud there's a beached rusted boat.

From the pub I predict I will be drunk when I die.

From the single bunch of flowers outside I predict I will be lonely when I die and that my death will be largely unmourned.

From beached boat I predict my death will come when all my plans are scuppered.

And from the barking dogs in cages I predict that I will die like an animal. Wounded, dirty, beaten, yelping and unimportant.

I get back in the car and start the drive to my next destination – Dead Lane.

This one is off Main Street in a little village in the East Ridings. On the corner I meet an old bloke and we get talking. He says he'll tell me the story of Dead Lane. He says it's a long story. He says that Dead Lane is the walk the prisoners took from the local prison to the gallows for execution. That's not a long story. They were hanged in a clearing in the woods just ahead. I haven't marked the clearing on the map – it's just by the church. I walk to the woods and find something like a clearing. I predict my death will be a hanging. I know the place I'm standing in is probably not the real clearing where they hanged people but still I don't like to be there.

I'm hopeful that my third death – the last Dead Lane – is going to be a bit more cheerful. When I get there 200 miles away Dead Lane, Essex is a very complicated scene to read. It's another country lane, and seems to be a shortcut of some kind because there is a lot of traffic and it's all going fast. Halfway down the road there's a set of tyre skid marks that go on for 20 feet or so before they disappear into a hedge. From the map you can see there's road-kill at regular intervals – a squashed fox, a squashed hedgehog and the flattened remains of what might once have been a squirrel. There's a members only Holiday Club campsite and a few houses scattered on its length with names like The Well House and Puzzleden. In a field there's a combine harvester and a whole bunch of crows.

From the skid marks I predict my death in car crash, and from the campsite I predict that this car crash will be on holiday. From The Well House I predict my death by drowning. Maybe the car will go off over a bridge as I am swerving to avoid a fox, a squirrel and a hedgehog. I predict that after my car has gone over a cliff my body will be washed up on the shore and eaten by crows. The only witness to the accident will be a man driving a combine harvester.

The house called Puzzleden makes me smile. I tell myself that my death will be a mystery, an enigma, an ambiguous suicide without note, or maybe I'll be someone that just disappears – maybe I will just leave the house one morning like normal and I'll never come back.

TE   I'm going to London to think about the future. I'm headed to Time Park. My plan is to find a male escort in London and hire him for an hour of his time. Or maybe half an hour if an hour is too expensive. I'm going to take him to a hotel as near to Time Park as possible and while I lie on the bed I'm going to get him to talk to me about time, and to make predictions for the future.

On the train I have a book called The Ladies Oracle – a book for predicting that mainly seems to offer affairs and romantic intrigues. I'm looking through the index to pick out questions.

My favourite is number 90:

Are they thinking of me in the place that I am thinking of?

But I think number 22 is the most relevant to a trip like this one: shall I have many adventures?

I do the Oracle just as the book says and I'm actually quite excited about what the answer's going to be. I ask shall I have many adventures? And the answer is:

You will have so many that you will be disgusted.

On the way to Time Park the train is delayed and delayed and delayed. There are floods everywhere and outside it's turning into night. When we get to London it's already late and we're kicked off the train in a part of London I don't know. In a bar I ask about hotels and all they say is 'don't go North – it's dodgy'. So I leave and I start walking North. Outside on the street there's a lot of lightning and families with rucksacks and bags of salvaged possessions and mops because of the flooding.

Somewhere walking in the rain I admit to myself that I'm not going to Time Park tonight. It's too far. It's too late. I'm lost. I don't have anywhere to stay and I'm soaked. There won't be a map of this place. I ditch the escort plan too and make a new plan. I'll find somewhere to stay. I'll ask everyone I meet about time and the future. And I'll try to stay up all night. I'm improvising. I'm off the rails. Up ahead there's a pub that says 'Budget Accommodation'. I'm pleased and relieved but when I ask the barman how much it costs he says £10, £12 or £14 depending on whether you're sharing with 10, 8 or 6 people. I ask about the future but don't get an answer.

From here on in it's a blur. I'm outside a Marriot Hotel a mile away, soaked and realising that I can't afford the £129 for a room there. I ask about other places and all they can say is don't go East it's a red light zone – very rough. I'm back in the dormitory pub getting told that they don't have any rooms free in any case. Then I'm talking to some bloke – Andrew, a musician – whose just won the karaoke competition singing a Stevie Wonder song called *Maybe* and he's talking about the future (it's going to be good) and the past – months last year flying from Glasgow to London rehearsing with his band. He says back then time was really elastic from the flying and the moving and it helps that the drugs were good too.

I'm looking in the karaoke songbook at all the song titles that have the word Time or the Future in them. There are only two with the future – *Future's So Bright I Gotta Wear* by Timbuk3 and *No Future in The Past* by Vince Gill. As far as time goes there are lots and I don't know most of them, so I'm glad I don't have to sing.

Any Time At All by The Beatles. *Are The Good Times Really Over* by Merle Haggard.

I'm quite drunk by now. Andrew says I can stay at his place. On the sofa. He says neither of us are virgins. It'll be ok. I'm thinking 'maybe' but when we're on the street together gone midnight in the rain he stops to talk to some other bloke, a taxi comes round the corner and I hail it.

I tell the cab driver to head for the first cheap hotel we come to. We seem to drive in circles a bit but soon I've checked in (£ 39 a night) and I'm out again by 1 o'clock – trying to stay awake and looking for more people to ask my question about time and the future. We're at Kings Cross. I recognise it. I find another karaoke place – very dodgy – and before long I'm sat at the bar again with Vodka and Red Bull and looking at the song list, at all the songs with 'Time' in the title –

Bad Time by Grand Funk Railroad

Big Time by Peter Gabriel

A Wound Time Can't Erase by Stonewall Jackson

A bloke introduces himself as Dave – a carpenter. I ask Dave about time and he says he works a 4-day week and at the weekend he looks after his little girl. Dave says the funny thing is that the weekends feel like a week. Dave buys me a drink. Dave owns property in Ireland. Dave's working on a mansion nearby. Dave's been here, there and everywhere. Dave also says the future's going to be good. When they kick out the karaoke almost 4a.m., Dave says don't take this the wrong way but I'm walking you to your hotel and I say I'm not going to take it the wrong way Dave.

As we walk towards the hotel, Dave's conversation becomes more urgent in a way I don't get. He's telling me about breaking up with his wife and that he wasn't totally honest when he said he was a carpenter and he's asking me about clubs and drugs and if I've ever done drugs and there's a real urgency behind this line of enquiry but it's not about sex. I can't really work it out at all.

And outside the door of the County Hotel, Dave does something with his fingers that I've never seen before. And it's something really professional I can tell. He produces this wrap of coke, it's like a kind of magic trick, just flicks his fingers like that and there's a wrap of coke and I'm laughing and I'm thinking about something Jerry said the other week back in Sheffield – that not doing something doesn't make a story – and I can't work out if Dave is selling me the coke, giving me the coke or inviting me back to his place in Sloane Square and it's gone 4 o'clock in the morning and he hugs me and he gives me the coke and he's gone.

Part Three: The Stories

RI Of all the roads in the country's *A-Zs* perhaps the ones that seemed to promise most were those marked Story Street, Story Park or Story Gardens. There were six of them – a story-place waiting for each of us. It seemed a perfect fit – too neat and too tempting to avoid.

JO 12.09.02. Again drawing destinations from a hat – a lucky dip of Story Streets to determine who gets the longest journey. Richard draws Story Street in Hull. I draw Story Road in Chichester. Terry gets Story Road, North London. Jerry, Stories Park in East Linton, on the East Coast of Scotland. Claire, Story Lane in Broadstone. Cathy, Story Gardens in South London. 90 miles for Richard. 200 for Jerry. A nice night in London for Terry and Cathy.

JE 13.09.02. I had set my alarm for 7 and I'm out of the house by 7.45.

CA I'm also up early and gone.

CL I take my daughter to nursery, then I leave at 9.

RI I sleep in a bit. I leave around lunchtime.

JO I leave at 10.

TE I leave at 11 and when I turn into Story St, London, a few hours later I say 'oh', without meaning to. It's a short street with empty council flats and lots of graffiti. The flats have grilles on the windows. There's a dumped fridge by one side of the road. I take a seat on the kerb and try to think.

Stories here will be about broken consumer goods (including fridges) and the different places they end up after they've become useless. Stories about graffiti and the people that write it and the reasons they write it. Stories about the people that design, market and manufacture security products.

JO Close to my destination I meet a postman who tells me that Story Road, Chichester does not exist anymore. It's not the first journey to a place that does not exist and I try not to let the news from the postman get me down. I head for the place where it should be, hoping to pick up what I can from the ruins or whatever has replaced it.

I find a half-built estate with some streets completed, others not. The whole place is housing for old people and I soon locate the office of the housing association that runs it. The man there contradicts the postman.

He says Story Road does exist. They moved it a little and rebuilt it but it's here and on a map he shows me. Stories about roads that have moved. Stories about postmen that tell lies and are caught out in the end, thanks to the decency of other citizens. Stories about things that are not exactly where they should be.

RI   I think that Story Street in Hull might also be hard to find but it isn't. It's right in the centre, about the fourth street from the train station. easy stories and stories with big letters and stories about things that happen really near train stations.

TE   I'm still sat on the kerb when some builders in a white van arrive to work on the nearest empty flat. I get talking to them. One bloke, the friendliest, says come in and have some tea. Stories about kindness. Stories about chance encounters between strangers. Stories which start with the offer of a drink. Inside the empty flat on Story Street there's a Barbie room – bright pink with a Barbie border – and a younger boy's room with non-specific toy-patterned wallpaper. Stories about children, stories told to children, stories about people that have moved.

CA   I don't go to Story Gardens in West London, like I am supposed to. I'm up late the night before and I start to have other ideas. I'm searching on the internet, drifting from map site to map site entering words at random, just seeing what's there. I don't know why I am looking or what I am looking for. There are no FICTION STREETS, no FICTION ROADS, no Fairy Tale Avenues, no Fantasy Roads. There's no CATHY ROADS, no CATHY NADEN ROADS although there is a NADEN ROAD. It's late. I'm drifting. Then with no expectation, I search for STORY BOOK and after my long line of bad luck this one comes up good. It seems that in the far edge of Scotland is not a street but a *place* called STORYBOOK GLENN. STORYBOOK GLENN it says – the place where stories come to life. Theme Park and Themed Outdoor Play Park. Suitable for all ages. It's hard to know what this actually means but when I leave in the morning it's at 7 and I'm headed, not to STORY GARDENS in West London but to Scotland and STORY BOOK GLENN.

JE   I'm standing on the nice grass by the nice houses and waiting for something to happen in Stories Park, East Linton. I don't care if it takes all day. I've got time. I can wait. Eventually a mobile fish shop arrives selling fresh fish. This is not exactly what I was hoping for but I have to take what comes. I buy two fish cakes and start talking to the fish seller. Stories about fish. Stories about men who sell fish. Stories about men that buy fish. I tell the man I'm here for stories at Stories Park and he spreads the word to his customers who are friendly and don't seem to mind talking for a few minutes.

I learn that the houses were built for workers at a nearby nuclear power plant but that there's not many of them left living here now. They all moved out because their wives couldn't stand it here. It was too quiet. No stories. They wanted something faster, something riper, so they moved to the nearest town – Dunbar. Stories about debauchery in Dunbar. Stories about relationships that don't work because the wives want something different than their husbands and stories about dangerous sources of energy.

RI   Story Street is strictly one way. It runs from Zen Audio/Hi Fi at one end to a pseudo McDonalds-type place called Yankee Burger at the other. I think stories here are about people who travel from one place to another, from the East to the West – Zen to Yankeeland. Stories about immigration and emigration. Stories about culture, trade and culture clashes. There are speed bumps so it seems as if any stories here are going to be slow ones, stories deterred, stories held in close check. Stories about difficult journeys. Stories about obstacles that need to be overcome. Stories about laws and restrictions.

CL   It's gone 2 in the afternoon by the time I get down to the South Coast in England. I walk Story Street in Broadstone several times. It is tree-lined and very quiet – looks like a long time since it's seen any action. There is a library on it, as if all the stories were rounded up and corralled in there, safely in the pages of books and not open on Wednesdays. I think the presence of the library here on Story Street is clearly some kind of a clue that must not be ignored – I give up my thoughts of having an actual adventure and go inside.

I start with the facts. The first card in the alphabetical index is for a book by ABD Al-Kadir called *The Horses of the Sahara and the Manners of the Desert*. The last card is for a book by C. Zwikker called *Fluorescent Lighting – A Review of the Scientific & Technical Fundamentals of the Fluorescent Lamp and Its Accessories*.

I don't think I can stand the excitement.

Headed for Fiction, I end up in the Reference. I'm looking at Atlases. Maps. Borders. Rivers. Roads. Lines. A political atlas from the late 1980s with a Europe already badly dated. A world atlas with the globe in diverse projections – the shapes and relative sizes of the countries shifting, stretching, shrinking. A book of ariel photos. Hard to locate myself. Looking at the maps.

I read something on the early map makers. The time before triangulation, the time before the ariel view, before satellites. Back then a map was made from stories – the certain ones and the rumours too. Some guy comes back from a journey and tells the stuff he's seen. All that gets added to the map. Each map a new mix of stories, each mix a new version of the world. I'm thinking that that's how we are working. On the ground. Building space out of rumours.

JE   I'm still at the fish van. I learn that Stories Park was named after the vet John Storie who owned the yellow house and that this land used to be a paddock for the sick animals. Stories about animals. Stories about sick animals. Stories about the different uses that a patch of land is put to. Someone tells me the street had been opened by some politician whose father had been the first person to fly an aeroplane over Mt Everest. Stories about politics. Stories about death-defying stunts. Stories about sons that grow up feeling they should compete with their fathers.

CA   On the train to Story Book Glenn there's a drunk bloke behind me whose 'entertaining' the passengers with a rolling commentary of bad jokes, snatches of songs and his speciality – mock Scottish accent. 'Aye me goin t' drink drink drink in Scotland! Put a sporran up yer bum!' The kids in the carriage are laughing.

When this doesn't get laughs anymore he takes to blowing raspberries.

We've been badly delayed and now we're speeding through a thunderstorm. The carriage is silent. It feels like we're all looking out, trying to see past the needles of rain into the fields and trees beyond.

Drunk man starts to speak. 'Rain, rain, rain', he says 'Same as Africa, where I come from. I come from Africa and as I said to the buffalo on the plains in Kenya.'

He doesn't finish the sentence.

'Look out there', he says. And we're all looking out. It's nice round here, by the look of it.

'Look there', he says. 'There's Jack.' We're all looking and we're all listening to his story now.

'Our Jack lives out there.'

He starts to talk about people we can't see, but who, perhaps, are travelling with him.

'There's Edith. She lives out there in them trees in the woods. And Joseph lives out there.'

Drunk man blows a long soft raspberry.

'We don't talk to Joseph. He lives on porridge and tree roots.'

RI   There's a stationers on Story Street, which I think is a good omen. I go in and buy two pens and a notebook. Then I go and sit in Yankee Land. I start to make a list of true stories – stories that have happened to me.

TE   I'm in the kitchen of the derelict flat on Story Street. One guy's stripping the wall and another man's hanging a door and the old bloke, the friendly one, hands me tea.

CL   I'm in the library. I've escaped from the maps and I'm headed for the fiction index.

JO   I'm headed for Story Street, now I know exactly where it is. The bloke from the housing association has told me that the old people who live there are sure to have stories to tell me. He's very optimistic.

JE   I'm still at the fish stall.

CA   I'm on the train. I'm watching the rain.

TE   When I ask about stories in the kitchen there's not much enthusiasm and the bloke stripping the wall congratulates me on how I've managed to shut up his colleagues. Nice to get some peace and quiet. I should come through more often. We're all laughing. It feels OK. The radio plays. Time passes. Next time the quiet bloke, the youngest, whose been hanging the door is the one who breaks the silence. He's hardly said a word until now but without warning he goes into a story. A long one. About a death. About his baby son that died. The diagnosis (a rare syndrome) the hospital (chaotic), the turning off of a life-support machine (hard to describe).

When Quiet Bloke stops speaking the old bloke says now that's a story for you that's true, that's a true one that is. Stories about death. Stories about children. Stories about the failure of medical systems and the bad communication of doctors.

CL   I'm at the index. The 800's in the Dewey Decimal System.

800 is Literature & Rhetoric

802 is Miscellany

810 is American Literature in English

811 is Poetry

812 is Drama

813 is Fiction

818 is Miscellaneous Writings

819 is Not assigned or no longer used

What I want is 813.

TE   Now that the story has finished there's silence again. I'm looking at my tea and the other blokes have stopped what they're doing, though I feel sure they must've heard the dead son story before. Quiet bloke continues 'we scattered his ashes at Glastonbury' and I feel I've got to say something so I say 'why Glastonbury?' and he says 'because it's a nice place' he says 'we did it at the top of a hill and the ashes flew straight back into our eyes because it was windy that day'.

He says 'we go every year' and for some reason I think he means to the Glastonbury Festival but he carries on – 'we put flowers down and the sheep eat them.'

Stories about funerals. Stories about silences that are awkward. Stories about strangers that intrude into other peoples lives and then regret it. Stories about men working together. Stories about Glastonbury, including stories about the festival and stories not about the festival. Stories about animals (including sheep) that eat important things.

CL   The first fiction book, the first A, is: *Abbey of The Lost* by P. Thacker.

While the last Z stands for *Zorro, The Masked Man* by Steven Gray.

I go to the shelves. It's late and I like the sound of Zorro best. I want to find it.

RI   I'm still in Yankee Land working on my list of stories that have happened to me.

The first one I think of is the time my mum took me to the doctors and when the doctor told her I needed an operation to remove two of my toes she just took me straight out of the room.

The second one I think of is the time I broke my leg and then fell in love with a doctor.

I sense that a medical theme is emerging.

The third one I think of is having to tell my dad that my mum had died. This was when his short-term memory was gone and I had to tell him the same news, the same story every day for two weeks.

By the end of the second week I had a neat and well-polished way of telling him the story – a version that I almost knew by heart.

Stories about stories that have to be told again and again.

JE   I'm at the fish stall.

CA   I'm still on the train, watching the rain.

CL   I've found it. Tenth shelving unit. Top shelf. The Zorro book:

> 'AGAIN THE SHEET of rain beat against the roof of red Spanish tile, and the wind shrieked like a soul in torment, and smoke puffed from the big fireplace as sparks showered on the hard dirt floor.'

'Tis a night for evil deeds!' declared Sergeant Pedro Gonzales.

The Library is closing. I have to read fast if I want to get further.

> 'Tis a night for evil deeds!' declared Sergeant Pedro Gonzales, stretching his great feet in their loose boots towards the roaring fire and grasping his sword in one hand and a mug filled with wine in the other.

Last call at the Library.

> 'Devils howl in the wind, and demons are in the raindrops! Tis an evil night indeed' the big sergeant said, and drained the mug without stopping to draw breath.

JO   Like most of the old people on Story Street, Chichester, Mr Chapel does not want to talk to me. As though he has heard rumours of the evil night mentioned in the Zorro book he will only open his door the tiniest of cracks. 'Hello Mr Chapel.' I say the people at the housing office said he might have some stories. Does he know any?

'No' says Mr Chapel. 'Not really, no.'

He says, 'there's nothing that comes to mind as I stand here now.'

I say 'I've come a long way.'

He says 'Nothing outstanding. Nothing that was not happening elsewhere in the world.'

'Nothing?'

'No' he says. 'I was working you see. Most of the time.'

Stories about working. Stories about age. Stories about stories and people who are looking for them. Stories about things that happen everywhere in the world at exactly the same time.

RI   I'm still in Yankee Land, trying to add something more cheery to my list of stories that have happened to me. For some reason I think about a long journey I made with Terry more than 10 years ago. Driving to Poland and going through Berlin just at the time the wall came down. An exhausting journey through terrible fog for hundreds of miles, in a right-hand drive car on narrow left-hand drive roads. I don't know why I think of it even. It's nothing to do with the medical theme and what I remember of the trip is mainly incidents involving other people. Not too much to do with me – a confused spectator at the fall of the wall. I'm only in the story while I'm driving in the fog. I add it to my list in any case – right after:

THREAT OF LOSING TOES

BREAKING LEG – FALLING IN LOVE WITH DOCTOR

And

TELLING DAD ABOUT MUM

I write:

DRIVING TO POLAND IN FOG

JO   In a second-hand shop near Story Road, Chichester I'm buying a book called AMAZING STORIES, INCREDIBLE FACTS. I take the book to a pub. Over a pint or two I hatch a plan to ascribe some of the stories I find in the book to Mr Chapel. I figure no one will notice. Mr Chapel – The Largest Man in the World. Mr Chapel – Europe's Most Eligible Bachelor. Mr Chapel – The Medical Mystery.

I think – Mr Chapel has no stories so I'll give him some.

Mr Chapel – Braver Than Brave.

Mr Chapel – Inventor of the Post-It Note.

Mr Chapel – Codebreaker.

And then finally: Mr Chapel – Man or Myth?

JE   The fish van is leaving and with it goes my supply of people to talk to. It's getting late. The last woman I talk to is a woman with a black Labrador dog. She laughs at my stories question – there's not many stories at Stories Park unless you count the strange brothers who live together in one of the houses. I ask her to say more. Their garden's totally overgrown and they hardly ever go out and when they do they don't speak to anyone. I ask why they're like that and she says 'Oh, you know. They had a bad war'.

Stories about brothers and about families and about gardens that are untidy. Stories about wars and what happens in them and what happens after them and what happens before them.

CA   When I was a kid I wanted imaginary places to be real and now – here at Story Book Glenn – they all are. In this river valley of pine trees Snow White's House and the Fairy Castle and Goldilocks' Cottage are all as real as real can be, but I'm too big. I'm Gulliver in the Land of Lilliput. Alice when the potion wears off.

I have the whole place to myself. No other visitors, no kids, no one around. I bend to push the door of Snow White's House and hold it open with a finger to peer inside. A tiny table with a tiny tea-set, tiny bunk beds with tiny rumpled sheets.

I'm walking. Past the Ice Castle, past the Gingergbread Man and the Yellow Brick Road. Everywhere the scale is fucked. Huge fluorescent fish jump from tiny ponds. 4ft blackbirds are nailed into trees. The scale keeps shifting, stretching and shrinking but however it changes it's never quite mine. I'm Gulliver in Lilliput. Alice when the potion wears off.

I turn and turn again. I take a wrong direction and find myself in an area of the Theme Park that has been left to run wild, a wilderness impassable with overgrown ferns. I pause for breath. It has started to rain. Up ahead is a sign. It says TROLL LAND. That's where I should go.

Discarded papers on the train this morning were all war warnings and human genes in copyright tangles, missing kids and streams of refugees, economic forecasts from bad to indeterminate. It is 13 August 2002 in a low-rent Scottish theme park called Story Book Glenn. I am alone. I am 40 years old and I have blundered into Troll Land. I don't know, by now, what on or off the earth I'm looking for.

In a clearing ahead I can see the Troll House and the troll himself stood by its stirring fibreglass bones in a fibreglass cauldron. Until now I have stayed out of these doll-house mirages, an observer to a landscape I know is not and cannot be mine. But now I must shelter from the rain. Gulliver in Lilliput. Alice when the potion wears off.

I slip past the troll, bend, enter and sit on the tiny wooden bench inside the house. In front of me three tiny chairs are arranged round a tiny log table. As I look at the chairs I know that others have been here before me, other shelter-seekers in this border zone between the real and the unreal – the chairs have each been graffitied in a blunt tracing of thick black marker pen. They read, Shelley's chair, Sophie's chair and Heidi's chair. Three girls. I am so very tired. I want to text Terry and Claire. I want to contact everyone, even though I know this is against the rules we have set. I want to contact the others. I want to send a text to say that I am sat in the Troll House. I know that no one can understand this at all. They think I am in London. But that doesn't matter here. Explanations can wait.

Surprised to find that there is a signal from this place I text – that I am sat in the Troll House and that I am constructing a list of stories and that I very much need them to help.

TE   I'm on the train going home from London when Cathy's text reaches me. I'm feeling good about my day. I send her the answer – STORIES ABOUT WOMEN ALONE ON A TRAIN AT NIGHT.

RI   I'm outside a fish and chip shop where I got some chips for my tea when I get the message from Cathy so I go into a bus shelter and I eat some more and think about it a bit. Then I send a message back that says: STORIES ABOUT MEN THAT CAN'T STOP EATING.

JE   I'm also going home. When I get her message I send Cathy the answer STORIES ABOUT PEOPLE TRAVELLING HOME.

JO   I'm in a hotel room watching PAY TV. I text Cathy back – STORIES ABOUT A GIRL AND TWO GUYS WHOSE VISIT TO A HEALTH CLUB LEADS TO A LOT OF RAUNCHY ACTION.

CL   I'm nearly home but I don't want my journey to end. I text Cathy. I send her the start of a story.

There were times when the landscape at night seemed more bearable than the too vivid landscape of the day. At night the country was inked out, edited, transformed by an absence of its own detail.

(I think you can just imagine me texting away like that can't you?)

At night the views were reduced to the glowing icons of lit windows in houses and towerblocks, the luminous rectangles of street signs and billboards, the fake orange supernova stars of streetlamps, the trailing lights of the tail lamps of cars and lorries, and the endless glow of tarmac rippling under headlamps, its surface like that of a sea.

My fingers get tired with the texting. I decide on a simpler . . . so I key in the message:

STORIES ABOUT YESTERDAY, TOMMOROW AND NOW

And then I press send.

An Essay

Christine Bacon and Noah Birksted-Breen

Ice&fire was founded in 2003 by playwright Sonja Linden. She was inspired to start the company because of some of the people she met while she was Writer-in-Residence at the Medical Foundation for the Care of Victims of Torture (now Freedom from Torture). Her first play for ice&fire was *I Have before Me a Remarkable Document Given to Me by a Young Lady from Rwanda* (*2003*), a two-hander based on the experiences of a Rwandan woman she had met at the Medical Foundation. The next play, also written by Sonja, *Crocodile Seeking Refuge* (*2005*), was based on five other clients and their experiences of the United Kingdom's asylum system. It was at this point, that we, as a company, decided that we wanted to tell more of these stories to more people than those who attended a limited run of a play and we wanted the stories to be told in the words of people who had experienced them. So we launched a project called Actors for Human Rights, a network of professional actors who donate their time to perform rehearsed readings of these testimonies, upon request, all over the country. The first script for Actors for Human Rights, *Asylum Monologues*, comprised three first-hand accounts from individuals who had sought asylum in the United Kingdom. There are now 11 scripts in the Actors for Human Rights repertoire exploring a wide range of human rights concerns and which reach approximately 10,000 people per year. The project has also inspired a German Actors for Human Rights network. As a company, we have developed an expertise in collecting, shaping and disseminating first-hand testimony which sheds light on contemporary, complex human rights concerns.

In 2009, we (Artistic Director of ice&fire Christine Bacon and Noah Birksted-Breen) started to become increasingly interested in independent media and alternative news sources. It became almost impossible for us to take the 'official version' of any event at face value. We started to understand how crucial independent journalists were to our world view and it was decided, that as playwrights, we wanted to explore what makes somebody a great journalist.

We wanted to speak to and write about journalists who we considered had done something significant in the context of their profession. That inevitably meant independent, investigative journalists and meant following the stories of real people. We knew it would be important to include a range of countries, not only those where there are clear limits on the media and where journalists have been threatened, attacked, imprisoned and killed for their work with impunity, but also those countries where the press is free in theory, but is subject to less visible forms of censorship. With this in mind, we chose five interview subjects from five different countries (Sri Lanka, Russia, Mexico, Israel and the United States). We found that the echoes and the contrasts between each journalist were fascinating – in terms of how they feel about what they do, why they do it and what role the state and the readership plays in their ability to continue.

Choosing these subjects was a process of discovery. We were greatly assisted by the publication *Index on Censorship* and its Editor, Jo Glanville, who helped us get in touch with various journalists we had identified through reading their work in Index. And like any such process, personal contacts, chutzpah and luck also played their part. We conducted in-depth interviews either in person, by phone or via skype with all of the journalists in the play and also gathered everything else we could find about them which would shed light on who they were, including: their work; other interviews they had done publicly; video footage and photographs.

We'd had the idea for *On the Record* in January 2009 and midway through 2009, ice&fire committed to producing it. We finished a first draft of the play in January 2010. The earliest draft had a few key ideas which would remain through to the final version, like the on-stage representation of Zoriah documenting the aftermath of the suicide bomb in Iraq as well as Lydia's on-stage abduction, but much of the rest of the play was still raw testimony which needed editing, shaping and dramatizing. This first draft was, in some ways, where the journey of the writing of the play began. We wanted to 'test' the play, not just on the page but as an artistic and performative piece of writing, so we approached the National Theatre Studio who gave us the wonderful gift of some time, space and actors in order to workshop the script. This culminated in a rehearsed reading of the play in the Studio for an invited audience of peers from the industry, who we asked for feedback afterwards.

We were keenly aware of the ethical demands of including real people as characters in a play but we decided – thanks to the discoveries we made at the Studio – that we wanted to go a step further in imaginatively recreating the stories of the characters onstage, concentrating more on capturing the essence of the people and their actions, rather than remaining too faithful to specific details. After some careful consideration, we felt it would be a good idea to include the journalist Lasantha Wickrematunge from Sri Lanka (who had been murdered in January 2009 before we interviewed his brother Lal) from the start of the play, so that the audience could experience a feel for the relationship between the brothers. We ourselves had never seen the brothers together, nor met Lasantha, but we felt as if we had met him through Lal's description of their relationship and we wanted to include Lasantha as a living character who the audience comes to know, only later to discover that these are memories of a murdered journalist, subverting the inherent expectations of a testimony-based play.

It turned out that we were even, sometimes, too timid in our approach. The only scene which was almost entirely invented (i.e. not based on anything we know to have happened) – a Skype conversation between Zoriah and his then girlfriend at the time he decided to go back for a second tour as a photojournalist in Iraq – had emerged from the rehearsal room process. The director, Michael Longhurst, and the actor playing Zoriah, Trevor White, asked us whether it was possible to include a scene with a personal backstory for Zoriah, since every other scene was directly linked to his work. We ran some rehearsal room improvisations and this prompted us to write a scene where we saw the toll Zoriah's job might take on his personal life – with a 'behind closed doors' conversation between his character and his imagined girlfriend. When Zoriah came to watch the production, we worried that he may take exception to this scene which had come from one passing comment he made to us about the strains on his then relationship – but he only grinned and said, 'You could have gone much further!'

We started the play in a way which would make it clear to the audience not to interpret it as a completely literal representation of reality. We included some quotations from the journalists themselves as a kind of prologue to the play including one from Amira Hass, the only Jewish Israeli journalist to live and work in the Occupied Palestinian territories, who told us 'I have one request. Now, because English is not my first language, it's not my native uh language . . . I would like, uh, my, usually when I speak, uh, I speak in you know, good, articulate language, I would like you to upgrade, to write it as if I spoke in uh, uh proper English.' We also felt the need to alter Elena's language as one of the two interviews we conducted with her was in Russian, and we had to not only translate that interview but also decide how 'foreign' to make it, using our second interview with Elena (which was in English – a second language) as a reference point. We started with Elena talking fairly neutrally – in something quite close to polished English – but through rehearsals, we felt we hadn't quite captured her quirky personality, and all the other characters (with the exception of Zoriah, a native English speaker) were speaking English as a second language – so we decided to work over her language in our play to approximate how she communicated in a second language, also using another English-language interview we found with her on YouTube which had appeared some time after we finished the rehearsal draft. The final version feels closer to the essence of who Elena is as a person, not just as a journalist.

The decision about what process to use was organic, as is hopefully clear from the examples above. In fact, when we began writing the play, we called it a verbatim play (i.e. where it would follow the lives of the journalists word-for-word, using only their own accounts of their work, through direct address to the audience). Soon, we had dropped this description and began calling the play testimony-based, as we started to shape and dramatize scenes. By the time the play was being performed, we felt it was most appropriate to say that it was authored by us, based on the real lives of six journalists. This evolution in the way we defined the genre of our play reflects the essence of our process – moving from a text which solely used real testimony into a play which is both dramatized and also intimately rooted in truth.

A further factor which shaped our approach to rendering real people into stage characters was an instinct that we should try, as much as we could, to use the journalists' own way of working as an integral part of the way each journalist is represented. This was particularly the case for two journalists, Amira Hass and Zoriah. Amira documents the daily realities of an occupied nation – not just the sensational stories but also the more mundane yet soul-destroying details of life under occupation. She has also written and spoken some profound truths about the nature of journalism. While we sought out dramatic arcs and highly dramatic moments for the other journalists depicted in the play, we let Amira tell her own story, almost entirely, like a series of articles – except spoken in an intimate relationship with the audience. Zoriah's photos do his talking, ordinarily, and of course we wanted to show those to the audience, in order to help tell the larger story of how and why the American military has a monopolistic control on what information leaves the war zones in which they are engaged.

At some points in the play, we combine verbatim and non-verbatim material in the same scene, layering real and fictional worlds. One clear example is Zoriah's sequence towards the end of the play, in which his actions, which had only been described verbally prior to that scene, were now embodied onstage with actual representations of his own work, that is, some of his photos, to deepen the audience's experience of the on-stage world with non-verbal documentary sources.

Figure 13 Courtesy of ice&fire theatre company. Photograph by Jon Hollway

Each journalist varied in terms of their enthusiasm for the project and their level of involvement. When we conducted the interviews, we had not been commissioned, the theatre had not been confirmed and no money had been raised. We approached our interview subjects saying: 'we want to write this play and put it on, but there is no guarantee it will go on.' Given that the people involved have extremely busy working lives, we had to be careful not to take up too much of their time, so the interviews were generally limited to two hours. In a couple of cases we went back later and asked follow-up questions. Each journalist was sent the first draft of the play and was asked to comment if there was anything which was inaccurate or which they felt misrepresented them. When the script was finalized for performance, we again wrote to all of the journalists letting them know what was happening and also letting them know we would be happy to share the script with them if they wanted to see it. No one asked to see it at either point – so we assumed we had their continued support. The play premiered at the Arcola Theatre London on 18 July 2011 and ran for four weeks. One of the journalists was able to see the play, Zoriah Miller, as he was living only a couple of hours away, in Amsterdam, at the time. His response was very positive and we hope that in due course, the other journalists may have the chance to see it also.

On the Record

Christine Bacon and Noah Birksted-Breen

Performance Script (20 July, 2011)

The play follows the real lives of six journalists. Direct address to the audience is drawn from first-hand testimony sourced from interviews and other material on the public record. All scenes are dramatised by the playwrights.

Characters

Lydia Cacho is tall and attractive with long dark hair. She has a warm voice with a mild Mexican accent. She takes great care with her appearance and wears figure-hugging clothes and high heels. She is 44 but looks younger than her age.

Zoriah Miller is American, tall, blonde, blue-eyed and well-built. He is 33 years old.

Amira Hass is Israeli, 53 years old and has an intense, focused manner. She wears round glasses, no make-up and dresses simply. She speaks with an Israeli accent.

Lal Wickrematunge is middle-aged, wears glasses and smart clothes and speaks slowly and thoughtfully, with an undercurrent of humour in what he says. He speaks with a Sri Lankan accent.

Lasantha Wickrematunge is 43, bubbly, curious. He dresses smartly. He speaks with a Sri Lankan accent.

Elena Kostyuchenko is 21 and fidgety, with a high-pitched voice. She wears simple, unremarkable outfits. She is mousy-looking. She speaks with a Russian accent.

All other roles are played by the cast.

Lasantha is sitting at his desk. He starts to type.

It's 6.30 a.m. Elena's flat. The doorbell rings. Elena appears in her night clothes, she goes to see who is at the door. Behind the door is a silhouette of a woman.

Elena   Coming. Coming. Yes?

OK

(*Elena opens one lock of the door* (*there are three locks*) *then stops and looks through the peephole.*)

Who's it from?

Pause

Just leave it outside.

(*struggling to hear*) What?

I can't understand what you're saying

Well, I don't recognise you.

Tell me from out there –

I don't care if the neighbours hear

Just go away – I'm not opening up okay . . .

(*Pause*)

(*Elena looks through the peephole and sees the woman go. Then she moves over to the window. As she does this, she picks up her mobile and dials.*)

(*On the phone*) Hey . . . I'm sorry to call so early/Yes/A woman came to my door and kept asking me to open it – and now she's out in the courtyard talking to a group of men/I don't think I should come in to work today.

Lydia   It's not that one day I decided to be heroic. And actually it bothers me that people think I'm heroic, that I'm sacrificing myself. I think that a sacrificial woman is something awful like Mother Teresa. She used to say 'give until it hurts', what's that?! I just think it's my right to talk, to be free, to write. I'm a good journalist and I will defend that right. So I . . . it worries me that people see me in that way because it just takes you away from the majority. It makes the majority think you are special and that's why you can do it. And that's a lie, I'm not special, I just decided to do this.

And on top of that, you know, I often wonder if I was fat and had a moustache, you know like . . . (*gestures for fat*), I mean like a really huge lesbian feminist, would they keep inviting me to all of these international events to speak? No way! But I fit perfectly with the cliché! This Latina woman (*she gestures – long hair, hourglass figure*). Anyway . . . I'm not politically correct, as I think you know by now.

Amira   I have one request. Now, because English is not my first language, it's not my native uh language . . . I would like, uh, my, usually when I speak, uh, I speak in you know, good, articulate language, I would like you to upgrade, to write it as if I spoke in uh, uh proper English.

Zoriah   I'm in favour of breaking any kind of rules. Centring your subject, shooting in the sun, using blurry shots, cropping, zooming, experimenting is important. So yeah, of course, a photo does often lie. It is a moment in time – it is impossible to tell the whole story in a sixtieth of a second.

Elena   Good journalism is investigation. Even if it is about 25 new sex positions, it's still investigation. When it's time to write the article, I say to myself, 'sit down, write the article' and then I say, when I finish, I will order a very, very delicious pizza. Also, I smoke, that helps me. A lot of people in the office, they smoke. Some drink to help them . . . actually I don't know the English word. Sorry for my English. It's not perfect.

Lal   I would like you to read this one first. And this is confidential. Keep this one off the record yeah? While you read it, I'm going to have a cigarette (*exits*).

Zoriah   It's kind of a silly story – I was doing some stuff for the Red Cross in New York. There was a blackout and people were stranded all over the city and we had this truck with 2,000 meals on it and there were like 4 or 5 thousand people who hadn't been home in days and were really hungry. But we weren't allowed to give out the food until we had a certain piece of paper signed. Ended up – the food rotted in the trailer and we couldn't even throw the food away because you needed to have a different form signed to throw food away! And it just clicked in my mind that I couldn't keep doing disaster management. Not too long after that, uh, the movie Salvador was on TV and I watched it and (*laughs*) that kind of made a couple more things click and then there was a bookstore down the street and they had a Salgado book on sale and by that point things were clicking real quickly (*laughs*) and that's when I bought my camera and my plane ticket.

Lydia   When I was a little girl, my mum used to take us to the slums in Mexico City. I remember I was trying to show this kid of my age, four or five, how to draw, right? And he would hold the pencil like this (*makes a fist*), I was like 'no,no,no,no.no, this is how you do it' and I would show him but he couldn't grasp the concept of drawing. We were driving back home and I asked my mum 'why can't he draw? Is he a bit . . .? And my mum said, 'He is really poor, he probably will never learn to read or write, or draw. Because you do have the rights you have, you have food, you have an education, you have to do something about it.' So that just stayed in my mind.

Amira   Very often I recall a scene that my mother told me about when she was transported by train to the death camp at Bergen-Belsen, and they were taken out of the carriages after 10 days. They were sick and some were dying. Then my mother saw these German women carrying baskets of food, looking at them, almost apathetically . . . with a sort of indifferent curiosity at this new delivery of people being led to murder. This image became formative in my upbringing. It's as if I was there and saw it myself. One of my worst nightmares when I was a bit older was that I would be in a situation in which I am the bystander.

I guess today I do not use this metaphor or this image very often because the problem, as I see it today is much less bystanders than collaborators. In Israel, we are all collaborators, even those who oppose the occupation, because we enjoy the privileges. The question is . . . how much we use our privileges in order to fight the regime of privileges.

(*Elena is smoking in a corridor of the Novaya Gazeta offices in Moscow.*)

Elena   When I was 14 or 15 – I bought an edition of Novaya Gazeta. It was the first time I see this newspaper. I open it and I saw a double spread of Anna Politkovskaya about what was happening in Chechnya. And I was just shocked. So I sat on the bench for long time reading the newspaper . . . well I dunno . . . I always thought that I am quite clever and well-informed person. I watched the TV news a lot, I read other newspapers, but I suddenly understand that I don't know anything about anything about what was going on in my country . . . Of course, I'd seen something about Chechnya on TV but nothing like this . . . .

Media in Russia is . . . how can I say it? OK, let me try to explain. All our TV is governmental, absolutely controlled by government, it's really shit. And that's how most people get their news. Newspapers are in an interesting situation because hmm . . . I don't know if you have self-censorship in the West but in Russia it's the main law of journalism.

When journalists pick a new topic for an article . . . 'no, I won't write about this because I don't want any problems and even if I write it, my editor won't publish it'. Most journalists – they know they're writing shit. Some start to find some reasons why they do it. 'Actually I'm doing in the interests of my government'. . . . 'I have children, I have a family, I don't want to get killed like Anna Politkovskaya'. . . .

(*Elena's mobile rings. She answers it.*)

Hello.

(*Pause*)

I understand but I can't really talk/You need to talk to – (/ *Loudly and emphatically*) – I understand but I can't talk right now, I'm not well/ What are you talking about! / I know how much I'm working Alla Victorievna. But you know that I can do an article quickly/ I can't talk now, call me later/OK – goodbye.

(*Elena hangs up*)

That's great! First they say, 'When are you going to finish this article?' and then, 'You shouldn't be working so much – you're going to wear yourself out.'

So . . . for now I'm in Moscow making new investigations. Eventually, it is my wish to work in Chechnya. But my editor feels that I have problem – he says I don't care enough for my life. But, in the future, one day, he'll hopefully say 'Elena now you're ready'. . . That's going to be the second happiest moment in my life after the moment when they told me that I am a special correspondent of Novaya Gazeta.

Journalist   Please don't smoke in the corridor.

Elena   Oh, ok.

(*Elena extinguishes cigarette and starts to tidy up what she was using as an ashtray – newspaper. She has made a mark in the table. She exits with the newspaper.*)

Oh shit. Well . . . let me give you the tour.

(*Elena starts walking along into the offices of Novaya Gazeta. She comes to a glass cabinet.*)

Elena   This is our museum with lots of interesting things. Here is the first computer of Novaya Gazeta . . . 16 years old! It looks really old now but probably it was very modern in those days. And here is first mobile phone of Novaya. Which Gorbachev gave to us. (*Moving along*) And here are all of our prizes.

Lydia   My former husband asked me for a divorce because of my work. He couldn't handle it. He'd be like – 'we need to hide' and would be like almost hiding under the bed! He was a dentist. We were together for 13 years. He was a nice guy.

Elena   When I came to work here, suddenly I have not many friends. They think I am crazy and don't understand why I have to do this. I realised my real friends are colleagues from Novaya. We just understand each other. It's very comfortable when I don't have to explain.

Lydia   I have great friends. I have my rituals with them. One of them owns a small restaurant and a bar, so we all go there and drink, we laugh a lot, we dance, we don't talk about serious stuff, we just talk about love, sex, anything except our problems. They know that, they understand, it's like a rule we've established. But my real escape is scuba diving. I go under the ocean and there's nothing . . . nothing . . . no talk, no noise. It's like being in the centre of the earth.

Amira   In general the Israelis regard me as some sort of a traitor and . . . are disgusted by the thought that I can live among Arabs. (*Screws up her face*) 'With Arabs?' 'Do you have friends in Ramallah?' I say 'If I lived in Paris, I would have French friends, no?' But this is something that is for some Israelis incomprehensible. Many Israelis tell me I'm extreme, I say no, it's the reality that is extreme. I'm not such a revolutionary as everyone thinks.

Zoriah   The life of a war photographer is a pretty solitary one. You travel most of the year and basically live in the shadows, struggling to make ends meet, having experiences that are difficult to talk about. The stress and exhaustion really take a toll on your body and your family and the people that are close to you – so I think that unless you really believed in it, it would be absolutely impossible to do this job . . . . and I use the word 'job' loosely because it, it doesn't feel like a job, it's more like a . . . I guess . . . mission isn't the best word, but it's the only one that comes to mind . . .

Lal   At the beginning, my father was . . . he felt quite proud, and as things started getting a little hot, he became worried. My wife and children have been supportive of course. We don't travel in the same vehicle, we do different runs. You constantly keep looking in your rear-view mirror, to see whether there is a pattern in the vehicles following you. You slow down, you go quicker. The fear factor, although it lurks at the back of your mind, it doesn't come to the front.

Elena   Here is a small exhibition about each of our colleagues who was killed. (*Pointing to a photo*) Igor Domnikov. The murderer . . . he used something like a hammer to Igor's head . . . in the entrance of his own home.

Lydia   I remember my guards telling me – if someone really wanted to kill you, they just need a bullet, a good aim and a couple of seconds. And I thought – that's true. So I started to worry less about having so much protection. As someone said – never underestimate the power of denial. If I didn't have a little bit of denial going on, I would go mad.

Elena   A few journalists here have bodyguards, but in Russia, if someone wants to kill you, they gonna kill you. This is typical Russian thing, they know they will never go to jail for killing a journalist. (*Pointing to another photo*) This is Yuri Petrovich Schekochikhin. He was poisoned.

Lydia   I don't have guards anymore, I don't trust them, but I am careful, and take precautions. Once a week I go to a mechanic I know and he checks my car to see if it has been tampered with. I never make an appointment by phone, or if I do I change the place at the last minute.

Elena   When you're going home, and you see there are men standing in front of your door and they're not smoking, they're just standing there, you get scared. Just for an instant the fear just hits you and then you need to just go into your flat and then it passes.

Amira   People always ask me if it's dangerous here, but I don't face real danger . . . I mean, okay, it is frightening to stand up to an Israeli tank and I don't know what it is going to do . . . or to sneak into Jenin, or when stones are thrown at me . . . of course, there are some levels of . . . ah courage . . . but you have people who go to war zones – I would never dare to do it . . . like in Iraq or Afghanistan. And I cannot tell you, I mean honestly, if there was danger that I would be killed or imprisoned and tortured, to stop me from writing, I think I would have stopped writing a long time ago.

Zoriah   Most photojournalists insure their cameras before they insure their bodies and there's a lot of us including myself who do this without insurance and uh we really keep our fingers crossed that nothing happens. I don't think you ever really know how close to death you are at any given point. There could have been dozens of mines I almost stepped

on, dozens of roadside bombs the vehicle I was in almost triggered . . .
who knows. Once you're on the ground, I don't think worrying does any
good, it's more important to concentrate on your safety. There's a million
things that occupy your mind when you're actually in a situation and
oftentimes it's only once you've left that it hits you . . . yeah, that can be
unsettling.

Elena   That was a notebook of Stas. The killer walked up to him
in daylight in a Moscow street and shot him in the back of the head.
(*Pointing at a book*) Nastya's book of Japanese martial arts. She was
walking with Stas, so she was shot too.

Lal   The threats began within the first year of setting up the paper. Of
course, every Sunday, the phone starts ringing at ten o'clock, because
that's when the paper comes out. They say 'you better find another
country to hide' (*laughs*). 'You are not safe in Sri Lanka anymore.'

Amira   Here's one. (*Reading an email on her screen in a neutral voice*)
'I hope you're not a Nazi but just a lunatic. Reading what you wrote
makes me shudder. Knowing that there are Jews like you in our world.
I wish you eternal life in hell with your friends the suicide bombers
who are celebrating in heaven. Devil woman. From me, an outraged
Israeli.' Another one . . . 'You are a whore'. . . 'Making your living from
lies'. . . 'Bitch'. Yeah, I get these kinds of emails all the time. There are
thousands.

Lydia   Mexico is a macho country. And if you understand that, then
you understand everything else. As well as my work as a journalist, I
founded a high security shelter for women and children who have been
victims of domestic violence and trafficking. The first time a guy put
a gun to my head I was outside my office and he came at me because I
helped his wife to go to register for a law suit against him. After that I
decided to put cameras outside my office and I developed this security
plan with my team.

Elena   Every two or three years we lose somebody and of course you
try not to think about who's next but you do think about it anyway.
Sometimes when you come to work you're thinking who's next, who's
next?

(*A man wearing a S.W.A.T. top is teaching Lydia how to disarm a
gunman. He holds a gun in one hand and points it at her upper body
while facing her. She tries to disarm him and doesn't do it properly.*)

Lydia   Oh . . . What did I do wrong that time?

Swat Man (*Hands the gun to Lydia and indicates to point it at him.*) OK – let's break it down real slow. So, the guy with the gun is going to expect you to put your arms up, so as you do that, you need to move your body off centre – out of the line of fire (*he demonstrates*). Then you need to push his arm with your right arm, and your left arm is gonna hit the wrist in a counter-clockwise circular motion (*he demonstrates*). Then the other hand is going to move the weapon up towards his head . . .(*demonstrates and pushes other arm down at the same time – and takes the gun away and points it at her.*) Then you need to step back immediately, at an angle (*demonstrates*).

Lydia OK. Let's try it again.

(*They do it again, slowly*)

Swat Man Perfect. OK now, speed it up – and remember, body off-centre

(*She does this.*)

Lydia Woah. (*Laughs*) Welcome to Mexico!

Swat Man OK – new scenario, you get into the guy's house, and he points the gun at his wife. What do you do?

Elena (*in a hushed voice as if in a library*) That's where Anna used to sit and here is a photo of her.

(*There's a kind of shrine to Anna with her books by the photo.*)

It was a Saturday . . . somebody told me 'Anna Politkovskaya was killed'. I didn't want to ask again, because I was absolutely sure, totally sure, she couldn't be killed. But in fifteen minutes, the internet news starts to publish about it. I realised that I would never have any chance to tell her that she was the person who changed my life.

Swat Man Good. Now, let's do the gun to the head (*he puts a gun to her head*)

Elena (*whispering*) Right . . . let's go.

(*Lydia disarms the S.W.A.T. man*)

(*Elena goes further down the corridor, turns left and then right into an office.*)

Elena (*Points at a corner sofa*) You always find somebody sleeping here when new edition is about to come out . . . Today there is no one because an edition just came out yesterday.

This is the sports department. You see that red material hanging? That is where we keep our most valuable things. (*Laughs*) The vodka and the beer.

OK – here's my desk. Well you can see for yourself . . . (*it's very messy. She sits down at her desk. Her laptop is open. Points to whiteboard.*) This is where we put themes we gonna write about. I try not to write about ordinary situations, like when policemen hit people.

One investigation I was making for months . . . well, there was a man, Misha, his son disappeared. The prosecutor general and the police closed their case without results . . . so Misha, starts his own investigation and quickly understands his son don't just disappear. He ran straight to police and gives them his information but they not interested.

So he came to us. I took this investigation and I see from the files that the official version of this case was absolutely . . . shit. My friend in police said they are not allowed to finish the investigation.

Well, the main thing is I find proof of something that nobody knows before: that there is a gang of criminal men, traffic police and police. It is like this – the traffic police and police are responsible to find the owners of trendy, expensive cars who didn't have too many relatives and then they give the data to the criminal men. Then the owner of car happens to meet a pretty woman – she invites him to her flat . . . they kill the guy, cut his body into parts and sell his car.

(*Grainy CCTV footage plays showing people entering and leaving a flat. Elena explains what's going on as the images are shown.*)

Elena   OK – so, 8.50 p.m. two men enter the flat. /9.00 p.m. A woman leaves the flat. 10.35 p.m. a woman returns to the flat with Misha's son – you see him there? / 11 p.m. the woman leaves the flat. / Misha's son never leaves the flat. / Then the night after – at 1.31 a.m., two men carry many bags and boxes from the flat.

(*The film continues to play and we watch the man and woman carrying the bags and boxes.*)

Elena   I tried to be careful, but, somebody find out what I am doing. Some men tried to kidnap my younger sister . . . they tried to pull her into a car – she managed to fight and get away. Well, I can't say 100 per cent for sure that there was a connection – maybe they just thought she was good-looking (*laughs*). Then some other strange things . . . I discover I am being watched from building opposite of my flat. Finally, some people came to my newspaper openly and told me not to publish the article and to say it was a lie or something. I said 'no, I won't do that'. I never change what I write. Never. Never. I don't own a flat, I don't have money – the only thing I have is my name to sign my articles with.

So we published. You probably think they were all arrested – happy ending! That is a funny idea for us. I thought this was a real chance to do something. But unfortunately the judges of investigation saw my evidence and they said 'you don't find anything new'. That's absolutely the usual case for Russia. Actually I think I did a good job because now we know the names of the murderers. But right now, they all do same jobs in the police.

Amira   I never studied journalism. I learned on the job. I started as a copy editor, at the bottom of the ladder. This was in 1989. And I got some very good advice from one of my colleagues that accompanies me to this very day. She said 'don't write clichés – clean them all out.' Stylistic clichés are dangerous – but the mental clichés are much more dangerous – writing in formulas according to what other media think about and talk about. Which shows that you have given up your own independent thinking. In general, journalists adopt the version of reality as it is presented by those who are in power.

If I was to be lenient with this type of journalism, I would say it is due to the socialisation that in a way, each of us goes through. In the sense that we all copy from each other until we stop knowing that we are copying from each other. We accept rules, we accept realities and events as if they were axioms, as if they were the sun and the moon.

Israeli media is quite. . . . uh . . . free. In the sense that Israeli journalists can criticise many aspects . . . and expose all kinds of embarrassing incidents between officials. But there is a consistent editorial policy that does not dare to contradict the ways in which the army and the bureaucracy want to present reality. Look at this. (*Picks up a newspaper on her desk*) The vocabulary used by the Israeli media is copied almost word for word from army reports. Every day, Palestinians are 'arrested' or 'detained' while an Israeli soldier captured by Hamas was 'kidnapped'. The army is 'operating' in Palestinian cities . . . but the Palestinians have 'attacked' Israelis, doesn't matter if the Palestinians are shooting at a force that invaded their village, and they are always 'terrorists', even when they are facing soldiers, armed to the teeth, who break into their homes in the middle of the night without invitation. Certainly, I know that real information about the occupation that my paper Ha'aretz gives reaches very few people – those who want to know.

Zoriah   One thing you see all over in Iraq is mainstream media who literally do all of their reports from their hotel balcony and once a month will embed with the US military. At one stage I ended up stuck in the Green Zone . . . and every morning you hear all the journalists calling the military press office from their hotels asking what happened that day, what's the news for that day, rather than finding out on their own. There's obviously reasons, I mean journalists are rightfully scared to do their work but I mean it's sad that the information they disseminate is from this single source. Most of the marines I spoke to when I was there feel that the media has completely failed them. They want their stories to be out, in a true and realistic way and not in a hygienic and ah . . . you know white-washed way. It's better with the European media . . . . the French are a kind of a photographer's best friend, they'll publish anything whether it has a need to be published or not. Germany seems to have an interest as well, but the United States is the worst, there's more censorship here than just about anywhere else I've seen, and most of it is from advertising dollars uh . . . because the media's become a corporate entity, it, basically, it's a business, not news any more, it's an entertainment industry. It's the whole adage of nobody wants to sell a watch opposite a page of someone dying. . . .

Lydia   After Iraq, Mexico is the most dangerous place in the world to be a journalist. The Mexican government is a really good faker. Some people fake orgasm – the Mexican government fakes that we have a good justice system. And people think that because we speak Spanish and we are under the United States, we are more developed or more democratic than we actually are. Out of every 100 crimes that are perpetrated in my country – only two of them get investigated. I mean since its origins, the criminal justice system is not only corrupted but it's colonial, from the Spanish. When they left, it stayed like that. So justice in Mexico is only for those who can pay for it. And most of us cannot.

Ever since I was born I was afraid of police men. I remember my mum telling me when I was a little girl, if something happens to you, never run to the police. If you see a police man, run away from him and go and knock on somebody's door and ask for help.

(*20-year-old woman enters.*)

Lydia   My colleague said you wanted to talk to me?

Woman   Yes. You are Lydia?

Lydia   Yes.

Woman   The journalist?

Lydia   Yes.

Woman   I heard you on the radio. That's how I knew about this shelter. I couldn't believe it . . . really . . . that there were people to come to, who would protect us.

Lydia   Well, we are really happy that you came here.

(*Pause*)

Woman   I want to ask you . . .

(*Pause*)

Lydia   It's OK.

Woman   I want to ask you to listen to my story. Then, I want you to write it down and talk about it. Will you promise to write it down and put it in the newspaper?

Lydia   Have you thought about talking to a therapist?

Woman   No.

Lydia   There's wonderful doctor here.

Woman   Oh. Thank you. OK, maybe I should talk to a doctor.

Lydia   I really think that's the best thing for you right now. If you go back to the office, let my colleagues know and they will arrange an appointment for you. OK?

(*Woman silently nods, and slowly gets up to leave. Before she exits she turns back to Lydia*)

Woman   So, can I come back to you after I have talked to the therapist?

(*Lydia struggles to respond.*) The police told him I reported him. He called me last week, saying he was gonna kill me. He said, 'You are really gonna suffer when I find you.'

(*Lydia Then gets up and walks over to woman and hugs her.*)

Lydia   OK. OK. I'm not sure what I can do, but I'll try.

(*Lydia indicates to woman that she should sit down.*)

Let's start with his name.

(*Pause*)

Woman   Succar Kuri. He runs the whole thing from a hotel he owns very close to this office, you probably drive past it every day. He is . . . in my mind . . . he is the devil. He abused hundreds of kids.

Lydia   Hundreds?

Woman   The first thing he did was buy us things and treat us like he was our nice uncle or something . . . we used to swim in his pool and stuff like that. When he raped me the first time, he said this is what all fathers do with their children and I didn't know about it because I didn't have a father. He filmed it and then made me watch the tape. He said he would kill my mother if I told her.

Lydia   (*takes out her notepad*) It was very brave of you to come forward.

Woman   He filmed us having sex with the men who came into his hotels and then sold them the tapes. Some of the kids were so small, the men would have to like . . . lift them on to the bed first.

(*Sees that Lydia is listening and continues.*)

Woman   There are lots of men involved. Some of them come from the United States and Canada and Europe to have sex with us. Some of them protect Succar because he is you know, laundering lots money for them. One of them is called Mr Emilio Gamboa – I think he is a politician.

Lydia   Yeah . . . yeah he is.

Woman   And another one is called Mr Kamel Nacif – a very rich guy . . . I used to see him on TV a lot.

(*Lydia is taking notes*)

Woman   Succar will keep doing this. He knows he can always pay the authorities and that's it. There is lots of evidence – I can help you to find it. His wife is an expert with technology and she puts all of the videos and the photos on his computers. There was a black one in his bedroom – that's the one with everything on it.

(*Lydia nods and writes this down.*)

Woman   Will you make a promise to me that you will investigate this? I will tell you about everything, I will answer all of your questions, I can help you find other children to talk to, but you have to promise me that you will write the names of all of the men involved so they cannot do this anymore. Can you promise?

Amira   I decided to cover the Israeli occupation, to monitor it as a journalist. And where else would I know what it feels like, what it is like, if I didn't live under Israeli occupation in the occupied territories. There are two peoples here and I feel attached to the two peoples. I am part of the Jewish Israeli people, but I also feel a belonging to the Palestinians who are, for me, I mean we grew up in the same you know, landscape, so the smells, and the voices and the sky, the colours, are the same. So I feel this affinity with them.

Once, I was at an Israeli military checkpoint and a soldier examined my identity card, then he stared at me. Then he examined the card and stared at me again (*eyes boggling*). He said 'But you are a Jew, what are you doing here?' I was very pleased with myself for my reply . . . 'You are also a Jew, the question is what you are doing here?' (*She smiles*) So, I was even more pleased when he said – 'Believe me, I have no idea.' This response I preferred to the more common response that I would get from soldiers at other checkpoints . . . they say 'we are here to protect you from terrorists and you should be thankful to us'. And they always say it in this typical paternalistic patronising tone, though I am probably older than their own mothers.

Yeah, OK no other Israeli Jew lives here. I have a kind of an obsession to get the taste or the flavour of things from the inside (*gesture – like she's touching cloth and assessing its quality*). To know what it is when a soldier aims a gun at you not knowing you are an Israeli. To know what curfew is like at night, to know what it is to have curfew in the middle of the day, all of a sudden. Or, when soldiers are searching the houses – going from one house to the next. I felt that as an Israeli, I needed to experience it on a daily basis. Not as a visitor once a week, not as a . . . you know, butterfly, but as someone who lives here.

The Israeli occupation . . . is like experiencing violence all the time. It's like battered women. It's to be a battered woman every single minute of your life. It is like an ongoing rape, an ongoing violence . . . and then there is the humiliation and the anger, the suppressed anger, because you cannot constantly react because you also want to live normally.

Life in Ramallah, it is a prison for the Palestinians. It is fine for me, I can leave when I want to. I can go from Ramallah to Jerusalem and my neighbours cannot do that. I can drive on roads which are for Jews and Israelis only. For me it's a 20-minute drive to Jerusalem. For most Palestinians, it is as far as the moon. But I'm a Jew and the taste of privilege is disgusting.

(*Lydia arrives at police station. A plain-clothes police man is sitting behind a black computer. He looks up at her.*)

Policeman   It took me three days.

Lydia   Photographs?

Police Officer   A video. He had it cleaned by a professional. I was just about to give up.

Lydia   Thank you. Thank you. What do we do now?

Police Officer   We need to show this to the mothers, you'll need to bring them here –

Lydia   Are you crazy? I'm not –

Police Officer   So they can make a positive identification –

Lydia   If I was a mother and I saw that, I would never recover from . . . They're still dealing with the shock of it. To know it's happened is one thing – but to see it . . .

(*Pause*)

Policeman   Well . . . you interviewed all the kids, didn't you?

Lydia   Yeah . . .

Policeman   You could watch it and I could take your statement.

Lydia   Oh, OK. This is really the only option, isn't it?

Policeman   Are you sure you want to do this?

(*Lydia sits by the computer*)

(*Lydia indicates she is ready. Policeman plays the video. They both watch for 20 seconds.*)

Lydia   Yes, that's one of the girls. That's her (*gets up and walks away*). OK, stop it.

Policeman   Wait – there are two more.

(*Lydia walks over and watches for five seconds.*)

Lydia   Yes. I know them as well.

(*Policeman stops the video.*)

Lydia   Will that be enough?

Policeman   You saw it. This is going to put Succar in a federal prison.

Zoriah   I shoot all of my stories from as intimate a position as possible, so I'll sleep in the same places as the migrant farm workers, or in a refugee camp, then all of sudden, the story is going on all around you, you're living in the middle of it and I think the people really respect the fact that you're there and you eat one handful of beans a day with them and they really see that you're putting more into it than the person that hops out of the humvee and takes the shot, which I see a lot of other photojournalists doing. When you live like they do, people will say 'oh, did you know our neighbour stepped on a cluster bomb and blew his leg off, would you like to take his picture?' That's when you really start getting deep into people's lives and into the story.

But when I'm in Iraq, I do all of my work embedded with the US military. I think that a lot of journalists have a problem with the idea of embedded journalism, they see it as censorship, and also that you're reporting from the military perspective. But it's basically the only way to work in Iraq right now. The situation is so volatile that you effectively cannot work as a disembedded journalist in Iraq unless you have the money to have a private army in the form of a private security force.

It was hard to decide to go the first time but just kind of knowing the experience, what it feels like to be there . . . I mean this job is extremely uncomfortable and you know we're sick a lot, we're exhausted a lot, you, you know, your emotions go from, way up to way down, I mean it's really, you kind of have to be used to . . . really living in peaks and valleys to do this work and, I mean, Iraq is that times fifty. It's probably one of the scariest places in the world – to deliberately go back and do it again, also to realise that there's a relatively decent chance you'll end up dead or missing limbs or severely injured in some way, and you really kind of go back and forth on, you know, is it worth it? I mean a mind-fuck is the, you know, the nice word for it.

People were shocked by the relatively mild images I brought back from my first tour in 2007. . . . I began to realise that the general public – when they hear on the news that X number of people died in a shooting or bomb blast – they don't have any idea of what that looks like . . . I knew the war was escalating but at the same time becoming more invisible. Editors were telling me that my work was some of the best they had seen during the war, but then the inevitable . . . 'no one will publish something this depressing' . . . 'people have compassion fatigue' or asking me if I had some lighter stories – on nightlife in the Green Zone or obesity in the army! I realised that my work in Iraq wasn't finished.

Lal   I played in the Sri Lankan under-25 cricket team, I opened for the bowling and batted, too . . . an all-rounder . . . Then I joined the police department for seven years because they were recruiting sportsmen. It was a good grounding but at the end of that period, I felt that my future lay elsewhere. So I got out and joined this printing company . . . and in five years I ended up buying that company. I was thinking of going into newspapers because I felt that was the future.

By then, that was in 1994, my youngest brother Lasantha, had come back from university in England and he was practising as a barrister for the President's Council and he was also writing. I suddenly found that he had a lot of politics in him and a feel for news.

Lasantha   I can take six months leave to help you get it off the ground . . . and then we can see where it goes.

Lal   We don't have enough capital to go for market share yet, but it should happen quickly.

Lasantha   How political are you willing to go?

Lal   Well – it will be up to you.

Lasantha   (*smiling*) Complete editorial freedom from the management?

Lal   Granted. I'm thinking that we could start with columns like the one you've done for The Sri Lanka Times, going to the insides of the Cabinet . . .

Lasantha   Ha! I've already got three stories The Times would never touch . . . a few files have landed on my doorstep . . .

Lal   (*to audience*) As soon as we started, as a marketing ploy, we went into the other side of politics, the other life of the politicians, for example Chandrika Kumaratunga, the President at the time, she was married to a very famous actor, he was from our school. And even though he was the husband of the President, he gave us a tip-off about her past and we wrote to her about it.

(*Lal reads out a letter to the former President.*)

Lal   (*reading*) Madame President, you presented your educational qualifications to the Parliament and to the Commonwealth Heads of Government but we have certificates to prove that you went to a finishing school in Paris and not the Sorbonne as you claim. So if you're kind enough to nominate a time and place, we can share our information with you and you can tell us if we are wrong.

Lasantha (*reading from a letter*) 'Dear Editor, letters to Her Excellency the President will be entertained only when they are from human beings and not when they are from animals, like you. We have put your letter into the dustbin although we feel that even that is too good for your letter.'

Lal (*to audience, laughing*) We reproduced both letters on the front of the newspaper . . .

Lasantha By now, people were queuing up to buy the paper . . . We started by distributing the paper ourselves by car, in our shorts and rubber slippers in the morning like delivery boys.

Lal In the beginning, we were sometimes slightly late and the shop owner once said 'you go and tell your boss, that they must bring the paper on time! People are waiting here – you can see the queue for yourself!' So I said (*laughing*) 'I'll tell him!' . . . We had just eight staff . . . only two computers . . . and Lasantha and I used to sit at the computers and key in the copy, do the layout ourselves . . .

Lasantha A famous story was the one we wrote about the President having an exclusive party for her and her ministers at the Hilton while there was a curfew because they said there would be a Tamil Tigers attack and the whole of Sri Lanka was in darkness, because there were also power cuts. She told the general manager of the Hilton, 'if this gets through to the Sunday Leader, you'd better go and find another job'.

Lal But we found a way – my background as a police officer helped. The story we wrote contained the menu . . .

Lasantha Smoked salmon and caviar . . . what everyone was wearing, the fine French wine they were drinking . . .

Lal And even the songs that the bands played and who danced to which song. The President went on television and took the newspaper to task, and we included her words in the article, so she really helped us to market the paper . . . (*Laughs*).

Lasantha We became number two in the market. When we felt people were watching us and reading us – that's when we started going into graft and corruption.

Lal (*Looks at watch*) Did you say this would take two hours? Because I'm hoping that I will catch *Billy Elliot*. I'm very sorry to have missed it the last time. I always catch a musical when I come to London. On my way out last time I saw *Mama Mia* and *Chicago*. I've seen *Hairspray*.

I saw *Les Miserables* with the kids once. . . . *Starlight Express*, when it was running, and I've seen *Grease*. Shall I draw the curtain? It's getting too hot. (*Draws curtain*) Is that okay?

Lasantha   So, it was in two thousand and uh . . . two thousand. The government started censorship of war news . . . they appointed a competent authority to check all the news that went in all the papers.

Lal   – Yes – (*to audience*) you had to send it to them before it was printed. And they used to run the red pencil through it. Some of the stories just came blank. Virtually. The newspapers started carrying blank stories, saying 'this has been censored, censored'. So we thought – how do we get around this?

Lasantha   We started sending him everything, even the sports stuff and he was getting a little fed up with this and said 'unless it's something serious, don't send everything'. So we thought, how do we write a story that isn't serious? So, we carried a story in banner headlines about a Tamil Tigers attack on the air force base in Palali – something the government was very embarrassed about.

Lal   But we did it in a different form.

Lasantha   Two bombs did *not* fall into the hangar. Three bombs did *not* damage the airstrip.

Lal   Two soldiers did *not* die from shrapnel wounds.

Lasantha   The next day 200 army guys came and sealed our press.

Lal   They pulled Lasantha from his car . . . masked men.

Lasantha   They smashed the car up and thrashed me with poles – you know, the kind of poles that have nails driven through them?

Lal   Another time they fired at Lasantha's house with semi-automatic weapons . . . they bulldozed the front part of my house once. Luckily no one was hurt.

Lasantha   Burned down the press a couple of times.

Lal   You become immune to it after a while . . .

Lasantha   We exposed the tsunami foreign aid story – I found that the current President, Mahinda Rajapakse, who was actually a good friend of ours – we knew him at high school, opened a bank account and close to a billion rupees, two-thirds of the foreign aid given to Sri Lanka to rebuild after the tsunami vanished into that account to fund his Presidential campaign. We wrote about it and he had to give the money back.

Lal   The police started an investigation which was halted, of course.

Lasantha   Then, do you remember – The President's wife created a scandal in India – and the Indian officials told him: 'I can keep this quiet here but in Sri Lanka I don't know – a paper like The Leader might carry it.'

Lal   We actually hadn't publish anything – but because the President's English wasn't very good, he thought we had! So he called Lasantha on his mobile – when was that?

Lasantha   2006.

Lal   He chose his words carefully from the finest available in the Sinhala language.

Lasantha   'Fuck your mother, you son of a bloody whore!'

Lal   'I will finish you!'

Lasantha   'I treated you well all this while. Now I will destroy you. You don't know who Mahinda Rajapakse is. You watch what I will do to you!'

I told him – 'We haven't published anything like that. . . . Someone's feeding you porky-pies.' But we did get an article out of it . . . I recorded the President's call and published it. They made it really difficult for us to publish after that . . . threats, lawsuits. But things have become a lot worse for journalists in the last two (*looks to Lal*). . .?

Lal   Yes, two to three years.

Amira   Power, any power, has to be suspected. Maybe my inclination by nature is to cast doubt on everybody who is important or likes to be considered important. There is a misconception that journalists can be objective. We always have a certain angle that is determined by our life, our gender, our economic situation, our history, by the mood that we woke up in the morning – everything.

When we know we cannot be objective, we are much more careful to be fair in the way we present the facts . . . and other voices – even those that we don't like.

We are not, as Robert Fisk says, in a football match, acting as a referee to decide between two groups. Did we expect journalists in South Africa not to have a stand about apartheid? Or people who covered the Soviet Union not to have a stand about the oppression there? Being fair and being objective are not the same things. What journalism is really about is to monitor power and the centres of power. You have to put questions to power. That's the main test of journalism.

And if we cannot challenge power or change something, at least let us annoy power. This gives a lot of satisfaction I must say – when we annoy power.

(*Lal and Lasantha are watching a video. Lasantha is bubbling up with excitement. Lal is stunned.*)

Lasantha   You see!

Lal   – Does anyone know we have this?

Lasantha   – The President. I asked him if he wanted to comment.

Lal   – Did he shout and scream?

Lasantha   He hung up. No comment.

Lal   I can't see him shaking this one off, 'President linked with plot to murder General' – we need to get it out quick –

Lasantha   How quickly can we verify? We won't get it today, maybe by Thursday if we're really lucky –

Lal   We'll publish the General's letter to start with, showing he was afraid he would be killed –

Lasantha   Yes, and in the meantime, we find this guy (*points to the screen*) to confirm his statement. Can you try to trace him?

Lal   If we're lucky he's in India or the United States. I doubt he'll talk unless he's got asylum . . .

(*Pause*) What?

Lasantha   If they're going for me, it'll be now.

(*Pause*)

I've put all of my important papers in an envelope in the cupboard over there . . . I was thinking of writing something strong – you know, a call to arms . . .

(*Sonali appears as Lasantha is talking.*)

No other profession calls on its practitioners to lay down their lives for their art save the armed forces and, in Sri Lanka, journalism. In the course of the past few years, the independent media have increasingly come under attack. Countless journalists have been harassed, threatened and killed. I have been in the business of journalism a good long time.

Indeed, 2009 is *The Sunday Leader's* 15th year. Many things have changed in Sri Lanka during that time, and it does not need me to tell you that the greater part of that change has been for the worse.

Sonali   Since we married two weeks earlier, um, it was perhaps the most carefree and happy that he had ever been . . . we were going out more and really sort of giving a lot to our relationship . . .

Lasantha   *The Sunday Leader* has been a controversial newspaper because we say it like we see it: whether it be a spade, a thief or a murderer, we call it by that name.

Sonali   We both had ties that bound us to Sri Lanka – the newspaper, the cause. It was not in my husband's psyche to ever say enough is enough and leave. On the contrary, he would say enough is enough and do something about it. It was very difficult for us to think about doing anything other than fighting for the causes we believed in.

Lasantha   The irony is, unknown to most of the public, the President and I have been friends for more than a quarter century. Hardly a month passes when we do not meet, privately or with a few close friends present, late at night at President's house. There we swap yarns, discuss politics and joke about the good old days.

Sonali   We knew he was being followed. There were two men in black helmets, black fatigues whizzed past our car on huge black motorcycles, the kind used by members of the security services. We immediately got inside the um . . . into . . . you know, inside our house and ah, I told him he should not go out, I begged him to stay, but he felt he had to go, it was the busiest day in the office – he had to write his columns and he said – 'Look I will handle this.'

Lal   It was around ten twenty on the morning of 8 January 2009. He was driving to work and uh . . . he was followed by motorcyclists.

Lasantha   Mahinda, when you became President in 2005, nowhere were you welcomed more warmly than in this column. So well-known were your commitments to human rights and liberal values that we ushered you in like a breath of fresh air. Sadly, for all the dreams you had for our country in your younger days, in just three years you have reduced it to rubble.

Sonali   I knew his cause, I couldn't do anything else. No one could tell him differently.

Lasantha   Why then do we do it? I often wonder that. After all, I too am a husband, and the father of three wonderful children. I too have responsibilities and obligations that transcend my profession.

Lal   There was some traffic in front, there was a bus and he had to slow down . . .

Lasantha   Is it worth the risk? Many people tell me it is not. Friends tell me to revert to the bar, and goodness knows it offers a better and safer livelihood.

Lal   There were hundreds of people on the road who witnessed it.

Lasantha   There has never been a serious police inquiry into the attacks against me, and the attackers were never apprehended. In all these cases, I have reason to believe the attacks were inspired by the government. When finally I am killed, it will be the government that kills me.

Lal   Four motorcyclists came close to his car, two came in front and blocked, two came on the sides –

Lasantha   There is a calling that is yet above high office, fame, lucre and security. It is the call of conscience.

Lal   – They shattered the two uh windows. . . . then put a gun against the head and shot.

Lasantha   Our newspaper is there for you, be you Sinhalese, Tamil, Muslim, low-caste, homosexual, dissident or disabled. Do not take that commitment for granted. The free media serve as a mirror in which the public can see itself sans mascara and styling gel. Sometimes the image you see in that mirror is not a pleasant one. But while you may grumble in the privacy of your armchair, the journalists who hold the mirror up to you do so publicly and at great risk to themselves. Whatever sacrifices we journalists make, they are not made for our own glory or enrichment: they are made for you. For you.

(*Pause*)

Whether you deserve our sacrifice is another matter.

Sonali   About 40 minutes later I received a call from the office saying that his car had been seen on the side of the road and that it was damaged and he had been taken to hospital. So I rushed to hospital.

Lasantha   Mahinda, you will never be allowed to forget that my death took place under your watch. As anguished as I know you will be, I also know that you will have no choice but to protect my killers: you will see to it that the guilty one is never convicted. You have no choice. I feel sorry for you.

(*Lal takes a blue plastic bag from its hook and takes it with him as he sits back down on his armchair.*)

Lal   The, the whole of the western province was numb after this happened and uh . . . the funeral itself attracted fifteen thousand people, it was bigger attendance than something seen for a head of state. And every Thursday even to date there is a vigil.

(*Lal lights the first candle in the vigil.*)

People just come, light lamps, stand there for about half an hour.

Sometimes I feel he's just going to walk into the office, there are times that you think like that. And I have to pass the place he was killed every day on my way to work, so it's tough. (*Indicates the blue bag*) I keep this in my office. Every morning it inspires me and the staff here to continue. It contains the trousers which he was wearing, the belt, his shoes and socks.

(*Zoriah is holding a thick pile of papers in his hand. He flicks through them. He dry-retches.*)

(*Lydia takes her car keys out of her bag. A plain-clothes police officer approaches her.*)

Man   Lydia Cacho? You're under arrest.

(*Man presents Lydia with a piece of paper.*)

Lydia   You haven't sent me any kind of subpoena. What is the charge?

Man   Just come with us to the station.

Lydia   No, I would like to – (*Sets off car alarm*) – call my lawyer.

(*Man pulls out a gun and they exit.*)

(*Zoriah is at his computer. Sound of Skype call being made.*)

Zoriah   Are you there?

Zoriah's Girlfriend   Hi honey –

Zoriah   Oh hey – I was about to give up –

Zoriah's Girlfriend   Have you switched your video – oh, I got you. Hey.

Zoriah   Hey. Did you just get out of bed?

Zoriah's Girlfriend   Thanks babe.

(*Zoriah laughs*)

Zoriah's Girlfriend   You're still flying in tomorrow night? You better not be bailing on me again.

Zoriah   No, no . . . just thought I'd say good morning, you know, make the most of being in the same time zone.

Zoriah's Girlfriend   Yeah – but I want your ass over here with me.

Zoriah   I touch down at 6:30 . . .

Zoriah's Girlfriend   Can't wait. Hey, I can't talk for very long . . . Freak face wants me in an hour early.

Zoriah   Oh OK – uh, I've got some news.

(*Pause*)

Zoriah's Girlfriend   You got the papers.

(*Zoriah nods*)

Zoriah's Girlfriend   How soon?

Zoriah   Two weeks.

(*Pause*)

Zoriah's Girlfriend   You said a month minimum.

Zoriah   Yeah.

Zoriah's Girlfriend   Two weeks? And then another three months of this?

Zoriah   You know . . . I mean, you knew . . . Don't be pissed with me, OK?

(*Lydia is in the back of a van. Man is sitting opposite her.*)

Lydia   What are the charges against me?

Man   I should be at a Christmas party right now. My wife's been planning it for months.

(*Lydia moves her hands from behind her head.*)

Man   Hands! (*indicates Lydia should put her hands back*)

Lydia   I'd like to make a phone call. It's my right -

Man   Sure, soon as we come to a store – I ran out of credit. (*His mobile rings*) Yes? No. Yes, boss (*hangs up*).

Lydia   Where are you taking me?

Man   You're going to be with us for a while.

Lydia.   People are looking for me. They know where I am. You are violating my rights and you won't get away with this.

Man   Nothing is going to happen to me.

(*Pause*)

Why'd you mess with Kamel Nacif? You think you're bigger than him?

Lydia   Do you want to know why I wrote the book? Do you have children?

Man   Two girls, what's it to you?

Lydia   OK. Picture a man taking your little daughters and using them for pornography and raping them.

Man   All your fucking talking! The boss wants you to write a statement – admit you lied and that's the end of the story.

(*Later*)

Man   Are you hungry?

(*Pause*)

If you want to eat, you need to do me a favour (*stands up and touches his genitals*). You must really know how to suck cock – a beautiful woman like you.

Nacif showed me a picture of you in your bikini and I thought – well that's a nice little gift. (*Spreads Lydia's legs with his gun*) I looked you up on the internet. I know where you live in Cancún . . . all alone in that apartment, very nice place, right on the beach. Lots of beer in the fridge, and all of your tiny bikinis. The gate in front of the building is so easy to open.

(*Phone rings*)

(*Rolls his eyes*) Mother . . . fucker. (*He puts phone to his ear*) Yes boss? No, Okay . . .

Man   Open up your pretty mouth.

(*Lydia is silent. He holds gun up to her lips. He pushes it in then makes semi-circular movements with the gun and pushes it in further.*)

Careful. It might go off.

(*Lydia closes her eyes*)

Hey – open up!

(*Lydia opens her eyes*)

(*He pushes the gun in and out of her mouth*) You like that don't you slut? A big hard thing between your lips. (*He eventually pulls it out. She's dribbled on the gun*) Ugh. You want more? (*He unzips her jeans and puts the gun inside*).

Lydia   Please don't do that – I really need to go to the bathroom.

Man   This is what you get for making up stories. I'll have my turn, then the driver will come back here and have his.

(*He keeps doing it. Lydia urinates. He pulls his hand away.*)

Ugh! You pig! . . . didn't your mother teach you to piss in the bathroom?

(*Later. It's much darker outside. Man bangs the side of the van.*)

(*calls out*) Stop here.

(*Van stops. Motor cuts out. Sound of waves.*)

Do you like the sea?

Lydia   Wha–?

Man   Do you know how to swim?

The sea looks really pretty at night

(*Lydia stays seated.*)

I'll just wait here. (*Pulls out a packet of cigarettes*)

(*At the army barracks in Iraq.*)

Soldier   So you're the journalist?

Zoriah   Yeah – Zoriah. Hi

(*Zoriah extends his hand and they shake hands.*)

Soldier   We've got you on a mission tomorrow morning.

Zoriah   Oh great. What's happening?

Soldier   (*looks at his clipboard papers*) Uh, it's a local city council meeting. There'll be a bunch of officials there . . . uh . . . local tribal sheikhs and us.

Zoriah   Oh right. Well, it's just that I've been to so many of those kinds of meetings, the photographic opportunities are pretty limited, you know, I just – really don't want to photograph another meeting.

Soldier   These guys are part of the uh (*looks at clipboard*) 'awakening council', they've taken up arms against al Qaeda here and we're backing them.

Zoriah   Yeah . . . but you know – I'm not here to document these kinds of PR exercises for the military.

Soldier   Well, that's what we've got for you.

Zoriah   I just . . . I can't do it.

Soldier   You're already assigned to a vehicle, you're already assigned to that platoon.

Zoriah   Well, I really, I just don't have any interest in it. Is there anything else that's going on in the morning that I can do, other than the meeting?'

Soldier   (*consults the clipboard*) Well, if you're that desperate . . . there's a security patrol that's going to be just down the street from the meeting. You can go with them but you're going to be sitting on the street all morning.

Zoriah   Fine. Thank you.

(*Zoriah is standing on the street. He has two cameras with him and a backpack. One camera is poised – ready to shoot. There is the sound of a blast. Zoriah turns towards the place the sound came from.*)

Fuck.

(*Silence. We hear a radio message.*)

Radio   All units – Suicide bombing at the council meeting. We have one KIA and two WIA . . . stand by.'

(*Zoriah quickly grabs his gear, throwing on body armour, Kevlar helmet, gloves, ballistic goggles, utility belt.*)

Zoriah   We jog down the street as the soldiers aim their weapons at moving cars, screaming for them to stop. People are running past us in panic. As we get closer – a hand on the ground. About five feet away, bone shards and a chunk of scalp with hair on a palm-sized piece of skull. The air smells of burnt flesh.

(*Zoriah is panting after the run down the street and tries to go into the courtyard – he can see beyond the Platoon Leader what the scene behind him is.*)

Platoon Leader   Hey – hey! You are not allowed in there.

Zoriah   Why not?

Platoon Leader   (*distracted by other things going on – to someone offstage*) Hey – watch the journalist. (*Points to Zoriah*) Watch the journalist! (*To Zoriah*) I gotta bring you over here (*starts to move him off*).

(*Zoriah sees the scene behind Platoon Leader and resists being taken off*)

Zoriah   When are you guys gonna let me in?

Platoon Leader   I don't know, I don't know what's going on – you just have to hold tight.

(*Radio message comes through for Platoon Leader who gets distracted by it.*)

Radio   Three KIA now. Repeat – three KIA.

Zoriah   (*getting restless*) I'm sorry, I gotta go in, you – you do what you have to do.

(*Zoriah walks in*)

Twenty civilians, three Marines and several interpreters are basically just lying in pieces in the courtyard of this building.

(*Zoriah starts to take photos.*)

I have to be very careful of where I am walking. I don't know what type of device has been detonated, I don't know if there is going to be a second detonation. Sweat is pouring off of my body. It is about 11 o'clock in the morning so the light is difficult to work with.

One of the marines is vomiting. People are screaming and crying, running as if they have something important they have to do, only they can't figure out what that important thing could possibly be.

I know the soldiers don't want me in the building photographing their dead friends. I also know that, in case of a secondary blast, my time to document the scene will be extremely limited. So I have about five, maybe ten minutes to take pictures.

(*Platoon Leader runs over to Zoriah.*)

Platoon Leader   OK – you need to leave the scene.

(*Zoriah continues to take photos.*)

Zoriah   Look, can you please radio higher command in Baghdad – they will verify that I am allowed to be here.

Platoon Leader   No arguments – it's for your own safety. There could be another blast any moment.

Zoriah   I'll sign something – have you got something for me to sign?

Platoon Leader   We've got word, you're not allowed to be here. We're locking you in a vehicle until further notice. I'm really sorry, man, my hands are tied right now.

Zoriah   There's gotta be some way you can allow me to stay here. I'm a photographer – This is my job. I'm here to document.

Platoon Leader   I mean, I promise when this gets a little more under control, I'll try and call somebody and get you permission to come back out – but I'm juggling a lot right now, so let's go.

Zoriah   I watch from the window of the humvee as soldiers collect body parts from the street and place them in bags and buckets.

Amira   People describe what happened in Gaza in 2008 as a war – but war is the wrong word to use. I went to Gaza after the Israeli army withdrew and I stayed for four months. By being there, of course, you learn a lot. My first impression when I entered Gaza, was that this had been a huge training ground for the soldiers, but with live ammunition. And this is by the way what the organisation Breaking the Silence noticed when they spoke to Israeli soldiers afterwards. Trying out all of the sophisticated, almost science fiction weaponry that Israel has – against what I see as like Native Americans with their arrows. It's not very politically correct, but if I'm asked to make a comparison this is it. That's why I cannot use the term war.

And the rockets of Hamas? I mean, really, it's even tiring to discuss it. So, everybody knows about the Hamas rockets. People have the impression that history started with the rockets. Look, Israeli officials have the talent always to reverse everything. I mean, it's Israeli policies of occupation which are the beginning. And then everything is a

response. Whether it's clever or not is a different question. The thing here
when we concentrate so much about the rockets, really we forget, we
completely forget the daily – not daily, the minute by minute violence,
when borders are closed, when all exits into and out of Gaza are closed,
it's like a black hole. Everybody – this isolation reduces people's lives
to basic concerns. Will there be electricity? Will there be water? Will we
find candles in the shop? Is there gas for cooking? This is violence, this
is daily violence.

(*Takes out a notebook*) Some of my notes from when I was there . . .
I interviewed a lot of people on the ground. Everyone I met had a
tremendous need to tell their story. In minute detail. Again and again.
A young father from Gaza City told me 'Although it was not my usual
custom, I made a point of kissing my children every night. I never
knew which of us would still be alive the next day, and I wanted to say
goodbye properly.' A mother repeatedly tells her children – 'All I hope
is that I die before I see something happen to you.' A young woman:
'When I wake up I am surprised. I know it's only by chance that I am
alive.' (*Consulting her notes*) Taleb, in a tired voice – after 12 days in
which he had lost all contact, the bodies of his sister and her son, riddled
with bullets, were found in their home. Four members of the Haddad
family, parents and two children, got into a car and fled the army that
was approaching their neighbourhood. A shell incinerated the car. Their
neighbours were able to identify the four scorched corpses only by the
license plate of the car. Imad Aqel Mosque in Jabalya refugee camp,
bombed and strafed shortly before midnight. These are the names of the
glorious military victories Israel achieved there – (*holds up a photo of
five girls*) Jawaher, age 4; Dina, age 8; Sahar, age 12; Ikram, age 14; and
Tahrir, age 17, all sisters of the Ba'lousha family, all killed in a 'precise'
strike on the mosque.

(*Same day as the suicide bomb. Zoriah is in his bunk. He's editing his
images. Soldier comes in with a phone and hands it to Zoriah.*)

Soldier   Public Affairs.

Zoriah   (*Takes phone*) Yes.

Voice of Marine   Mr Miller, I'm gonna need you to hand over the
memory cards from the cameras you were using today –

Zoriah   I'm sorry I'm not going to do that –

Voice of Marine   You need to hand over the cards – or delete the
images.

Zoriah   I'm sorry but the contract I signed is very clear that you don't have the right to delete any film, or confiscate any – just check with higher command, they should be able to –

(*Sound of phone hanging up. Zoriah hands back the phone.*)

Zoriah   (*to Soldier*) How's everyone doing?

Soldier   It's just really quiet.

Zoriah   Were you there?

(*Soldier shakes her head no*)

Soldier   I was joking around with Dan right before he left. He kept making comments about my ass.

(*Pause*)

Bet you're glad you talked yourself out of that meeting.

Zoriah   Yeah, that was . . . yeah.

(*Soldier turns to go, then stops*)

Soldier   Can I see them?

(*Pause*)

Zoriah   Sure.

(*Soldier sits next to Zoriah and they look at the photos on his laptop.*)

Zoriah   Can you recognise any one?

(*Soldier shakes her head no*)

(*We see Lydia curled up in the van. Man is clearly tired and frustrated*)

Man   What kind of crazy bitch are you? Two words. I lied. Huh? No?

(*Pause*)

OK. Time for a swim.

(*Man drags Lydia from the van. Lydia struggles to get away. Man pushes her towards the sea. Lydia resists. The sound of the ocean. Lydia shuts her eyes.*)

(*Faint sound of Man's mobile ringing. It gets louder. Lydia opens her eyes. She is completely calm. Man answers phone.*)

Man   Yes, no, yes, yes, fine. (*He hangs up*) Change of plans. You're famous. You're on TV. Lucky you. (*Leans over her*) Keep your mouth shut about this and we'll leave you alone. We got a deal?

Lydia   Yes. Of course.

(*Zoriah presses 'post' on his website. He then sends an email.*)

'Hey mom, sorry it's been a while. Hope you're doing great . . . Paris is great. Can't stop taking photos. The students I have here are much better than those crazy Germans last year. I'll give you a ring in a few days. All is well, x, Z.'

(*Lydia walks out of the shadows looking pale and tired. LADY drapes a jacket around her shoulders and leads her to a microphone which has been set up on a stand.*)

Lydia   (*to Lady*) Thank you.

(*It is evident that there is a small crowd of reporters and general public there to listen to her. Someone takes a photo of her.*)

It's good to be free.

As you know, I was abducted from Cancún two days ago by police who were bought off by one of the richest men in Mexico – Kamel Nacif: N-A-C-I-F. For 20 hours, the worst 20 hours of my life, I was made to believe I would die if I didn't say that all the evidence in my book was made up and the girls were liars.

I thought about the girls and I kept remembering that they all said they would tell their story to me because they didn't want other girls to be raped or abused. I thought that was so brave and so powerful that they were willing, after being exposed to these terrible things, to go through their own pain in order to protect other girls they didn't know. And if they were willing to do that, then I have done a good thing – I have written the names of these guys down, and they will not be able to do this so easily now.

I know I am messing with organised crime. My father asks me why I refuse to accept the idea of living in another country for a while. But I believe in my rights. I have the right to a life free of violence and a life of happiness and I think if somebody has to leave my country – it should be the mobsters – why me? If I gave up and left, I would not only lose all my vital energy, it would be a betrayal to all the people who talked with me and told me their stories.

I want to thank all of my colleagues and friends who worked really hard to save my life and each of the 40,000 people who marched on the streets of Puebla for my freedom. I know that for 100 years there hasn't been a public march like that here. The marchers did not know me before, but they were holding up these huge cards saying 'We are all Lydia Cacho.'

Sixty-four journalists have died in Mexico and not one of these murders has been explained.

(*We hear the distorted sounds of a telephone call between two men. A few lines are distinguishable.*)

'-My precious Governor.

-Yesterday I gave that old bitch a fucking good slap.

-These journalists, they think they can play God . . . with their pen they can cut you to pieces.'

(*A group moves towards Lydia. They place a number of microphones in front of her.*)

Reporter   Lydia, Lydia – how what is your response to-

Lydia   (*ignores the Reporter*) And if one day – I hope not – but if one day, they do get me, I want you to be very, very sure that they did not win. They will never win.

(*A sudden flurry of flash photography. The group descends upon Lydia. One of them fixes her hair, another removes her coat and outer garments to reveal a 'No paedophiles, no corruption, no impunity' singlet top.*)

(*Photos/video of Lydia looking glamorous, talking to the press start to fill the space. The sound of the muffled phone conversation gets louder. We catch a few more pieces of the conversation:*)

'- I am going to drive her mad until the lady begs for mercy.

-When she gets here, she will find out that lies and slander won't be tolerated in my state of Puebla.

-I want to thank you, Governor. I have this amazing cognac which I will send to you.'

Reporter   Twelve secretly taped conversations between Governor of Puebla Mario Marin and Mexican tycoon Kamel Nacif were handed over to newspaper *La Jornada* today.

(Somebody applies lipstick to Lydia's lips and helps her into some high heeled boots. Photos are being taken of her the whole time.)

Reporters   Lydia! Lydia!

(Lydia emerges from the crowd looking composed.)

Lydia   *(chooses a Reporter)* Yes?

Reporter   What is your response, now that you know the Governor and judge of Puebla are implicated in your abduction?

Lydia   All of Mexico can listen to these conversations and hear for themselves how corrupt some of our politicians and officials are. I intend to take my case to a federal court and file a suit against the Governor for bribery, conspiracy to rape and abuse of authority.

Reporters   Lydia! Lydia!

Lydia   *(chooses another Reporter)* Yes?

Reporter   Are you worried about your safety?

Lydia   I mean, these guys are enemies for life. They know I'll keep talking, they know what I know, they know I'm writing another book. As long as I live, I will continue to write and writing will keep me alive.

(Zoriah is asleep. The Soldier comes in and wakes him up.)

Soldier   Hey, Zoriah . . . *(hands him the phone)*

Zoriah   Yes?

Voice of PA Officer   Military Press Officer Keith Alfreds here. I've been asked to call you.

Zoriah   Oh, OK. Is there -

Voice of PA Officer   Mr Miller, I need you to take your blog off-line immediately.

Zoriah   I, uh, can I ask why?

Voice of PA Officer   You've depicted Marines killed in action and that's a breach of your contract -

Zoriah   Well, there are no identifiable features. I made sure of that -

Voice of PA Officer   The Marine corps have a different policy to the army – we don't allow photographs showing any kind of clothing that could be identified as Marine clothing. In several of the photos you could see the Marine's cammo and their boots.

Zoriah   Well, that basically means no photographing the Marines! I didn't sign any agreement like that.

Voice of PA Officer   Mr Miller, that is absolutely in the contract you signed.

Zoriah   Well, if there's a different contract from the Media Hold Harmless Agreement, I was never asked to sign it. I know what I signed, so you are mistaken -

(*Sound of phone hanging up.*)

(*Later. Zoriah's phone rings. Soldier is sitting in Zoriah's room with him.*)

Voice of PA Officer   Mr Miller, I'm asking you for the last time to remove your blog.

Zoriah   I'm sorry but I'm not going to do that.

Voice of PA Officer   Do I understand you're refusing an order?

Zoriah   Correct.

Voice of PA Officer   As of this moment, your embed is terminated.

(*Later. Camp Fallujah. A detention cell. Zoriah's on the phone.*)

Zoriah   (*To Soldier*) You have no right to detain me. I haven't broken any rules. I want to speak to your superior.

Voice of Commander   You're gonna have to sit tight until we can arrange to get you to Baghdad.

Zoriah   I'm being held against my will –

Voice of Commander   General Kelly wants to arrange a meet –

Zoriah   I've done everything within regulation – you have to let me out of here!

Voice of Commander   Sure, I'll get one of the Marines to let you out of the gates into Fallujah and you can make your own fucking way home.

(*Later. Zoriah's on the phone. His laptop is open and his blog page is displayed.*)

Presenter 1   You're with KPFK – 90.7 FM in Los Angeles and 98.7 FM in Santa Barbara County . . .

Presenter 2   And we're back here on Radio Active on this Tuesday, 2 July 2008, already in the month of July, look at that . . .

Presenter 1   I know there's a little bit of a delay and the connection is not a very good one . . . I really thank you for being on the programme – I know it's about 2am in Iraq . . .

Presenter 2   We're speaking with Zoriah Miller, an American photojournalist who has come out from behind the lens and into the spotlight. So, you claim you've been censored by the military?

Zoriah   Yes, I took pictures of something they didn't like and they removed me. Deciding what I can and cannot document, I don't see a clearer definition of censorship.

Voice of High Command's PA Officer   Zoriah, General Petraeus has asked me to call you. Your credentials are in jeopardy.

Zoriah   What a lot of people don't know is that during the entire Iraq war, only five images have been published showing dead US service members.

Presenter 1   Sorry, you cut out for a second there. Did you say five?

Zoriah   That's correct. And two of those are mine. The photographers of the other three were also disembedded.

Soldier   The last time I was home, I couldn't believe what I was seeing on the news. A total whitewash.

Voice of High Command's PA Officer   You've shown complete lack of respect for the Marines who were killed and for their friends and families.

Response to Blog   I'll be sure to send the pictures of you in a body bag with a camera lens sticking out of your forehead to your mother and see how she appreciates it. Posted by: Buddha.

Soldier   It's fucking war. Give them a dose of reality.

Zoriah   I've been consistently prevented from going to places where anything big is going down . . .

Presenter 2   Well, Iraq is a dangerous place Zoriah . . .

Voice of High Command's PA Officer   You posted your photos online before the families of the soldiers were notified –

Zoriah   I'm one of only nine journalists embedded with the military at the moment and there are 150,000 US soldiers on duty. So with such a small number of storytellers covering these important events, how is the public expected to make educated decisions about this war?

Presenter 1   So now you're fighting PR stunt with PR stunt?

Zoriah   Speaking out about this isn't the greatest career move I've ever made. But this may be a situation where I can do more good being the news rather than being the photographer of the news.

Response to Blog   You inserted yourself into the story to cover an agenda you wish to push. Do not claim otherwise. And now you get to reap that whirlwind. Posted by: Bill.

Voice of High Command's PA Officer   I accept that the timing of your post was within regulation, but you have still provided the enemy with an after-action report on the effectiveness of the attack, putting the United States and Iraqi forces at greater risk for harm.

Soldier   If I was an Iraqi, I'd join the insurgency. You know, if this was my country and a bunch of people came in and were occupying it, you know hell yeah, I would be fighting against them.

Zoriah   The really disturbing thing is how incredibly easy it is to remove an embedded journalist . . . It basically gives the Department of Defence free reign over what information comes out of Iraq.

Voice of High Command's PA Officer   The Marine Corps high command is pushing to have you permanently blacklisted from reporting, or even setting foot in an area controlled by the US military.

(*A projection on a screen which says 'Amira Hass – Winner of the Women in Media Lifetime Achievement Award 2009, Waldorf Astoria Hotel, New York City.'*)

Amira   Shalom. Marhaba. Allow me to start with a correction. How impolite, you'd rightly think, but anyway, we Israelis are being forgiven for much worse than impoliteness.

What is so generously termed today as my lifetime achievement needs to be corrected. Because it is failure. A lifetime failure. Come to think of it, the lifetime part is just as questionable. After all, it is about a third of my life, that I have been engaged in journalism. Also if the lifetime part gives you the impression that I'm soon going to retire, then this impression has to be corrected as well. I'm not planning to end soon what I am doing.

But as I said, the real correction lies elsewhere. It's not about achievement that we should be talking here. But failure. The failure to make the Israeli and international public use and accept correct terms and words – which reflect the reality. Not the Orwellian Newspeak that has flourished since 1993, which blurs the perception of real processes that are going on: a special blend of military occupation, colonialism, apartheid, Palestinian limited self-rule in enclaves and a democracy for Jews.

It is not my role as a journalist to make my fellow Israelis and Jews agree that these processes are immoral and dangerously unwise. It is my role, though, to exercise the right for freedom of the press, in order to supply information and to make people know. But, as I have painfully discovered, the right to know does not mean a duty to know.

Thousands of my articles and zillion of words have evaporated. They could not compete with the official language that has been happily adopted by the mass media, and is used in order to dis-portray the reality. Official language that encourages people not to know.

Indeed, a remarkable failure for a journalist.

Elena   It can be very difficult . . . sometimes you feel depressed . . . it's hard basically, you get tired. You get exhausted, like that's enough. Or sometimes you're getting heavy pressure on you. Then, like what happened this morning, some little old lady calls, and says 'I lighted a candle for you in the church today and I will light one tomorrow.' (*Smiles*).

Lydia   Only the other day, as I was pushing my trolley along the supermarket aisle, two older women approached me – one of them threw herself at me for a typically Mexican-style embrace, and told me that her granddaughter wrote an essay at primary school on her chosen heroine. 'Why did she choose me?' I asked, and she answered: 'Because we are all a little bit like you, and you remind us of it, when you refuse to give in, when you won't hold your tongue, and when you smile and tell us that the world is also ours.'

Elena   When I'm writing articles and they threaten me, I'm not scared at all. I'm writing, writing, thinking about nothing only what I'm writing. I'm on a high.

Amira   There's the depressive side – which is an interwoven thread throughout life. A feeling that there's no purpose in life. And there's the militant side, these two things are always interwoven in my life.

Lal   We feel that what we are doing is of a higher calling. . . . It's like a duty. (*Smiles*) But there is also another side to this. Man's greatest high is power over another man. That's a fact. Journalists know that when they take the pen and write, they also have that power.

Zoriah   It's an old war photographer's saying that everybody wants to get an image that will stop a war but ah . . . I don't think anybody's managed to do it yet.

Lydia   There was one time I was on the same plane as Nacif going to London – he goes there a lot because he's a professional gambler and he's been banned from the United States. I couldn't believe it. I saw him at the terminal – a woman recognised him from the media and started pointing and shouting – paedophile, paedophile!

I saw him again when we got off the plane. He looked over at me at the baggage reclaim and I thought wow – there he is. A man who wants me dead.

But . . . I could see . . . there was this look in his eye. When I collected my suitcases, I walked right in front of him, and he kind of . . . stepped back (*demonstrates*) – it was like a reflex. (*Smiles*) Maybe he thought I was following him through London gathering evidence about what he was doing . . . rather than him following me. And that made me relax. I could feel it. He was scared of me.

Introduction to *Seven*

Seven is a ground-breaking work of documentary theatre that captures the remarkable lives of a diverse and courageous group of women leaders around the world. A collaboration by seven award-winning female playwrights, the play is based on personal interviews with seven women in the Vital Voices Global Leadership Network who have triumphed over enormous obstacles to bring about major changes in their home countries of Russia, Pakistan, Nigeria, Northern Ireland, Afghanistan, Guatemala and Cambodia.

As Vital Voices Global Partnership President Alyse Nelson said, '*Seven* is a commanding reminder of the transformative power of women's leadership in our world.' The lives of these women provide a portal through which audiences will be able to experience a diversity of cultures while bearing witness to the varied ways to which seven individual women have overcome seemingly insurmountable hurdles to justice, freedom and equality.

Seven, it is hoped, will travel around the United States and the world to spread the word about the transformational power of women's leadership when they receive training to build their capabilities, connections and credibility in their home countries. Since its founding in 1997, Vital Voices Global Partnership, a non-governmental organization, has empowered and built a powerful network of more than 1,000 experts and international leaders who have trained more than 5,000 emerging women leaders in over 150 countries in Eastern Europe, Asia, Africa, Latin America and the Middle East.

Vital Voices has seen time and again how its investment in women has a huge 'multiplier effect' in remote communities across countries and continents. After participating in Vital Voices' training and mentoring programmes and networking with successful and influential women, thousands of emerging women leaders from around the world are inspired and empowered to fuel the engines of progress in their countries and mentor other women in the process.

The women in whom Vital Voices invest, in turn, 'pay it forward' by returning home to train and mentor more than 100,000 women and girls in their communities, founding their own businesses, serving their countries by participating in government and promoting a civil and just society through non-governmental organizations.

As a result, over the past decade, more and more women are leading positive change in developing countries by taking the reins of government, achieving unprecedented financial success, and safeguarding the human rights of their countries' most vulnerable.

For more information about Vital Voices Global Partnership and how you can get involved, please visit www.vitalvoices.org. More information about the play can be found at www.sevenplay.org.

Seven

**Paula Cizmar, Catherine Filloux, Gail Kriegel, Carol K. Mack,
Ruth Margraff, Anna Deavere Smith, Susan Yankowitz**

Production Notes

Seven is a documentary theatre piece based on verbatim extracts from personal interviews with seven extraordinary women who are working to effect change in the world.

Hafsat Abiola, Nigeria interviewed by Anna Deavere Smith.

Faridi Azizi, Afghanistan interviewed by Ruth Margraff.

Anabella De Leon, Guatemala interviewed by Gail Kriegel.

Inez McCormick, Northern Ireland interviewed by Carol K. Mack.

Mukhtar Mai, Pakistan interviewed by Susan Yankowitz.

Mu Sochua, Cambodia interviewed by Catherine Filloux.

Marina Pisklakova-Parker, Russia interviewed by Paula Cizmar.

Seven was created to be performed in any number of ways, including on a bare stage with no set. All parenthetical descriptions of settings or physical locations in the script are included to evoke a sense of place, mood and atmosphere. Much of the text is direct address, and movement is optional and up to the director and production. The other media – projections, sound effects, music – are indicated in the script as options that might enhance the work. In addition to songs and music from cultures around the globe within this theatre piece, a sampling of the original language of the seven women would also enhance their tales.

Seven was first presented on Martin Luther King Day, January 21, 2008 at the 92nd Street Y, in New York City as part of the Unterberg Poetry Centre's Reading Series Event. It was directed by Evan Yionoulis; the lighting design was by Burke Brown; the sound design was Sharath Patel; the production supervisor was Linda Marvel; and the stage manager was Melissa Spengler. The cast was as follows:

Hafsat Abiola	Danai Gurita
Farida Azizi	Heather Raffo
Anabella De Leon	Mercedes Herrero
Inez McCormack	Joan MacIntosh
Mukhtar Mai	Mahita Kakkar
Mu Sochua	Christine Toy Johnson
Marina Pisklakova-Parker	Linda Edmond

Seven was subsequently presented at Sidney Harman Hall at the Harman Centre for the Arts in Washington DC, on November 12, 2008. It was directed by Evan Yionoulis; the lighting design was by Burke Brown; the sound design by Sharath Patel; the production supervisor was Linda Marvel; and the stage manager was Melissa Spengler. The cast was as follows:

Hafsat Abiola	Rachael Holmes
Farida Azizi	Heather Raffo
Anabella De Leon	Mercedes Herrero
Inez McCormack	Terry Donnelly
Mukhtar Mai	Mahita Kakkar
Mu Sochua	Mia Katigbak
Marina Pisklakova-Parker	Betsy Aidem

Characters

Hafsat Abiola:
Nigerian. Tall, thin, dark-skinned, speaks quickly, softly, few pauses, light-hearted, very attractive, highly educated, 30's.

Farida Azizi:
Afghan. Beautiful, private, and highly intelligent, rarely revealing her emotional scars, 40's.

Anabella De Leon:
Guatemalan. Glamorous and theatrical, with inborn confidence, uncompromising conviction, 50's.

Inez McCormack:
From Belfast. Highly educated, speaks eloquently, passionately, with feeling and ready humour, 60's.

Mukhtar Mai:
Pakistani. Illiterate peasant woman, modest and delicate, becomes increasingly articulate and fierce, about 30.

Mu Sochua:
Cambodian. Graceful, intense, with both humour and sadness visible, youthful 50's.

Marina Pisklakova-Parker:
Russian. Empathetic, intelligent, with a sense of destiny, operates softly, using her wits and logic, 40's.

Note: The actors occasionally form an ensemble and become voices or characters in one another's stories (e.g. Caller, Mrs Posada, Mony, etc.). Their 'roles' are to be assigned by the director. The actors most often speak directly to the audience but at times also engage with another 'character' in the stories they recount.

Each actor steps forward and introduces herself.

Hafsat   Hafsat Abiola, Nigeria

Sochua   Mu Sochua, Cambodia.

Anabella   Anabella de Leon, Guatemala.

Inez   Inez McCormack, Northern Ireland.

Farida   Farida Azizi, Afghanistan.

Marina   Marina Pisklakova-Parker, Russia.

Mukhtar   Mukhtar Mai, Pakistan.

(*Lights blink. Inez steps forward.*)

Inez   So now we're sitting 'round together in North Belfast in a small dark room in a community hall, sewage coming up the sinks and all these women, they've survived the worst, y'know, and we're reading the Declaration of Human Rights out loud 'til we get to the word 'inalienable' and it's hard to pronounce, so they start laughing and think I said 'alien' and maybe I'm talking about outer space, and I say, it's hard to *spell* too!' 'But what does it mean anyhow?' one woman asks me. That word inalienable, it means all these rights we're reading, they're part of every human being! 'What do we have to do to get these rights?' They're yours, I tell them! She looks at me amused. 'Well that's the best fuckin' kept secret in the whole world's all I can say!' (*Lights blink. Telephone rings. Lights then come up on Anabella in her office. A line of people wait to see her.*)

Anabella   On the days I give audience, Monday and Friday, my God, you can't enter my office. A line, groups of twenty, forty people are waiting for me. They come from all over the republic. (*To Mrs. Posada*) Go on tell me your problem.

Mrs. Posada   (*Handing her the prescription*) Necesito la medicina para mi madre que es may vieja.

Anabella   (*To her assistant*) Mary please get me Director of General Hospital because Mrs. Posada needs medicine for her mother and they didn't give her any. (*Mary gives her the phone*) I have a phone without wire. (*On the phone*) El director del hospital? Anabella de Leon. How are you? Fine? Okay – Everybody answers my call because they know I am not playing! Here is Mrs. Posada. You didn't give her medicine for her mother. She is presenting to me the prescription this moment. I

need you to solve this problem. Okay? You say you are going to send
me the medicine? No, she is going to go there now and you will give her
medicine. Okay? Okay, thank you very much because if you don't give
her medicine I am going to call you to the plenary, Okay? Bye bye. (*To
Mrs. Posada*) Your problem is solved. Please call me when you have
your medicine. Okay, the next. Please what can I do for you . . . ? (*Sound
of wind. Fareda walks downstage wearing a burqa.*)

Fareda   In the night wind when I think of home, I think of mountain
shadow, as I hide in the borders of Afghanistan to walk so many times at
night. It is the faces of the women that will always move me, guide my
footsteps through the landmines . . . I see a woman giving birth all by
herself because, under Taliban, male doctors are forbidden to treat women
and women cannot be trained as doctors. (*Re-experiencing*) I see her
face as she dies in front of my eyes. And I cannot stay calm. What can I
do? The only way to bring basic health care to these women is to walk.
Sometimes at night to regions so remote, so I smuggle myself and my two
small sons under my burqa to try to bring healthcare. The burqa can be a
good thing to disguise myself. When I feel the mujahedeen watching me
across the mountains, I find they are not all against women. Sometimes
they tell us where the landmines are or not to go a certain way, there might
be thieves! (*As Fareda crosses stage, a telephone rings. Marina picks up.*)

Marina   Crisis centre for Women. How may I help you?

Caller   I heard you on the radio.

Marina   You did.

Caller   I heard you on the radio. You were telling my story.

Marina   Yes?

Caller   My husband – my husband is beating me – he has beaten me for
twenty six years.

Marina   Where are you?

Caller   I am in bed. With a broken back. From his beating me.

Marina   Tell me your address.

Caller   I heard your voice. You sounded like someone I could trust.

Marina   Tell me how to get to you. So I can send help.

Caller   Girl, my husband is very powerful. He's in one of the
government agencies.

Marina   I will come and bring the police.

Caller   You know girl. You don't understand. If you call someone, he will find out –

Marina   Tell me –

Caller   Before you can get to me, I will be dead.

Marina   (*To audience*) She calls for about a month. Then she stops calling. She is one of the ones I could not save. (*Sochua appears in a pool of light. She has a string in her hand, winds it around her wrist thoughtfully.*)

Sochua   *Khmuc* are malicious spirits and the *pralung* is the soul. All those years I did not know that in our culture, in Cambodia, we are supposed to have nineteen souls. Every part of our body has a soul: hair, feet. I ask victims of trafficking, when did you lose the soul? They say their souls left when the trafficker took them away from their families. That their souls are still in the rice field. When you are raped you lose your *pralung* – someone takes it away. I've been working with trafficked women since I became Minister of Women's Affairs in 1998. Until that time only men held the position. The first thing I did was challenge an old Cambodian proverb 'A man is gold, a woman is white piece of cloth.' Think of it. If you drop a piece of gold in the mud, you can clean it, and it will be shinier than before. But if a piece of cloth is stained, it is ruined. If you've lost your virginity you cannot be a piece of white cloth. Each year more than thirty thousand Cambodian children are forced into prostitution. Girls as young as eleven are tricked – promised jobs, to help their poor families – then taken away to become sex workers. I'm working now with one of them, a girl called Mony. (*Hafsat talking into a microphone to an unseen interviewer.*)

Hafsat   How did I come to speak out? Well I was living in the US and you know how American society is – I mean, very nice people but often they don't know a lot about any other place, even other parts of America, or Canada! Their nearest neighbour! So what is the chance that they're going to know about Nigeria and care? It was 1995 and I was at Harvard in my second year. I just finished class when I see students petitioning and I know it will be something really ridiculous like the right of students to walk barefoot on campus on Sundays, and I am trying to avoid them, but they are very persistent and stop me and only because I am black. Then they say to me 'We have a petition. The elected president of Nigeria is in jail, and we are getting signatures.' And I say to them 'Don't you know you're getting signatures for my father?' And of course they don't know but they get excited and say, could I speak to their group on campus about the situation in Nigeria. I thought I'd be speaking to a vacuum, that nobody would hear, but they cared and they listened and that is how I began to find my voice. (*Inez steps forward*)

Inez   My father took me away from school at sixteen and put me to work as a clerk in his one-man printing business. It was very constricting. I wanted to go to university and I knew my family wouldn't let me. So I left home. I got a bedsit and applied for a lowly civil servant position. At the interview I am asked:

Questioner 1   What do you think of homosexuals?

Inez   What – ?

Questioner 2   What would you do if your brother married a black woman?

Inez   Offensive questions, that are not the real question, which is 'What do you think about Catholics?' I am from a Unionist Protestant background. I wouldn't have known a Catholic until I was eighteen – I remember a conversation in the office about a Catholic who'd gone for promotion and how you have that because Catholics couldn't be trusted. And that's when I realise the conversation could only take place because there aren't any Catholics in the office! . . . Northern Ireland was a profoundly unjust place to live. It still is. It's a very cold house for the poor. In the North if you challenge injustice and you're not on the side of the status quo, you have to be on the other side! A very rigid power system. I remember a relative of mine saying:

Relative   Inez, you've no right to upset us like this!

Inez   (*to relative*) And you've no right to live in a way that upsets others! (*Anabella takes out a piece of paper, unfolds it and holds it up.*)

Anabella   Here is a chart I made up: 1954 I was born, you see here. I call it 'darkness'. That is followed by 'sorrow', my childhood, then 'basic knowledge' when I learn everything. And here, I call it 'enthusiasm' and here 'courage' and 'no playing' that is my school days. I won excellent grades which help me to win a scholarship to study law. 'Discrimination' is that period of my going to law school. My scholarship was to private university. When I got there, my classmates discriminate against me because they have money and I am poor people. They say to me 'You must go to public university. You are not our circle.' I tell them: 'Just because you say to me that I must not go here? No! Forget it! Bye, bye!' I don't know what it is to be silent. I must all the time defend my rights. 'You do not have the same as I have between my ears,' I tell them. 'If you discriminate against me for being poor or being woman, I am going to discriminate against you for being stupid!'

(*Sochua hold string in hand and picks up a ladle.*)

Sochua   We go through the Calling of the Souls ceremony now for Mony. She has just been rescued from a brothel. (*Sochua brings Mony forward, Everyone else forms the Community.*) I hold a ladle to call her souls into a small fishing basket. You have to call nineteen times . . .

Community Members   (*chanting*) Oh precious *pralung*, what you see today to be the river bank is actually total darkness. You must beware of all the trees which harbour evil spirits in disguise.

Sochua   We wrap her wrist with nineteen cotton strings for each of her souls . . .

Community Members   (*continuing to chant*) I am tying strings around your wrist, and around mine, to unite you with your relatives, old and young, grandmothers and grandfathers. May each string bring back your soul and may your mind and body be whole.

Sochua   The entire time, she says almost nothing. She is only a kid – a beautiful child, that smile and everything. But she is lost. You can see it. Just by looking at her you know that she is soulless. It is a form of emptiness, depression. When you ask about that moment, that painful moment when she was penetrated, forced – she just keeps saying:

Mony   (*deadened*) I lost my soul. He took away my soul.

Ensemble   I am finishing my call, oh nineteen souls, come back all together now . . . (*Lights shift to Hafsat with her microphone.*)

Hafsat   Oh yes I think it matters, the nature of your soul. I think of my soul as light-filled. Not that I'm some kind of psychic person, but I believe there's much more light than darkness. It matters to me that I shouldn't be vindictive or harbour ill will for other people. When you experience brutal events you can start feeling very hostile and bitter, and there's a lot of dark energy I don't want.

(*Lights shift to Marina and two women.*)

Marina   At my son's school – Peter was seven years old, first grade – we mothers let the kids go in and then we would stand around and talk about school, other things. I was assigned to the Institute of Socioeconomic Studies of the Population at the time, and one morning,

I am talking to two other women – one is homemaker, the other is a computer programmer. I say, you know (*to the women*) I am doing a survey at the institute and we have these letters coming in, women talking about domestic violence.

First woman   Domestic violence?

Second woman   What do you mean?

Marina   (*Aside to the audience*) When I was growing up in the Soviet Union, no one talked of such things. We did not even have words for it. So I explain that it is . . . (*turning to women*) when husbands are controlling, jealous, when they put you down and won't let you speak to other women or your family, isolating you. And the emotional abuse, the psychological pressure slowly comes to physical abuse. And sometimes not so slowly. (*To audience*) After I explain to them, both of them – both of them – say their husbands are abusing them. One for six years. One for ten – I feel something sinking inside me. Later the one who is a homemaker calls me crying.

First woman   My husband was putting on his suit. And a button came off. And he picked up his shoe and slammed me in the face. In front of the children.

Marina   (*Aside to the audience*) Her face is bruised, swollen, for a week. (*To the woman*) Why don't you just leave him?

First woman   (*A long beat, lost*) You know, where would I go?

Marina   (*To audience*) So I start calling social services. I call different agencies and I ask: Who can help a woman in a situation like this? And everywhere the answer is 'No one. It's a private matter.' Well I am not ready to accept that. So I get an office and a phone and set up the domestic violence hotline – actually I call it a 'trust line'. Because all the women could do is trust.

Anabella   Ah, it is so hard. I am all the time declaiming, denouncing, but they don't investigate anything! Impunity is the queen of Guatemala. When the law has no consequences, then everyone thinks 'I can do what I want. I can steal, I can murder, I can beat up my wife.' The domestic violence is going to be a crime very soon because we are pushing to create this law. But we need the judges to comply because we need to stop (*Slaps hands*) the violence against women. This year, twenty-five hundred women have been murdered. They were born, they were good, and now they are dead.

Marina   In Russia, fourteen thousand women every year are killed by their husbands. One woman every hour. (*The telephone rings*) For a long time it is just me alone. On the phone. Counselling people. Trying to help them find legal aid. And I can't do what a normal hotline can do. I am the only person doing this in all of Russia. (*She picks up phone. Lights on Farida, alone, walking in the mountain, carrying a pack.*)

Farida   If there is no clinic, no hospital, no transportation, there is nothing. So we need to train the women on vaccination, sanitation, nutrition . . . (*Kneels down, opens her pack, putting together the kit.*) We make a basic midwife tool kit with nailcutters, soap to clean hands, gloves, a plastic sheet for giving birth, the scissors to cut the umbilical cord, things for measuring the fever. Even we coordinate with Taliban. I always tell openly what is this project, how it benefits the women, what is the budget, impact. And the Taliban say, 'Well, okay, we will let you have your project if you will teach the women the Quranic verses, about the prayers. And we want to see your material, to be sure there is nothing against Islam. We don't want Western ideas to be enforced.' So we say, this is fine. So they accept us. We place materials inside the midwife tool kits, how to pray, how to clean the houses, how they respect their elders, how to make their husbands happy, how they can prepare the food, the women have to know these things. (*Sochua wraps up the string to put it away.*)

Sochua   The Calling of the Souls ceremony, I do it, because you know, it's part of my culture. But do I really believe in it? I don't think so. I love my culture, my tradition, but it tells you that if you've lost your soul, you deserve it. If you have been tortured, raped or battered, it's your karma. So if you believe in this you, you may as well say, that's it, that's the end of my life. The most painful part for me is when the children say 'Give me the soul back.' I translate that into a fight for justice. I say 'Help Mony with the case against her trafficker. That will be justice!' And she does win. The trafficker and the brothel owner are found guilty and go to jail – but the man who first raped her has never been found. So in that sense, Mony's soul can never return to her. These victims will be whole again only when they feel free from being raped again, sold again, that the man won't come back and harm them – but if the man lives next door? We gave Mony everything. She came and lived with us . . . but she couldn't. She ran away, cut herself off from her family . . . now she's somewhere in some other brothel. (*Hafsat speaks into the microphone.*)

Hafsat   In my society the name they give you at birth show you how much they value you. So my name, 'Hafsat' means 'the treasured one'.

My dad, he called all his daughters 'supergirls'. But I had big self-esteem issues! My mum was a legendary beauty. She was one of four wives and there were nineteen children! And you know, there are many elements of growing up in a polygamous family that are wonderful because you have readymade friends, but it is inevitable that you get compared. Everyone knows how brilliant my father was, I mean very genius. And there's my sister Aiyo, who was kind of walking in his footsteps, and then there's me. Average. I think once I came out of Nigeria I realised its okay to be different. I used the time away to build my own sense of who Hafsat is. (*Spotlight on Mukhtar, sitting in her house, embroidering.*)

Mukhtar   My great aunt had the honour of naming all the children in my family. She called me Mukhtar, which means 'powerful' or 'self-respecting' and that always was strange for me because I am very thin, and in my culture, a thin person is considered weak. My village is Meerwala in the southern part of Pakistan, one of the poorest areas of the Punjab. We are from the Gujars, a peasant tribe of low caste. Like other girls, I played with dolls and climbed trees, but all daughters must learn special jobs so they will be useful in the family. I was taught to do embroidery. People brought fabric to me and I would design and sew their shirts and trousers. I also grew flowers and plants and this something I still love to do. Last year, I planted a jasmine and started some fruit trees, too, but the goats came. They ate up the mango and lemon trees, and so I replanted them – but the goats came again. And again. They did not know that I am just as stubborn as they are! Whenever they do, I am going to keep on with the plantings, and one day I think the goats will just give up and my trees will have the victory. My village had no school, and no one in the family could read or write. I learned the things my mother had learned and her mother before her: how to do housework, fetch water from the pump, make *chapattis*, hang the clothing to dry on palm trees. I did not have any idea that in other places girls were being educated. I did not know that I had been taught nothing about the world . . . No I was taught something – all girls were; I was taught silence, I was taught fear. I was taught that some people are high up and some are inferior. I learned to hide my face and bow my head, to submit, to agree, to obey my parents, and stay away from boys. That is all what I knew. But time caught me, it gave me a lesson –

Sochua   The war in Vietnam – we never thought it would come to Cambodia. We were listening to the Beatles . . . And then it came. My mother and father put me on a plane to France. I left the family. I was eighteen, and I was so, so desperate. Like 'This river is bending but which rock do I hang on to?' There was no rock, and it was going very fast. I never went back. From an innocent teenager to a refugee. Hopeless and an orphan.

Farida   If you start from 1980 in Afghanistan where I was born – I was there until the age of nine. We had everything. But because my father was a doctor, we were in danger. He tried to help too many women and children crowding into our house under Russian rocket fire until one day there came a hole into our living room. We had to flee Kabul and flee the Russians. And then to flee the Taliban in 1993. We panicked by the thousands that time, pushing to escape, no transportation, all the roads were either closed or blown up. We saw some people drenched with blood, not from their own wounds but from walking over the bodies of the dead. We could only crouch down in the sewers until there was a ceasefire. How could I know my family would live in a Pakistani refugee camp for fifteen years – the best years of my youth?

Marina   My husband and I are on our first vacation in years, in Finland. We go mountain skiing. And he feels tired. He says, I'll go and take a nap. And suddenly I realise his nap is getting too long. When I find him he is still alive; but in the emergency room they are not able to save him. Heart attack. He is thirty-seven. I am thirty-three. He was the only one at the time who was understanding and supporting my mission. I am alone. I wonder: Do I have the strength to do this work?

Anabella   My mother, my brother, and me lived together in a small dark room. From a little window I could look out and see *mi madre* cooking. I still remember when I was very young, watching her stooped over a pot cooking a meal for us; each night we eat black beans; frijoles with tortillas. I saw a woman go over to our little outdoor kitchen and throw dirt in the pot my mother was stirring. Our family's food for the day was damaged – our only meal – and my mother began to sob. I was young, but I knew I wanted to get out of that world; a world where the women being so angry and hopeless they throw dirt in your food; or like my mother, all the time in the silence, praying and crying. It is the beginning of my life that is responsible for my way of being. (*A distant drum beating like thunder. Louder. Then stops.*)

Inez   The city of Derry is on this hill, surrounded by walls, with cannons overlooking the Town Square. And at the bottom of the hill was the collection of streets known as the Bogside. Long ago, it would've been for very poor people, Catholics coming in from rural areas, the poorest of the poor. Families lived in one room, the damp coming down the walls . . . I remember being told, looking down at the Bogside from the hill of Magee:

Neighbour   (*Whispers*) You don't go down *there*.

Inez   And now I am married to a Catholic from 'down there'! It was the summer of 1968 when I met him. I went to London. I walk into this bar and there is this guy with a Derry accent selling drinks. I buy a drink. And I'm still married to him! He was much more politically aware. Listening to him talk about the North? I began to glimpse this other, darker world. We hitched to Portugal. On TV at the youth hostel we saw the first huge civil rights demonstration in Derry. I saw my husband's face go white. People were beaten off the streets. We hitched straight back home. I was in the same physical landscape, but I'd crossed over into another country!

(*Under following section: Urdu prayers*)

Mukhtar   Some men of the Mastoi tribe come to our house and say that my twelve year old brother, Shakur, has committed a *asina* with a girl from their clan and will go to jail. This crime they put on Shakur means rape or sex before marriage and is punishable by death. My family is sure that the accusation is false, and later we out we are right; my little brother is the one who has been raped! – and by the same men who are laying blame on him. But what can we do? The Mastoi are a higher caste than we are, they are landowners, so whatever they say is law. The men of the jirga, our village council, meet to discuss the situation and decide that I, Mukhtar, must ask forgiveness for my brother. If this will free him, I am happy to do it. (*Starts to walk*) It is twilight when begin walking toward the farm of the Mastois, holding my prayer book to my breast. My father and uncle go with me. We enter their compound with its high walls. The clan-chief, Faiz Mohammed, and four other men are standing there with rifles, and behind them are many more men of their tribe. I lay down my shawl as a sign of submission. (*Spreads her shawl on the ground and kneels.*)

Praise be to Allah, Lord of the Universe.

The Compassionate King of the Day of Reckoning,

These only do we worship and of these only do we ask help.

Guide us unto the right path . . . Amen.

Then I look at Faiz and say: If my brother has offended you, I beg pardon for his action and beseech you set him free. Faiz glares at me with wild eyes and now I understand! He will not forgive our family, he wants only to humiliate someone – and as always it will be a woman. But never did I imagine what happened next. (*Begin Yoruba prayers for the dead.*)

Hafsat (*Into microphone as if answering a question*) . . . Well, I'd gotten a message early that morning that something had happened in Nigeria, and I thought it had to do with my dad. My older brother was in DC so we all congregated at his home, waiting for word. (*Phone rings; she picks up, puts down microphone.*) Then I got a call from my sister Aiyo.

Aiyo's voice Have you heard anything?

Hafsat No.

Aiyo's voice Your mother was in an accident.

Hafsat (*To audience*) That was my mother, her stepmother. I wasn't worried because I knew my mum was very strong. I was waiting for word about the extent of injuries, what they wanted us to do. And Aiyo called me again later –

Aiyo's voice Have you heard anything?

Hafsat No.

Aiyo's voice Hafsat, your mum is dead. (*Hafsat puts down the phone and sits, shaken. Urdu and Yoruba prayers mix.*)

Mukhtar Four men pull me by my hair and arms and drag me into a windowless room. I am thrown onto a dirt floor . . . a stable. The only animals there . . . the only brutes . . . are those men. I scream for them to release me, but one man shows me his gun and the others hold me down. For more than an hour, I was raped by those four men of the Mastoi tribe. Men with shotguns forced my father and uncle to wait outside. I can still see them standing near the door, helplessly, while the men took turns, one after the other. Day and night, I tell you, night and day, every girl walks in terror of what happened to me. By the time we are eight, we know that a man can grab us whenever he pleases, take us to some dark place and push us down . . . break our bodies . . . destroy our childhoods and our futures. Inside our homes, we feel safe – but when we go out, the fear takes hold of us, day and night, night and day. It is like a vulture flying just above our heads while we walk or work or play. And when it happens, it is beyond any nightmare.

Hafsat My mother wasn't in an accident, she'd just been assassinated. She was driving to a meeting with the Canadian ambassador because of the work enrolling our allies for the democratic movement. This was in 1996, my father was still in jail, and my mum had become the voice of the movement. She was driving in the streets when the car that had been tailing her – was with soldiers – they overtook, shot her driver, and then shot her. In the head. Point, ah yeah. But I don't know that she knew what was happening because it happened so quickly. You know, she probably would have been thinking that the noise was a flat tire or something, and then they killed her. (*Mukhtar wraps herself in her shawl; a gauntlet forms and walks down the aisle of the villagers.*)

Mukhtar   When they are finished with me, I am thrown outside. My clothes are torn and I am nearly naked. I lie on the ground, alone with my shame. My uncle and father help me to my feet and walk home with me, past hundreds of townspeople. No one says a word to me as I go by; they all lower their eyes or stare at me with disgust. Now I am unclean and dishonoured – in the eyes of the tribal elders, my family and the villagers. In that one hour on the stable floor, my life has been destroyed . . . (*Prayers segue into drums. The villagers transform into marchers.*)

Inez   On the final day of the ninety mile Burntoller March, just outside Derry on a narrow road. There is an ambush . . . – a hundred men come down the hills on the right hand holding clubs with nails in them, others come up from the river side on the left, and the police block us front and back to allow them to come at us! People start running, screaming . . . (*Re-experiencing*) Now I'm in the front, but I mean all you could do was keep walking, y'know? And then, just as we come into Derry on a small narrow street . . . stones are lobbed down on us and the police block the street so we have nowhere to run! I try to get into the doorway of a shop and of course it's locked, and I'm screaming as blood runs down my face . . . but the shop assistants are just standing inside . . . and they are laughing! And they're people from my background, you know? I mean, you'd have to dehumanise any group of people to demean them that way! . . . Now I experience, from the inside, this, this paralysing sense of powerlessness that comes from humiliation! I'm hit by a couple of men wielding heavy branches like clubs – when I go home my neck and shoulders are badly bruised. My family were distressed, but then comes the classic remark:

Relative   If you hadn't been there it wouldn't have happened!

Inez   I was suddenly an outsider in my family. I crossed a line. That much changed the shape of the rest of my life! (*The marchers change mood – marching now in line, as refugees in the Khmer Rouge camp.*)

Sochua After nine years of exile I took the first chance to return to Asia in 1981 with the International Rescue Committee to work in the Thai-Cambodian camps. With my team I travel into the jungles to bring supplies of food and clothing. We reach a refugee camp on the top of a mountain, still run by the Khmer Rouge. The refugees are told to come outside the camp to collect the supplies we brought them. They are not allowed to speak. They march out in line, dressed in the black pyjamas the Khmer Rouge insist they wear . . . Just seeing the Khmer Rouge soldiers in their uniforms brings back the war . . . my parents . . . friends . . . all gone . . . I never said goodbye. It is hard for me to keep quiet – I want to free these refugees! I now have a raging struggle to continue working in Cambodia, helping its people recover! I know from this moment on my life is going to change! (*The marching refugees freeze in place.*)

Mukhtar (*In her room, embroidering*) For the next few days, I lock myself in my room. My mother brings me food but no one speaks to me about what happened, and I speak to no one. In my country, women do not talk about such degrading things with others. I know about three other rapes that had taken place before mine. One woman complained to the police, but they dismissed her case. Another stayed home and never mentioned it again. And the third woman killed herself. She swallowed a bottle of pesticide and died right then. (*Increasingly agitated*) Is that what I should do, I ask myself? In Pakistan, staying alive is seen as more cowardly and shameful than the rape itself. But in my heart I do not believe that anyone in my family really wants me to die – especially my mother, I can see it in her eyes, I can feel in her touch that my pain is hers, that she suffers with me and wants me to go on living. But if I don't commit suicide, what will I do with my life?

Farida All the time in the refugee camp, I dream to go to school to learn to be a doctor, like my father. But we couldn't go outside the tent or they might kidnap us or sell us to the warlords. We saw the windows of the school shot out and shut down. Finally I am so happy when I hold my first book in a refugee school, it is coming to me from the University of Nebraska . . . (*The freeze breaks. The actors transform into children and a teacher in the classroom.*)

Students (*Individually reciting*)

Five bullets times five bombs is equal to twenty-five weapons.

The orange colour is the rocket and the blue colour is the Stinger.

The green is the Kalashnikovs.

Teacher   Answer these questions in your notebook. If one mujahideen kills four Russians, how many mujahideen wake up, pray and go fight and kill the Russians? What do you think of the Russians? Draw an airplane bombing on your house.

Student   (*Holding up a painting which might also be shown on screen.*) Here you see the house is burning. The man is hurt and the children are fearful from the fire.

Farida   Many million dollars spent to bring the message of violence into refugee schools. There is not a lesson of what is a mother, what is a brother. My first school is the propaganda to become a warrior.

Sochua   We got over six hundred million from the West to repair the country, but no matter how much you bring, you cannot restore the soul. The war is never over. It's like you put acid on a person. The scars will always be there. You can build roads, you can de-mine rice fields, but you cannot reconstruct the face. How can you put back together a family that has been destroyed?

Farida   We need to start from scratch – the younger generation – and I say education yes. You can build a building very easy, but it is better first to build the minds and then the building, so that building should be safe in the minds. (*Marina holds a large book with the title Domostroi in Russian. On the screen, the words 'Household Rules' appear.*)

Marina   When I started my work and would speak to the police, they would say 'Oh come on, women don't feel loved if they're not beaten.' I was astonished! 'He beats you, therefore he loves you.' It's a Russian saying that comes from the sixteenth century – from *domostroi* household rules – written rules stating how a household should be run. (*Each of the rules appears in turn on the large screen in Russian.*)

Ensemble (*Each line in a different voice*)

The man is master of the house.

Everybody else is his servant.

A man should punish his wife to make her more obedient.

Don't beat her on the face, because you won't be able to show her in public.

Don't beat her on the stomach if she's pregnant.

It's better to use the whip rather than the stick because it will be more painful so she will learn her lesson better.

After beating her, show how much you love her so she will understand the lesson deeper and appreciate you more.

Marina   He beats you therefore he loves you. Since the sixteenth century it has been an excuse.

Anabella   My father left our little rooms when I was only three, but I always love him with all my heart. He was very emotional like me, a handsome man, brave and strong looking. But there was always trouble in his life, drinking and women. When I was twelve years, my father came to our house. 'I have a new woman', he tells my mother. 'I am going to introduce you to her. But don't say that you are my wife, only that you are the mother of my two children.' When he brings the woman to our home, *mi madre* says: 'I am only the mother of his children; we don't have any relations.' I was very angry. 'You are both going to be punished for this because you are not saying the truth!' And to my loving mother, 'You don't have dignity as a woman!'

Mukhtar   One idea keeps pushing away the others. Maybe I can help the women of my country. Yes, yes, that should be possible . . . So this is how I am thinking when I learn my rape is not just an evil plot of the Mastois but was ordered – ordered – by my tribal elders, the very men who are supposed to deliver justice and protect all women as if we were their daughters. Before my rape, girls were kidnapped off the streets, or a man would force sex on a woman – but this time, the entire council had decided I would be gang-raped. They called it an 'honour revenge'! Nowhere does the Quran say that Islam supports violence against women. This is why the Imam tells the congregation in his Friday sermon:

Imam   The village council has sinned greatly in ordering this violation of Islamic law. The criminals responsible for the rape must be brought to justice. Mukhtar Mai and her family should go to the police and file charges immediately.

Mukhtar   I had never heard of the Constitution or realised I was a citizen of Pakistan, and that citizens, even if they are women, have legal rights. In my whole life I had never talked to a lawyer or a judge or a policeman. But this Mukhtar was not the same woman who had kneeled down to the Mastoi. (*Puts down embroidery*) Now, whatever happens to me, I am going to speak out. (*Telephone rings. Hafsat answers.*)

Hafsat   (*On the phone*) Which newspaper did you say?

Journalist   The New York Times. What is your reaction?

Hafsat   Excuse me. To what?

Journalist   You don't know?

Hafsat   No. What is it?

Journalist   Your father is dead.

Hafsat   You are mistaken. (*Puts the phone down, heartbroken.*) But he wasn't mistaken. My father was dead. He had been in solitary confinement for four years since the election. He was supposed to be released within days. He died in a meeting with US State Department and Nigerian Government Officials – probably poisoned. His presidential campaign had been called 'Hope '93. Farewell to Poverty.' Our country was then one of the poorest in the world because of the corruption of leaders. For the first time in Nigeria's history, people had voted for the man. For the promise. But the military government didn't want to leave. They offered money, access to oil fields, but they couldn't find the price that my father would accept. He wouldn't betray his democratic mandate from the Nigerian people. They took his life. The same as with my mom.

Mukhtar   Eight days after the rape, I travel to the police office in Jatoi, many miles away, with my father and brothers. (*Entering the police station.*) The policeman is sitting at this desk when I enter. He does not even lift his head to look at me.

Policeman   Yes? What do you come to tell me? Your complaint.

Mukhtar   I was . . . Faiz Mohammed . . . from the Mastoi . . . He ordered . . . four men to – to rape me –

Policeman   No! This cannot be your report. You must not say you have been raped! We know what happened. (*He waves a piece of paper at her*) You must just sign here.

Mukhtar   But I . . . I . . . I don't know what it says.

Policeman   (*Grabs her hand*) We know. Sign, I said!

Mukhtar   I can't – I don't know how to write my . . .

Policeman   So? Use your thumbprint, like the other women! (*The other women gather around to watch as he presses her thumb into an inkpad, then onto the bottom of the page. From this point on, the women begin to engage with one another from time to time in their speeches and response.*)

Mukhtar   This is when I understood why we must have knowledge. If you are educated you can fight for your rights. But when you are illiterate, how can you stop the injustice that falls down on you?

Hafsat   We don't really know what happened. Maybe we'll never know. And to be honest with you, it's not so important to me how they died. The most important thing is how they lived! And I am making up their legacy. I've named my organisation after my mum, Kadirat. In Arabic it means power. I am working to show young women that they can have power and teach them how to reclaim it. (*On screen rain, fields of fruit and vegetables; later snow, the sea . . . music of Ramayana.*)

Sochua   Now that I again live in Phnom Penh, my childhood memories flood back; this is where I learned how to bike, that's where I learned how to swim . . . When rain came down in buckets, flooding the streets, my brother Song Lee and I caught fish to put in huge jars on our third floor balcony. I used to accompany my mother to Psa Tmei, the large, yellow central market, where the stalls spilled outside into the open air. I loved to wander through the long rows, staring at the huge piles of fish, fruit and vegetables. I spent a lot of time in the kitchen, helping my mother cook. At night on the radio we listened to the opera. Music of Ramayana plays for hours.

Anabella   My brother used to play in a big hole, like a trench, that surrounded the zona where we lived. He didn't like school. I was all the time thinking I need to study. I need to prepare. I tell my mother: One day I will have *la gire* villa, a swivel chair, and many people under my command. My mother laughs and says 'Esta bien para sonar.' It is okay for you to dream! Now I am three times elected and sitting in my swivel chair!

Marina   My father was a military pilot. My mother was a nurse. I grew up mostly in the northern part of Russia, in the polar area. Murmansk. In winter, I would go skiing with my friends. For us to go three, five kilometres in the wild forest, that was normal. Really we were afraid of nothing. In the summer, I would spend time with my grandparents who lived on the Black Sea. For me, swimming in a storm, jumping under big waves, swimming as far out as I could where you could almost not see the shore – that was normal. I was the first grandchild, first niece, first everything for everybody, so I got a lot of attention. I loved it. When you grow up, when you have a happy childhood, you think that is normal. You don't realise, you know, that there is a different world out there . . . (*And a field of bright red poppies, from which Farida emerges.*)

Farida   When I walk along the border of Afghanistan . . . I see so many red and pink flowers – both sides of the road. I think, oh yes, my country is so beautiful. Then I see that it is the poppies for the opium. I see the women in the poppy fields, side by side with the men, cutting the cane until the milk comes out. And the opium blows through their dresses, hair, mouth, until they are addicted. In the north, the mothers give small pieces of the opium to the children to calm them down, so they can weave the carpets for ten hours a day. That's how the children start their own addiction. So we try to give them an awareness of the consequences. How it can destroy them!

Mukhtar   I am brought before a judge. He sees how tired I am and brings me a glass of water. Then he asks me to describe every detail of what happened in the stable. I tell him things I have not told my own mother. Before I leave the courtroom, he tells me to hold fast to my courage. And the next morning when I wake up there is such a racket outside my house! (*Sounds of dogs barking, chickens squawking, cameras click and flash.*) Reporters call out for me, women's groups, civil rights groups – from all over the world. The Pakistan Human Rights Commission has demanded a full investigation, and the press is supporting my lawsuit. But I hear that my rapists are laughing at the whole thing, they think it is ridiculous – a poor peasant woman trying to fight the influence of the land-owing Matsois!

Anabella   In Guatemala, corruption is in the police department, the ministry, the judicial branch, even in the Supreme Court. In 2001, Vice President Reyes used the National Printing Press to print false identity papers for his supporters so they could vote more than once. When the man who operated the printing press spoke out, his wife and daughter were attacked. When a key witness agreed to testify against him, he was shot dead. And when I denounced him, the Organisation of American States mandated bodyguards come to my house in the morning, and they are there with me until night.

Inez   (*As if viewing the site*) Ballymurphy – it was and is one of the most deprived housing estates in West Belfast – I was placed in a small welfare office there in the early 1970s. Deliberately sending me and my two friends, three barely trained young hippie Protestant women to an empty flat in the neighbourhood of a shooting war between the IRA and the British Army. Clearly designed to give them an excuse to close the office! We didn't know that. We knew nothing. We were known as the 'Well-Fairies'! All we did was – well somebody comes in, a woman who has two disabled kids, and she's pregnant, and her husband has no job, and I am about to counsel her on her inadequacies? You know? That's why we write lots of vouchers for food and for other things, so the costs of this office suddenly go from zero (*Sound*) zooooom! We're suddenly ordered to be transferred. Our office is (*mockingly*) too dangerous! We just keep on going to work. And someone says I better join the union. So I did and I'm elected shop steward of the Well-Fairies, just the three of us! Then I'm told to recruit more union members. And somebody's bothered with the part-time hospital cleaners, the school meals workers – women who'd go stand in front of tanks or shake down the bars of a prison to rescue their sons but won't take on a boss because they feel powerless, y'know? So I keep organising, and they keep joining the union. When they go on strike, all decent people close their shops and join the huge picket lines! (*Workers with Inez and Anabella stand in a defiant line, holding hands. The two union struggles interweave. One actor portrays both bosses.*)

Anabella   (*To Boss*) What is the reason you want to fire these airport workers? Tell me in front of them.

Boss   (*In Spanish*) We are doing construction at the airport. We have no more use of their services.

Anabella   They have worked in the airport for thirty years and you're going to fire them? No you are not. They have families. They have children. They need their work.

Inez   (*To Boss*) You want to cut the hospital cleaning budget? Why?

Boss   (*In English*) It is essential to good finance.

Inez   Are your pensions and your benefits going to be cut as well? Because one hundred of you would cost as much as ten thousand of the women!

Anabella and Inez   No! You must work out how these people can keep their jobs! (*Silence – until the Boss throws up his hands. Everyone cheers.*)

Inez   So much of my work came from these women cleaners . . . The idea of it: to enable people on the powerless end, the bottom of the heap, the invisible to be part of the making of change! That changes how they see themselves and, well, that changes everything, y'know?

Anabella   In my country, poverty has a woman's face. They are the most damaged of the population, the most low in education. Myself and thirteen congresswomen submitted a set of bills aimed at improving women's programmes. When it comes time for the vote, the men in Parliament hide in the bathroom. I open the door, the other women storm in, and we pull them out one by one! The male party members make me promise never to do this again. But the bills got passed!

Mukhtar   The rapists stop laughing when the court orders them to pay me an enormous fine and condemns them to death. Again the news flies everywhere, in my country and abroad. One day I am told to report to a local office where I am given a check for half a million rupees . . . about eight thousand dollars – by a government minister – a woman! She explains that it is a settlement for my pain, but maybe, I think, it is also a bribe for my silence. I am about to hand back the check when suddenly I feel that God speaks through me. 'I don't need money. I need a school.' I cry out. 'A school for girls in my village. They must learn to read, to write, to know their rights as citizens. Help me.' I implore the woman who has benefitted from her education. 'Help me build a school.' She says I may use the money in any way I choose. And so begins my new passion, my mission in life.

Hafsat   It is part of our culture in Nigeria to gather and listen to stories in our villages . . . 'tales by moonlight'. So let me tell one. A true story. About a girl named Zaneb. She was just fifteen years old when I met her, when she first rushed into our office. (*The girl runs over to Hafsat.*) She's thin, comes barely up to my shoulder, and looks like the wind could blow her away. And the words rush out of her!

Zaneb   My parents, they want me to marry an old man in Saudi Arabia. They betrothed me to him when I was born. I tell them 'No!' I want to go to university. I won't marry that man.

Hafsat   You must, the parents insist. And they bring her to Niger where they'll put her on a transport to Saudi Arabia.

Zaneb   Wait! You want me to meet my husband looking like this? No, if I am going, I must get my hair done to look good for him . . .

Hafsat   The parents agree and leave her at the hairdresser because you know those tiny braids that African women do?

Zaneb and Hafsat   (*Smiling at each other*) They take hours!

Zaneb   And that's when I escape!

Hafsat   And she comes to us! We give her shelter and funds for school, and for a whole year I try to speak to her parents and help them understand her dreams.

Zaneb   They will not understand. They say I have shamed them.

Hafsat   She wants to be reconciled with them. So I decide we must try to give them back their respect. On the birthday of the Prophet of Islam, Zaneb and I –

Zaneb   Hafsat and I, we travel together to my family's compound. Many people are gathered there reading the Quran as we enter. They all stare at us. And we kneel . . . (*They kneel*) And Hafsat says:

Hafsat   'On behalf of your daughter I apologise for any shame she has brought upon your household.'

Zaneb   My father stares but says nothing.

Hafsat   Please. Zaneb will return to help your community when she becomes a doctor . . .

Zaneb   But he just stares. They all do. And the silence is frightening. Then suddenly –

Hafsat   Suddenly her father reaches out – and hugs her!

Zaneb   And hugs me. And I am so happy.

Hafsat   And this story of Zaneb has spread far and wide. It is inspiring so many young girls to see how they too can choose their lives.

Sochua   My life, it seems like a river with many bends. And it bends all the time, this river. I'm now Secretary General of the Opposition Party, seeking a seat in Parliament in the next election. Our party's sign stands tall in the last stronghold of the Khmer Rouge. Landmines are still in the rice fields and forests, malaria is widespread – I lead a team of rural women leaders to every house in four hundred and eighty villages to bring the message of democracy and justice. On the trail we listen to stories of separation, stories of hunger and of fear . . . When I'm on the campaign trail I love it. Being on the motor-taxi, the oxcart, crossing a river on a boat, going to the temples, talking to the farmers, visiting Muslim communities . . . At my age I'm still discovering my own country. The Opposition Party can become the new government if the people of Cambodia fight for change.

Mukhtar   I set up the school in a field and go from house to house, pleading with parents to send their daughters to school. Every day more little girls arrive with notebooks and pencils. They learn math, social studies, the English alphabet, Urdu, and the Quran. But we also teach them that women are equal with men, that all of us are human beings and must be treated with respect in society!

Inez   You really accord human rights when you respect those with whom you disagree . . . Recently Israeli and Palestinian women came to Northern Ireland to share insights and devise strategies for peace-building. When they first arrive I can smell and feel the tension, the fear, and the anger. After thirty years of struggle in the North I learned you must not drown in your own pain. You must allow your humanity enough room to recognise the pain in the other . . .

Marina   When you grow up with love around you that gives you the internal freedom to share this love with others. It gives you an internal responsibility to share this love, and it gives you the ability to share it.

Farida   In the refugee camp, I worked in the Norwegian Church Aid Office, and we were supporting a small magazine for children called the Rainbow to spread peace messages instead of violence. And then a man came to the office . . .

Man   You know this rainbow on the cover has a pigeon on the top. And these two hands are a Christian sign. This shows a political agenda. They want the people to be Christian.

Farida   I am Muslim, I work here, no one forces me to be Christian. We work for human beings who suffer a lot, that's all.

Man   I know Islamic and Pakistani intelligence. I have their support, and I myself am from intelligence. If you don't stop the magazine, I will destroy your office. I can do anything to you and your family.

Farida   Here I am, whatever you can do to me, then do it! My work is for needy people, and you are not needy people, so get out of here!

Man   I will see you. I will do what I can to you! You will never enter Afghanistan again.

Farida   (*Backs away from the man, clearly frightened.*) The man keeps calling and calling and calling every day, and it was at that time I was told for the safety of my children I should leave Afghanistan – and this is what I do. (*At the same time, a phone rings. Marina picks up.*)

Stalker   (*On the phone*) Marina?

Marina   Yes.

Stalker   The entrance to your apartment is very dark.

Marina   Excuse me, who are you?

Stalker   I'm someone who was affected by your work.

Marina   Did I help your wife, your girlfriend – ?

Stalker   It doesn't matter. I know where you live. Aren't you afraid that your son is alone in the street?

Marina   (*To all*) I feel that somebody has struck a knife in my heart. He knows about my son. And it goes on for months. (*The phone keeps ringing as she speaks*) I don't allow Peter to answer the phone at home; I have my parents pick him up from school every day, or he goes to his friend's house, but he is never, never alone.

Stalker   (*Underneath Marina, continuous*) Aren't you afraid for your son?

Marina	**Stalker**
I am afraid to enter the building.	Aren't you afraid?

Stalker   The entrance to your apartment is very dark.

Marina   Sometimes I just pray that the elevator will go to the first floor fast. So I can just get in and go.

Stalker   (*Simultaneously*) If someone were to stick a knife in your back. Or worse, a needle – you'd never know who did it.

(*The women have been occupying separate positions on the stage. Increasingly their words begin to overlap and they move in proximity, becoming a community.*)

Anabella   Men, very strong, come to my office looking for me. They wear suits and coats to cover their guns. 'We are looking for Anabella. She is on the list. We know her death date!'

Mukhtar   I receive death threats. The government revokes my passport, forbids me to leave the country, places me under house arrest.

Inez   My car is surrounded by soldiers, paratroopers, my door flung open. I'm pulled out and thrown over the car and they're screaming: Who am I? What am I? What am I carrying?

Anabella   One them sticks a large gun hard between my legs and calls me a F-ing bitch . . .

Mukhtar   President Musharaff states: 'Since the Mukhtar Bibi case, all a woman has to do to become a millionaire is get herself raped and tell the press about it.'

Farida   Three hundred women set themselves on fire in Herat.

Anabella   My advisor is tortured. They break his fingers, burn his hands, take his eyes out, and they strangle him.

Farida   The husband pours acid on her face, the side of her neck.

Marina   The woman covers the baby with her body but the husband keeps beating her. She asks for a divorce, but he says: 'I'll kill you and tell everyone you ran away with another man.'

Farida   If she has abuse she has no choice. 'You can come out of that house when you are dead!'

Anabella   Hah, my God! I wouldn't care if I had to die in the fight. I have plenty of powerful enemies because those who fight corruption don't make many friends. Hah, sometimes, I feel the sorrow, but I feel proud I am a congresswoman. I feel proud too that I am not dead.

Hafsat   At the end of the day my father gave his life. And I think that is a very powerful message to give to people who feel disempowered, that . . . there is no price too high to pay to let you know there is sanctity in your voice . . . And my mother because she refused to stand for injustice in Nigeria, because of that her spirit will live on. (*Sound of wind*)

Farida   Now that I am far away from my home, I dream that I am walking with my children in the east and most remote part of my country. Where there is no road. The elder women call to me: 'Farida, you do not have to wear your burqa here.' Inside the village we are very safe. The women are coming out to solve things. (*All gather round Farida. Patterns of white flakes fall on stage/screen.*) And I dream of little bits of paper falling like snow. As I reach for them I see that they are prayers for me. So many women praying that I will not die, that I will escape what has come to harm me, to break my very heart. Like the black wind before the sun. I read each prayer and my strength comes back, and is how we will survive.

Marina   My favourite time walking, believe it or not, is when it is snowing. Snow makes it beautiful around Red Square. This is the time to put myself together. To come to some harmony with myself. Because if you are not in harmony with yourself this is a very difficult job to do. When I started, 1993, there was only me, only one crisis centre. Now there are one hundred and sixty crisis centres, shelters, organisations. A whole network.

Mukhtar   I have opened three schools in Punjab province and they are for boys as well as girls, because boys too must learn that under Islam, under the law, women have the same rights as they do. And in Meerwala, where I almost killed myself, I have built a real school house with a library and six classrooms. The children come from many tribes, from low and high castes – girls from the Gujars, and yes, we take even boys from the Mastois!

Marina   There is a story, we use it in training a lot. A guy is walking along the river and suddenly sees kids drowning. And he goes into the water and starts rescuing them. And another guy is walking nearby, and he's asking, what are you doing? The first guy says I'm rescuing kids. Help me. And that guy gets into the water and starts teaching the kids swimming. And a third guy comes along. And he turns around and starts running. And the two guys in the river say, wait, we need your help! Where are you going? And the third guy says, I want to see who's throwing the kids into the water in the first place! Right now we are rescuing and teaching, but we are not yet working with the cause. So it has to be deeper.

Anabella   I wake up very early in the morning, I take the shower, and go to the beauty parlour. Not for vanity's sake. My appearance is important because I must have a good face for los pueblos who are looking to me to speak out for them. When I was a child, I make a promise to myself: I am going to pull out my mother, my brother, and me from the poverty and leave this little dark room; and then I am going to pull out the women of Guatemala, the silent women, and the men who have no worth in their work. I say, they must not stay in silence. No more silence!

Mukhtar   I was the first student in my own school, and now I am in the fifth grade there. For the rest of my life I will never need to use my thumb to sign my name on my homework – or on anything! (*Writes on paper/screen, in Urdu and English.*) Mukhtar. Powerful. Self-respecting. Mukhtar.

Farida   We have a Farsi proverb we say: However high the mountain is, it must have a way on the top that you can reach it.

Hafsat   We shouldn't be resting, should be thinking we've tried our best. That just means our best is not good enough. We need to really step up. Women are the greatest untapped resource in Africa. We are the future!

Inez   If you put equal rights at the heart of things, you have to be sure everyone is at the table. You have to look and see who isn't there, who isn't being heard. And use your power to change that! Just take one small step forward. That first step is always the massive one!

Sochua   Every day I see a woman, whether she serves beer in a beer garden or sex workers or garment factory workers. They are my sisters, my friends, my teachers. When people say, how can you wake up and still do this after twenty-five years? I say you have to do it until people who do not have a voice, do.

Suddenly a phone rings. Each woman on stage instinctively reaches toward it – then freezes. The phone continues to ring as lights fade to blackness.

An Essay

María José Contreras Lorenzini[1]

Pajarito Nuevo la Lleva is a Chilean slang phrase, which is especially used by children to indicate that the last one to join a game has to play the worst part or role. Literally, *pajarito nuevo* means 'new bird', referring to the newcomer joining a game, and *la Lleva* means 'is it', referring, for example, to the person who has to tag the others in a tag game. Therefore, the literal translation could be 'the new bird is it'. The Chilean theatre play entitled *Pajarito Nuevo la Lleva* is based on testimonies of people, who were 5 to 10 years old during the state coup in 1973 in Chile or during the resistance protests in the 1980s. The title refers to the difficult position that children found themselves in during the dictatorship – a time when the majority of adults/parents were paralyzed by fear and often unable to provide explanations for what was happening to their children, who as

Figure 14 Courtesy of Teatro de Patio.

'new birds' were thus compelled to suffer the effects of the state violence without recourse to any meaningful frame of reference or clear rationale.

Pajarito Nuevo la Lleva resulted from an interdisciplinary research project at the Theatre School of the Pontificia Universidad Católica de Chile. This project was developed in 2008 under the guidance of María José Contreras (Theatre Director), Milena Grass (Theorist) and Nancy Nicolls (Anthropologist) and was titled *Theatre and Memory: Strategies of (Re)presentation and Scenic Elaboration of Children's Traumatic Memories.*[2]

The first phase of the work, directed by Milena Grass, included a theoretical revision and critical discussion of the existing bibliography on trauma and testimony. In the second phase, the anthropologist Nancy Nicholls collected testimonies from 13 people who were 5 to 10 years in 1973 during the state coup or who met the same age criteria during the protests that emerged in the 1980s. We decided to choose testimony givers who had not suffered directly from human rights abuses (in the first person or through their nuclear family) and instead we focused on those who represented any child swept up by the general sociopolitical situation in Chile at that time. However, after we had conducted the interviews it became clear that even those who did not suffer the direct impact of the dictatorship had and continued to experience the aftershocks and latent effects of sudden and traumatic cultural upheaval. The third phase consisted of a theatre laboratory through which we explored different modes of translating the original testimonies into an embodied performative practice. The following actors participated in this laboratory: Andrea Soto, Pablo Dubott, Carolina Quito, Macarena Béjares, Simón Lobos and Alvaro Manríquez, alongside the crucial collaboration with Ornella de la Vega, as assistant director. Over a period of four months we explored different ways to 'perform trauma': from reinterpreting trauma at a semantic level, through to physically translating the sonority of the voices and re-enacting the gestures of the testimony givers as observed in the video recordings.[3] Almost all of the testimonies were non-linear, fragmented, disorganized discourses marked by blank mnemonic spaces, whereby the witnesses acted out meanings for which words were lacking, often making gestures, grimaces and garbled sounds to evoke their memories of past experiences. We decided that the performance had to remain faithful to this pronouncedly incoherent way of communicating and as a result we came to rely on body language almost more than the spoken word. As a director, I concentrated on the performers' physical presence as a privileged site from which both the verbal accounts and corporal memory could be articulated. I decided to work with physical scores that didn't mimetically recreate the remembered anecdotes, but which allegorically and metaphorically approached the palpable pain of the testimonies and their articulation.[4] I hoped, in this way, to attain a relationship with the audience whereby '. . . the untranslatable and non-representational is transformed into communication, respect and understanding.'[5] This phase concluded with the creation and staging of *Pajarito Nuevo la Lleva* in October 2008.

We engaged in this project by responding to what seemed to be an ongoing and always urgent political commitment to our history. Hence, we thought that by understanding the children of the past we could better comprehend the adults that governed and lived in present-day Chile (Contreras, Grass & Nicholls, 2009). As mentioned previously, the understanding we sought was not only rational, but also seemingly irrational, inclusive of the embodied memories. In this respect we set out to bridge theoretical approaches (trauma studies, post-conflict studies, semiotics, oral history, anthropology and performance studies) with an embodied performative practice, so as to investigate a two-way synergy: how could theory contribute to the staging process and how could the staging process enrich theoretical accounts of trauma and testimony? We were also interested in exploring different layers of memory, that is, from the way children construct their memories (in this case mainly traumatic memories that lacked a semantic account – both because of the intensity of the events and because adults were usually unable to provide explanations), to how these memories are recalled by adults. Additionally since the actors were very young, our practice explored what Marianne Hirsch has identified as post-memory or 'the relationship that the generation after those who witnessed cultural or collective trauma bears to the experience of those who came before.'[6]

Teatro testimonial is a fuzzy notion used to describe theatre based on testimonies and personal memories, where words and experiences of real people are edited, arranged or re-contextualized for the stage. We, however, were not looking to reconstruct others' narrated memories, but rather to work creatively on the complex and paradoxical epistemological status of testimony. Instead of forwarding a unique truth that tried to take into account the 'true' stories of these sons and daughters of the dictatorship, we aimed at exposing the complexities involved in the restoration of traumatic memories, especially when these memories were imprinted during childhood. In order to evoke post-dictatorship Chilean society, where diverse interpretations about the past radically diverge to the point that there is still a portion of the population that speaks of 'President Pinochet' (instead of referring to him as a dictator), we decided to multiply the interpretative possibilities of the work. To do this we established different and distinct communication channels – one on stage (mainly the actors' physical scores) which was accessible to the entire audience simultaneously, the other individual to each spectator. With respect to the latter, we requested that each of the spectators attend the performance with a personal sound device with earphones (Walkman, mp3, iPod). Once the spectators arrived at the venue, they had to choose from two alternative soundtracks: 'A' and 'B' (this was a blind choice, since they couldn't really know what they were choosing). Both soundtracks contained different fragments of the original testimonies. The decision to make the original voices accessible to the spectators responded to what became our understanding of these testimonies – namely that the voices of the testimony givers, their intonations, stutters, pauses and especially silences spoke about the limitations we faced when attempting to recuperate a record of past traumatic experience. Therefore, instead of making actors 'perform' the testimonies, we made a concerted decision to share the Barthesian idea of conveying 'the grain of the voices', the material body language that emerged from the spoken testimonies to the audience. The soundtracks were mathematically synched with the actors' actions, so if a certain scene lasted 2'32" seconds, the audio fragment would precisely coincide with that time lapse. The soundtracks also included silent moments that matched the periods in which performers spoke on stage. This way, each spectator heard sounds and music both from the stage and from their individual audio devices. This format allowed us to produce two effects. The first was that of dividing the audience into two different groups which interpreted and experienced the performance differently according to the soundtrack they chose. This effect homologized each spectator's position to those of the children of the dictatorship (who only knew and understood what was happening around them depending on what they heard – or didn't hear – from adults.) The second effect was that of clearly making obvious the double status that the performance of the testimonies has, namely the 'immediate' original testimonies (the original voices heard through the audio tracks) and the 'mediated' interpretation of testimonies (the actors' voices). In this way the work self-consciously demonstrated both the raw testimonies and our own mediation of those testimonies, thus making evident the negotiation between the real and its representation in our own practice.

In 2012 we created a second version of *Pajarito Nuevo la Lleva*, with the original actors Carolina Quito, Pablo Dubott, Andrea Soto as well as three new actors, namely Luis Aros, Andrea Pellegri and Vicente Almuna. The re-creating process of 2012 was very interesting, since it meant remembering and restoring the first version. Thus, we created another layer of memory, that is, the memory of the artists remembering the memories of others, again. The 2012 version was both a repetition and a new interpretation, since we decided to change some aspects because the political scenario in Chile was, by that time, radically different. In 2008, under Michel Bachelet's government, there was a clear politics of memory, which was evidenced, for example, by the inauguration of the Museo de la Memoria (The Memory Museum) in Santiago. Now, in 2012, the situation is extremely different, as Sebastián Piñera's conservative and right-wing government has marked a pronounced disengagement from the politics of memory, whereby a state policy that insists on looking towards the future has displaced an earlier project to remember, let alone investigate Chile's unspoken past. The 2012 version of *Pajarito Nuevo la Lleva* includes new scenes (some of the original ones were disregarded) and three additional versions of the soundtrack, so we are now working with five different soundtracks. The new soundtracks do not only include the original testimonies, but also the actors' interventions as they express their own memories about the original performance. In addition, in the later version, the actors sometimes read the witness testimonies in a direct address form, reflecting our own increasing and ongoing uneasy awareness of the limitations of re-performing somebody else's trauma.

When coping with traumatic situations, what remains unsaid is even more important that what is finally spoken. This was very clear in the testimonies that we worked with, when, for example, the testimony givers incongruously laughed while describing something tragic, or when the disconcerting pauses threatened to dissolve the discourse in silence. Also we noted that by adding the voices of the actors into the soundtracks of the later performance, we actually creatively empowered the actors as second-degree witnesses, with yet another layer of testimony. Most of the testimony givers confessed during the interviews that they had never spoken about their childhood under the dictatorship before. They were recuperating (and constructing) their memories while being interviewed. Sometimes, they lacked words and just made sounds or gestures in an almost child-like manner to describe what they felt during the interviews. We encouraged these non-verbal accounts, which then became part of the physical and vocal scores of the performance. The gap between adults and children was also mirrored by the selection of the cast. In both versions I worked with very young actors, most of whom were not even born during the dictatorship. Therefore, the scenic translation again explores the gap between the voice of an adult describing childhood memories and the young bodies and voices of the actors who perform the testimony of such an adult, in a sort of post-memory performance. We also explored the gap between media and presence, as the audio device sounds intertwine with live actions on stage – creating multiple temporalities and spaces: *a here and now that recalls a there and then*. In this respect *Pajarito Nuevo la Lleva* highlighted a series of ruptures and fissures – the gaps between the said and the unsaid, between adults and children, between media and presence. These are results we would like to explore further in our future work on memory in performance.

The invitation to publish the text of *Pajarito Nuevo la Lleva* was exciting, troubling and problematic. How could we transcribe *Pajarito Nuevo la Lleva*? For the most part the actors on stage do not speak, and the words within the work are mainly confined to the soundtracks that by the time of the final version constituted five different sets. The difficulty of translating and transcribing *Pajarito Nuevo la Lleva* into a written text is intrinsically related to the nature of this memory work. Our memory-object, namely the traumatic memories of children, lacked words both because they are often painful to express and because they were experienced during childhood, when lucid verbal accounts are even more difficult to construct. Also much of the performance is sited within the corporeal memory of the actors and presented via physical non-literal scores. In addition, the encounter with the audience also relies on a very particular spectatorship that heightens the fissure between the collective and the individual experience of the past. The audio device enhances the awareness of the spectators' own bodies and individual presence. Therefore, the entire process throughout its diverse phases is profoundly based on embodied practices. In this respect, it could be said that publishing this text implies transcribing and translating a repertoire into an archive and this further voyage requires coping with what resists the trace at so many levels.[7] Our solution was to invent the use of a particular format that would somehow describe the performance, taking into account its kaleidoscopic, multi-sensory diversity. The format we chose was a three-column script: in the first column we included the transcription of a soundtrack, which includes an edition of the original testimonies and some interventions by the actors. In the middle column, we note the movements and physical scores of the actors (this implies the traditional problem of the verbal account of movement that is never enough). In the third column we include the transcription of another soundtrack. Once again, it would seem we encounter another fissure – the gap between word and action, script and performance – a hurdle we have attempted to partly overcome with the 'body of text' we have prepared. In this spirit, we hope that a trace of the bodily experience of *Pajarito Nuevo la Lleva* may be discovered within these pages.

Notes

1   María José Contreras is Ph.d in Semiotics and currently works as Theatre
    Director, Performer and Professor at Escuela de Teatro Universidad Católica
    de Chile. www.mariajosecontreras.com
2   This research was financed by Concursos de Cultura y Creacion Artistica
    (VRAID N 15/2008) granted by the Vicerrectoria Adjunta de investigación
    y Doctorado de la Pontificia Universidad Catolica de Chile and Laboratorios
    Teatrales 2008 of the Theatre School at the Universidad Catolica.
3   For a detailed account of the performance as research process in the
    laboratory, see Conteras, Grass and Nicholls (2008). 'Pajarito Nuevo
    la Lleva: estrategias de representaçao e elaboraçao cênica de memória
    traumatica infantil.' *Revista Aletria: Revista de Estudos de Literatura Artes
    e Culutra de Expressão Hispânica. Minas Gerais: Universidade Federal de
    Minas Gerais,* Vol. 17, January–June 2009, pp. 154–72.
4   By score I apply Eugenio Barba's notion of score: '– the general design of
    the form in a sequence of actions, and the evolution of each single action'
    (beginning, climax, conclusion); – the precision of the fixed details of
    each action as well as of the transitions connecting them (sats, changes of
    direction, different qualities of energy, variations of speed); – the dynamism
    and the rhythm: the speed and intensity which regulated the *tempo* (in the
    musical sense) of a series of actions. This was the metre of the actions
    with their mico-pauses and decisions, the alternation of long of short ones,
    accented or unaccented segments, characterized by vigorous or soft energy; –
    the orchestration of the relationships between the different parts of the body
    (hands, arms, feet, eyes, voice, facial expression). (Barba 2010: 27–8).
    Eugenio Barba, *On Directing and Dramaturgy: Burning the House.* London
    & New York: Routledge, 2010.
5   Irene Wirshing, *National Trauma in Postdictatorship Latin American
    Literature. Chile and Argentina.* NY: Peter Lang, 2009, p. 67.
6   Marianne Hirsch, 'The Generation of Postmemory' in *Poetics Today* 29(1),
    New York: Duke University Press, 2008, p. 106.
7   See Diana Taylor, *The Archive and Repertoire. Performing Cultural Memory
    in the Americas.* Durham: Duke University Press, 2003.

Pajarito Nuevo La Lleva:
The Sounds of the Coup

María José Contreras Lorenzini
Translation: Camila Le-Bert

Acknowledgements

Director	María José Contreras
Assistant Director	Ornella de la Vega
Theatre Researcher	Milena Grass
Testimonies collected by	Nancy Nicholls
Company	Teatro de Patio
Cast (2008):	Pablo Dubott, Andrea Soto, Carolina Quito, Alvaro Manríquez, Simón Lobos, Macarena Béjares.
Cast (2012):	Pablo Dubott, Andrea Soto, Carolina Quito, Luis Aros, Vicente Almuna, Andrea Pelegri.
Sounds of the coup was based on the testimonies of:	Leo Fernández, M.G.A., Claudio Pérez, Andrea Ubal, Jenny Henríquez, Mario Costa, Iván Navarro, Emilio Soto, Genaro, Marisol Pacheco, Doris Pacheco, Roberto Cofré, Daniela Zenteno.

The first versión of *Pajarito Nuevo la Lleva* was financed by Concursos de Cultura y Creación Artística (VRAID N° 15/2008) granted by the Vicerrectoría Adjunta de Investigación y Doctorado de la Pontificia Universidad Católica de Chile and Laboratorios Teatrales 2008 of the Theatre School at the Universidad Católica.

Pajarito Nuevo La Lleva: The Sounds of the Coup

María José Contreras Lorenzini Translation: Camila Le-Bert

Reading Instructions: The middle column describes the physical action onstage. This contains everything the audience sees and hears. Column n. 1 contains one of the soundtracks of the original testimonial recordings and/or the voices of the actors intervening over the original testimonies. Column 3 bears an alternative soundtrack. Every audience member will have access to column n. 2 and either column n. 1 or n. 3.

Upon entering the theatre, audience members will unknowingly choose one of the two soundtracks, without realizing the implications of their decision. It will be explained to them that when they see the 'Play' sign they should press play on their audio devices.

Column 1	Column 2	Column 3
A Soundtrack	Onstage action	B Soundtrack
	Assembly	
	All of the actors enter the stage from the sides in school gym uniforms. On a golden tray, covered with a doily, they carry a virgin figurine. They form into two lines facing the audience. They stare at the audience with a puzzled look.	
	All sing the version of the Chilean national anthem that was sung during the dictatorship:	
	'Sweet homeland, receive the votes, by which Chile, under whose altars you swore, that you shall be either the tomb of the free, or an asylum against oppression.	
	Your names, valiant soldiers, That have supported Chile, Upon our bosoms have been carved; Our sons shall know it too. They shall be the cry of death. . . .'	
	(A 'bomb' is heard and there is a blackout: the actors shriek in fear from onstage. The only light comes from the plastic fluorescent virgin.)	
	(A giant sign appears that says_ 'PLAY') (*this is the signal for the audience to press play on their audio devices.*)	

Column 1 A Soundtrack	Column 2 Onstage action	Column 3 B Soundtrack
Roberto	**The paintbrush**	**Claudio**
Now, looking back on my 46 years, I do think it affected me because I think I belong to an oppressed generation. It's hard to speak out against injustice, against something that is unjust, even though you can see it, it's like it's hard because I never thought that: the military would come and do whatever they wanted, I couldn't see it but I could hear it and whoever tried to take a stand was taken down. So, looking back, it made me this kind of a person, even though, I'm not that much like that because when something bothers me, when it bothers me, you can tell from a mile away and I just say it and I argue and fight. Actually, I'm really good at fighting at home with my wife and my son, at work, at my church, where I help out. I'm a little confrontational. I think I belong to that repressed generation, we don't have the freedom kids have now, they get to the point where they can be insolent, disrespectful, because they were raised in 'democracy', in freedom, they don't have a military officer pointing at them with a rifle; there are the politicians on the telly or just the empty seats in the senate, but they don't have that and they say so in the student movement, the 'penguins'. So, I didn't have that, no way.	*Luis, Vicente and Pablo stealthily get together and plan something in silence. Pablo doesn't seem convinced, they hide. Luis grabs a paintbrush and paints on the public high school wall. Vicente and Pablo watch out nobody comes by. They hear something and run off, desperately. They arrive to a safe haven and all stay motionless. Pablo is on the floor; he rises and comes over to Luis.* **Luis** Hey man, Where's my dad's paintbrush? **Pablo** (*sitting down*) The cops took it. **Luis** Man, my dad's paintbrush! **Pablo** Okay!!	The first time we wrote on the school walls, in 1986, 1987. . . There were three of us and, on Sunday night, we got together to write on walls and, all of a sudden, this civilian car pulls up and stops in front of the Liceo de Aplicación and one guy gets out with a gun and says 'stand over there', and I was holding a paint can and a paint roller and the other guy had a paintbrush and another guy was keeping watch out back so he stayed back on the other side of Cumming and we both looked at each other, looked at the guy who was pointing at us and threw everything on the ground, we had this reaction and we ran off. So we ran (. . .) we went through all of those streets behind the school, the alleys and we got away. Then, half an hour later, we met at the place where we said we'd meet if anything happened. We got there, frightened, because after that a lot of cops showed up. They must have been alerted because a lot of cops showed up in the area; and I was like 'hey, and what happened to the paintbrush?', 'What paintbrush?', 'The *paintbrush.*' 'I don't know I threw it at the cops.' And I'm like: 'that's my dad's paintbrush!!' I'm not very materialistic, if something gets lost, it gets lost, but about the paintbrush, I was like 'It's my dad's paintbrush. He uses it to work.'

Column 1 A Soundtrack	Column 2 Onstage action	Column 3 B Soundtrack
I don't remember the first scares with the police and the military kicking the polyclinic, those scares, but I just stayed normal, playing normal, I kept on, I don't remember the curfew restrictions. I do remember afterwards, when I was a teenager, we still had the curfew, I remember it then because it was a different period in my life, but years later, when I was 15, 16 years old; that's when I felt the oppression.		It was the paintbrush he used to paint the steel bars when he was welding, and I had taken it, so I had left him, from my perspective, so he couldn't work. And I made such a big deal that, an hour later, we went back to school to get the brush. The brush wasn't there; they had taken it with the paint. I was so worried (. . .) for me, it was like I had left him without a hand.
Moscow radio begins its daily program for Chile. 'Listen, Chile, to the news of what the Junta hides and prohibits. What happens within Chile and the voice of world's solidarity? Listen Chile. A Moscow Radio program.' (*Moscow radio music*) **Claudio** In that part of Caro there were bonfires all over; lots of people would get together. Everyone would shout out the typical cry against the dictatorship. Nor the police nor the army went into that area, it's like nobody went in there. To go fight you had to go to Avenida Central. A huge mob came out of Avenida Central. That's where we all went. The next day you would go to school and we would get to school and the Bata store had been looted and the	**Raid** *Two girls and a boy are listening to a makeshift radio. They try to tune into something until they finally tune into Moscow Radio. They are enjoying themselves until, suddenly, two armed military break in. The girls cry, the boy tries to calm them down. The military raid the house, they rummage through the furniture, they throw things, they make a mess with the books and end up lifting the flexi from the floor. They don't find anything.* *The military leave.* *The girls are left crying.*	**Macarena** . . .yeah, our house was raided. They came one day, in the morning, really early, my parents weren't there. And they looked for whatever we had and we didn't have anything, they broke everything and we had flexi floors in the dining room and they pulled up the flexi tiles to see if we had anything. . . nothing, they couldn't find anything, they never said what they were looking for, they treated us awful. I was about 9 and my sister must have been 16 or 17. Crying and what did they want. Where were my parents? We were crying, the women, and they were like calm down, calm down, trying for them not to break any more things. They broke in and we were like having breakfast, watching TV, ooff!

Column 1 A Soundtrack	Column 2 Onstage action	Column 3 B Soundtrack
Unimarc supermarket wasn't Unimarc. . . it was Unicoop, it would've been looted too, all of the local shops would've been looted as well.		We were by ourselves; we were left by ourselves, so we were really scared.
The way home from school in the morning was like a battle zone, because every corner had a bonfire of burning tires.		They asked us about dad, they told us to shut up, that they weren't going to do anything, that they were looking for material, like evidence; and there was this other guy who stood in the door and told us this was routine, 'nothing is going to happen to you, you're going to be fine', that it was routine procedure, but the guys left a huge mess, everything upside down.
It was shocking. That became routine.		
		What I feel was worse was that, afterwards, we were left alone, we didn't have parents that could give us an explanation or that could give us a hug and tell us it was all over; it was all really shocking.
Leo	**The Mummy**	**Claudio**
Real dead. That was the general opinion. I remember, back then, because there wasn't. . . there was never. . . my family was against, sometimes they would say real dead and sometimes they would say he was a communist, so to be a communist and to be dead was normal; maybe because of that kind of death, because he was up to something, it was always associated to the fact that he was killed that he was a communist. So, that made it justifiable.	*Andrea and Pelegri wearing little birthday hats. Everyone else sings happy birthday. Andrea gestures as if she wants to speak but cannot. When the song is over, Pelegri blows out the candle. Great revelry.* *Everyone puts mud on Pelegri, who plays 'the mummy' and chases everyone around the space. When she grabs someone she sinks their head into a tub of water. All laugh and celebrate.*	The kids used to like to come to my birthday, for example, because they would drink milk. Since my mom worked at the polyclinic, she always had powdered milk and she made it with chocolate and I remember when I'd go to the other kids birthday parties they were always pretty meagre, there was never any milk, none of those things; and maybe, in the passage we weren't the richest family but, in certain things, you could maybe see

Column 1 A Soundtrack	Column 2 Onstage action	Column 3 B Soundtrack
They didn't talk like that, like 'poor woman', but, instead, 'son of a bitch, let's hope they're all real dead.' I thought it was strange. I thought that association was strange. That to be a communist was the same as to be a terrorist and to be dead; nobody would've wanted to be a communist back then. If they had died then that went with being a criminal that was what would go out on the radio, in the papers. So, there was no sympathy, there wasn't. . .		some differences in the way we put value into certain matters. . . In my birthday parties there was lots of candy, it was February so all the kids were there, nobody went away on vacation, almost everyone had never been to the beach. All of the little tables and everything was in the living room and then on the street, the street was yours, a while there (at home) and then, everyone would go out onto the street. The birthdays yes, maybe, for some event, for September 18th, for example, and for Christmas and Easter were events for the entire passage. The gates would be closed to the passage, little lights were put up, the trees were painted, the sidewalk, everything.
Roberto	**Adjustment screen**	**Jenny**
. . . I remember there was a television set on the block and we would pay to watch it. . . Imagine a group of street kids sitting on a row of benches, the TV in front, up high and it was one of those Antu or Bolocco brand, in black and white and we paid about 100 pesos of today, something like that.	*Physical group score on the adjustment screen. All six actors move through the space making the characteristic noise that television sets made in the 1970s before they started their programming, when they were on the adjustment screen.* *They walk, sit down, act like they're watching television.*	They would cover our faces so we couldn't see any further or at least they covered my face, or else I would've found out everything about my dad but it was always like they were always trying to be like everything was ok. In the end, they wouldn't tell us anything, the grownups would talk among themselves and they would

Column 1 A Soundtrack	Column 2 Onstage action	Column 3 B Soundtrack
And, all of a sudden, a channel is going to show a Western and, on another (a different show), that's when the conflicts would start about what we would watch, until the majority won and we would put one on. And, usually, the naughty bunch would sit in the back, we would slap the kids in the front and a group of kids would just hang out; and I remember, dearly, but the way they were, I don't know what kind of technology those TVs had but, all of a sudden, the cartoons, the images, would get all crooked.	*Caro sits in front of an imaginary television set, facing down stage, and starts singing a typical song from 1970s television.* *One by one, everyone else joins in singing and moving their head from side to side.*	leave us watching TV, and they didn't make us part of what was going on. I wondered why the cops showed up, why did this happen, why are they shooting. 'But, Jenny, we're in a dictatorship.' that's all they would say. 'And when is it going to be over? When are we going to be able to go out?' The first thing my dad would do was cover my face, so I couldn't see what was going on, always like 'she's a little girl and she shouldn't have to know what's going on.'
(Silence)	**Persons** *(Pablo walks towards Andrea and whispers into her ear.* **Andrea** *listens and says:)* One of the things that happened was that they stopped him, they yelled stop! A military patrol car, and he, obviously, didn't hear them and they shot him, but the bullets didn't hit him, they shot at his feet to draw his attention and that's when they arrested him, searched him and, that night, he got home. We were frightened for quite a while. *(Then, Andrea goes to Pelegri and whispers into her ear. Pelegri overacts, you can barely hear her and she underlines the meaning of the text with her acting.)*	*(Silence)*

Column 1 A Soundtrack	Column 2 Onstage action	Column 3 B Soundtrack
	One of the things that happened was that they stopped us, they yelled stop! A military patrol car, and we, obviously, didn't hear them and they shot us, but the bullets didn't hit us, they shot at our feet to draw our attention and that's when we were arrested, searched and, that night, we got home. We were frightened for quite a while. (*Pelegri is exhausted; she has a sort of hysterical attack.*) **Carolina**, (*lying on a couch tells her version.*) One of the things that happened to me was that I was stopped, they yelled stop! A military patrol car, and I, obviously, didn't hear and they shot, but the bullets didn't hit me, they shot at my feet to draw my attention and that's when they arrested me, searched me and, that night, I got home. We were frightened for quite a while.	
Emilio	**The dogs**	**Jenny**
Obviously, there was a before and after: there was one neighborhood, a way of life that ended from one day to the next, not gradually, I wouldn't say that I went into my adolescence and that I was interested in other things, no, it was over because it was over,	*Everyone sits on the floor, they're all clearly bored. They start throwing stones into the empty space. Then, they cover their faces with their arms. They repeat this several times. They get up and walk towards the audiences, picking up the stones from the floor.*	I remember a situation really well that happened to us, when the curfew caught us on the street, we had gone to buy bread and my dad was on crutches and I was walking with him as if nothing was wrong, carrying the bread bag and, all of a sudden – anything that was

Column 1 A Soundtrack	Column 2 Onstage action	Column 3 B Soundtrack

you can't get together in the street or stay out until whatever time you wish; the rules changed completely, from one day to the next, (. . .) Before the street was public, it was part of the house and, from one day to the next, the street was the street, the doors were closed and we began to walk from one house to the other. (. . .) All day you could see military walking around, navy officers dressed for combat, carrying machine guns, you had them in front of you, all day and you could see them very close up so the fear was even bigger.

The street was the public space and, evidently, afterwards, when there was a curfew, the houses ended up close-up like the tops of submarines.

My parents wouldn't let us go out too far away, we had to be close, around the block, it's like the universe had shrunk, I remember that very well.

They provoke a pack of imaginary dogs, barking and clapping very loudly. They get scared, apparently, the dogs attack them. They run off hell for leather. After running they stop.

They look up, listening to the sound of low-flying helicopters.

They stare, defiantly, at the audience. They go back to sitting against the wall. They try to throw stones but they can't. They cover their faces with their arms.

military was gathered in the square- and they started running, and I, distinctly, remember that they knocked down my daddy's crutch and he falls, and swearing '. . .what are you doing here with the kid.' I left the bread and picked up the crutch and got him on his feet. We had two blocks left to get home, but they were really aggressive, but I didn't cry. I didn't cry, I got him up.

It's like I saw him in such a state, like they humiliated him there, on the floor, on top of everything they were pointing at him, so I got him up and we left, and we never talked about it; we got home and we never talked about it, we got home and we stayed in silence, the both of us and we never, so that's when we blocked it.

Daniela	**Pablo's bottle**	**Daniela**

I would say my clearest memory of that period I have, has to do with the kidnapping of teachers at my school in 1985. I was in the Latinoamericano school; Javiera Parada was my classmate, I, actually, knew her family really well, we would travel on vacation together with her dad, her mom and her brother,

Pablo has a water bottle in his hand. He takes out a packet of red powdered juice and pours it into the bottle. He shakes the bottle so the juice will dissolve into the water. He looks up, listens to the helicopters. He, desperately, drinks all of the juice, staining his white shirt. He smiles, mischievously. Walks

I would say my clearest memory of that period I have, has to do with the kidnapping of teachers at my school in 1985. I was in the Latinoamericano school; Javiera Parada was my classmate, I, actually, knew her family really well, we would travel on vacation together with her dad, her mom and her brother,

Column 1 A Soundtrack	Column 2 Onstage action	Column 3 B Soundtrack
and a memory I have is really incredible because it's been over 20 years and I have a very clear memory of that morning. We were in math class with a teacher, aunt Isabel, she was writing math symbols on the chalkboard and I remember I was drawing with a pencil, a notebook and a ruler whatever we were going over at that time and we hear a helicopter flying over very low; so we hear this helicopter noise in the classroom, screams and struggles at the school entrance and like shooting. That's when they take José Manuel away, Javiera's dad, who was talking to Manuel Guerrero, he was the school inspector at that time.	*towards the audience and sits down. Puts red juice powder in his right hand. He licks it, seductively. He laughs. He lays his head on his right hand as he looks up. A bomb explosion sounds. His cheek bears the mark of his fingers in red.*	and a memory I have is really incredible because it's been over 20 years and I have a very clear memory of that morning. We were in math class with a teacher, aunt Isabel, she was writing math symbols on the chalkboard and I remember I was drawing with a pencil, a notebook and a ruler whatever we were going over at that time and we hear a helicopter flying over very low; so we hear this helicopter noise in the classroom, screams and struggles at the school entrance and like shooting. That's when they take José Manuel away, Javiera's dad, who was talking to Manuel Guerrero, he was the school inspector at that time.
Back then, our classroom was right in front of the school entrance and, at that moment, our teacher, because they had started shooting, asks us to hide under our tables and, then, they got us out through the door that led to the kitchen and to an inner entrance to another part of the school, that didn't lead to the main entrance but to a stage the school had; they take us to these wooden rooms, that were part of an addition that had just been built. That memory, the sound of that helicopter flying low was a sound that I kept hearing over and over again and then, when I heard something I would go back to that scene.		Back then, our classroom was right in front of the school entrance and, at that moment, our teacher, because they had started shooting, asks us to hide under our tables and, then, they got us out through the door that led to the kitchen and to an inner entrance to another part of the school, that didn't lead to the main entrance but to a stage the school had; they take us to these wooden rooms, that were part of an addition that had just been built. That memory, the sound of that helicopter flying low was a sound that I kept hearing over and over again and then, when I heard something I would go back to that scene.

Column 1 A Soundtrack	Column 2 Onstage action	Column 3 B Soundtrack
(*Music: The ranchera*)	**Pee**	(*Music: The ranchera*)
Ivan	*Vicente, wearing dark glasses, drinks a glass of whiskey. A ranchera plays. He, maliciously, sways his hips.*	**Andrea**
I mean, the thing was the fear, in the end, the fear of the day, for example, an aunt, they would pass those fears onto us.		At home, I always had the feeling that I had things that I wasn't supposed to have: records, books. I always knew we had things that were kept hidden.
They were always worried, they weren't at ease and, maybe, she was a little paranoid, maybe they were exaggerating, I don't know. They always thought the worst, that they were doing this for a reason, they're following her because they know she had been a UP partisan. . .	*We see a woman enter the stage, facing upstage. She has a hard time walking, she looks drunk or ill. Vicente drinks his glass of whiskey. The woman pees herself, we see the pee dripping down her legs.*	I was absolutely sure there was an uncle but that we couldn't say there was an uncle. And he would stay with us some days. And this uncle would be kept hidden in a room on the first floor that was like a study, that's where they set up a bed and there he was all day long, he didn't go out.
So, they would pass that on to us and I think they passed that on to me, some of their hatred. With my aunt, and talking to other people that were close to her, they saw hate, something I had never seen as a kid, so much hate.	*We hear a deafening laughter from the woman. Andrea runs to Vicente, she gives him an effusive hug. She is, actually, drunk, she loses her balance and falls.*	And, one day, I was walking by that room and I tripped and fell and I cried and he came out to see me and, for me, that was like. . . I felt important because I knew that this uncle was hiding and that he couldn't come
. . .The thing is that she was very paranoid, when she would make friends, she would always think that, maybe that they were detectives and that they were trying to find out, through her. So, my aunt, above everything, tried to make sure that I never found out about certain things and she asked me never to tell anything to anyone.	*The two women fall down at the same time. They lie on the floor. Caro cries and Andrea laughs.* *Vicente goes over to Caro, pokes at her with his foot, checking to see if she's dead or alive.* *Then, he helps Andrea get up. He takes her away.* *Caro is left, lying defenceless, on the floor.*	out and that nobody could know that he was there and the fact that he came out to help me, because I had fallen, I felt like I was really important. I don't know how long he stayed there, (. . .) the feeling of keeping something hidden at home, a person.

Column 1 A Soundtrack	Column 2 Onstage action	Column 3 B Soundtrack
(*Silence*)	**Post memory**	(*Silence*)
	Vicente	
	My dad was always of the mind of telling us things in grown up terms because, then, when we are older, we would understand or we were going to listen and understand and the discourse was going to be coherent. He explained the entire political thing to us, what a coup d'état was, I was 13, but when I was older I understood what it was; always, when we were going to school in the morning, he would say 'don't look at a policeman', 'don't walk in front of the military', 'if a policeman is walking your way, cross the street' and, to this day, I'm scared to death of them. That's always caught my daughter's attention.	
	Luis	
	. . .so, at one point, we were very lost because, over there, the streets aren't octagonal and there were some policemen. And I said to my daughter, 'go ask the policemen!', and my daughter didn't want to, 'no', she said, and a policeman heard, and says to her 'come here, sweetie, I'm not going to do anything to you!' and he starts calling her to come over.	

Column 1 A Soundtrack	Column 2 Onstage action	Column 3 B Soundtrack
	My daughter is pale, she's 18 years old. We come closer and the guy is really nice 'what are you looking for?', 'what are you scared of?', he says to her and she's still pale and real quiet. Afterwards, I asked her why she was afraid and she told me.	

Andrea

...maybe because of you, because I remember when we would go out with you in the car and they asked you for your license and registration and you shivered. You would say you weren't frightened but you still shivered.

Luis

And well, I'm not scared of anything but they still frighten me, until this day. To have that feeling of somebody that has absolute power over you, and you don't have any chance of saying anything... you couldn't complain or tell anyone anything, they had absolute power over you; and I thought it was so surprising that my daughter, twenty years after the dictatorship was over, would be scared.

Marisol	**War**	**Genaro**
Hearing those shots made me terrified, I would cover my ears, my mom would cover my ears and she would cover us up, real covered up. My mom would play with us so we wouldn't hear, she covered our ears, but it was impossible not to hear them	*Luis starts the game yelling 'sooo', while he tries to catch his team members. Since he doesn't manage to catch anybody, when he runs out of breath, everyone kicks him. He falls to the floor. He tries again. They kick him again.*	From an early age, I was obsessed with coming back to Chile and fighting Pinochet. By the time I was 9, I was sure of it, when I was 12 all I wanted to do was leave and I left, I got here, I lasted a year and, by the time I was 14, I was

Column 1 A Soundtrack	Column 2 Onstage action	Column 3 B Soundtrack
because they would shoot right there, by your house. But she would take care that we all covered our ears somehow so we wouldn't hear; my mom cried a lot, I remember, my strongest memory from the days of the coup was that my mom was crying, crying, crying. Once, I asked my mom what was wrong and she answered, crying, that they had killed the president, and I didn't understand anything. And with time, she realized that he had killed himself. My mom cried a lot, a lot of sadness, for many days she cried a lot. My mom told me that Allende was a very good man, a very good person and that he helped poor people, so that hurt her very much.	*'He discovers a roll of toilet paper on the floor. He throws it at Vincent's head. Everyone reacts and get ino the toilet paper war game. They throw rolls of toilet paper at each other in the air. Everyone laughs and has fun. Pelegri distances herself from the group. She takes a glass bottle and starts making a molotov bomb. She, delicately, pours gasoline into the bottle, lights the fuse, puts it in place. While the rest play, she finished the bomb. She gets up, molotov in hand. Everyone stays still. She simply walks out of the space.'*	already a member of the party. I had gotten a cell, I had contacted an uncle, I was doing all kinds of shit, I was an informant, I would transport shit, I would do things, I was doing what I had dreamt of doing: in my kid's game fantasy, that had been very cultivated in Europe in terms of resistance and fascism and by a family completely inmersed in politics as well as the resistance. That was really intense because it's not what a kid should be worried about, adult crap. I think, what I find sad, is that Pinocho took up so much of my brain, for so long and that it was the obsession of a generation is also a pity. The good part, is being able to have gotten to know other parts of the world, other languages, cultures and that is priceless to this day, because it made us get to know other worlds beyond our desires, and I always saw that as a good thing, cool. The bad part is having spent so much time on shit when you could've been doing something more useful or educating for yourself.
Daniela I was 11 years old and I was in the sixth grade. In terms of emotions, it was part of a general sensation of great fear, fright. . . it was very evident at that time,	**Andrea's bottle** *Andrea has a water bottle in her hand. She takes out a packet of red powdered juice and pours it into the bottle. She shakes the bottle to dissolve the juice.*	**Daniela** I was 11 years old and I was in the sixth grade. In terms of emotions, it was part of a general sensation of great fear, fright. . . it was very evident at that time,

Column 1 A Soundtrack	Column 2 Onstage action	Column 3 B Soundtrack
we could feel it, but at that moment it felt very evident; there's this feeling that's something's wrong, that no one really wants to tell you, but you feel the anguish and the worried looks from these teachers, as an environment of fear where anything could happen. They take us to these rooms, the whole school is there; Estela, Javiera's mom, who had gone to drop off Javiera and her brothers, and José Manuel had stayed talking, she comes back, she comes back to the school, this appears shortly after on Cooperativa radio and she comes back to get Javiera. We didn't know her dad and uncle Manuel had been kidnapped, and it was like something was being rumored but we still didn't have any official information about what had happened.	*She looks up, hears helicopters. She, desperately, drinks all of the juice, spilling on to her white shirt. She smiles mischieviously. She walks towards the audience. She sits down. Pours red powder into her right hand. She licks it, seductively. She laughs. She places her head on her right hand as she looks to the sky. A bomb is heard. Her cheek bears the mark of her red stained fingers.*	we could feel it, but at that moment it felt very evident; there's this feeling that's something's wrong, that no one really wants to tell you, but you feel the anguish and the worried looks from these teachers, as an environment of fear where anything could happen. They take us to these rooms, the whole school is there; Estela, Javiera's mom, who had gone to drop off Javiera and her brothers, and José Manuel had stayed talking, she comes back, she comes back to the school, this appears shortly after on Cooperativa radio and she comes back to get Javiera. We didn't know her dad and uncle Manuel had been kidnapped, and it was like something was being rumored but we still didn't have any official information about what had happened.
Macarena I remember we would go out and bang on pots and things but then we would go to bed, but, then, with all the noise on the street it felt like lots of people screaming, crying, bullets in the air. I remember I always felt like there were lots of people sitting and yelling 'And he will fall', but a lot of people, I don't know, I imagined they were all sitting down, very much in order, maybe the way they sang was very clean and orderly and that they could	**Demonstration** *Children hidden under a blanket. They walk around with the blanket over their heads, as did the detained at the National Stadium.* *All of a sudden, they start banging spoons and pots. Caro takes a pot.* *Demonstration score.*	**Marisol** Because the military would shoot at night. And the master bedroom faced the street, so it was dangerous to hide there, so my mom would cover the windows with pieces of cloth or blankets and we would all sleep in the small room that had these. . . bunk beds. (. . .) I think that about 7 in the afternoon we would already be hiding there in the room, and all dark, we couldn't make noise, we would do everything in a

Column 1 **A Soundtrack**	Column 2 **Onstage action**	Column 3 **B Soundtrack**

have been singing in an orderly fashion, but I think it was a lot people that were on the streets singing 'and he will fall', like in the stadium (. . .) Imagine what that was like, for a kid, to be there but not be able to see it, so you start to imagine things and they're things like (. . .) like that at some point those people were going to come into the passage, I felt like it was far away but that, at some point, they were going to do away with everything, it was very strong, the energy was. . .

Me, lying in bed, everything dark, in bed because for the curfew, for the national protests, they would make us go to bed early with a candle, there wasn't electricity. Besides, with my brothers, we talk among us, 'imagine this, imagine that. . .'

We would start to count the shots we heard, and that they heard so and so's voice 'no, I know for sure it's so and so's voice', this neighbor's voice', 'no, I know it's Mrs Something, I can tell by her voice', but they didn't let us talk much.

hush: my mom would feed us in whispers, she would say, please don't talk, don't cry, don't yell out anything and, sometimes, we would peek out the window and we would see the military pass by. Because, when you're little, you're always a little curious, when my mom was away we would run and open the curtain to see.

Still, you felt scared, because I would think 'what if a bullet pierces through the wall and kills us'; I would tell my mom they were shooting, that a bullet was going to pierce through one wall and, then, through the other and kill us, or that a bullet was going to reach one of us. Thanks to the construction, the walls were thick, but, then, the following day, we could see holes in our neighbor's walls.

Roberto

Good Night

Mario

I remember it would get dark and the shootings would begin, the first days, and for me it was awful: I remember, for me, honestly, they had to give me a potty, I was horrified. I would hear the shots and I knew it wasn't a

Caro lies on a bed sheet. She lays her head on a pot. Simón is standing next to the sheet. A gloomy murmur is heard from outside 'and he will fall, and he will fall' Andrea, Pablo and Luis enter.

There was this rage that I didn't know how to express, it was very strong. There's this feeling of rage with the country, with the rest of the people; the people that supported Pinochet would say so, in public, very out

Column 1 A Soundtrack	Column 2 Onstage action	Column 3 B Soundtrack

good thing, as a kid, running or playing I'd never heard a bullet out in the open; so, to be restricted to home, getting dark and hearing shots, in my way, I was the youngest and that's what it produced in me, a great deal of fear at night. And you had to be in silence because I remember my older brothers would make me be quiet, and they would say, look there they go, there they go, and you could, actually, hear the footsteps of the military were supposedly walking around, I don't know if they were keeping watch, patrolling or checking something out. Those were the fears of the first days.

I would get into bed and nobody could get me out. My older brothers would go and peek out of the fence but I wouldn't, I remember, for me, it was fear, a lot of fear.

I am a fearful person, essentially I am a fearful person, I have a hard time doing the bad thing.

Very frightened, in fact, I ended up in the potty. I don't know how long that lasted for. The shooting would begin and my mom and my brother knew what they had to do, because my stomach aches were terrible. So, how long that went on for I don't remember, but the shootings, I remember, lasted for a long time; I listened, not always, but for many days, months later, you could hear the shots.

They sing 'and he will fall. . .'.

Everyone lies down. Vicente wakes up, agitated. Andrea plays and sings a song, the rest follow. . . Simón tells them to be quiet.

Vicente   Good night.

Andrea   (*imitating Simón*) Good night.

Everyone laughs and plays.

Vicente (*angry*) Come on!

Luis (*imitating Pinochet*) Good nigh'

(*Everyone laughs and plays saying good night in different languages. Vicente, abruptly, gets them to shut up:*)

Shhh!

They look at each other, behind Viente's back, and continue to play and laugh. Vicente stops them.

They hear a noise. The kids take refuge in a human pile. Vicente hugs them. Andrea sobs.

in the open, identifiable, it wasn't something that was kept hidden, it was showable; I had classmate's mothers that adored Pinochet, you could tell because when there was any act for this man they would go and get their kids, it was all very exposed. Also, a rage against them, because so many of they had triumphed, obviously, and they made that known, you could see it.

This feeling of rage, of accumulating like various feelings of resentment and the feeling there was. . . how do I build something that will allow me to survive, (. . .) beyond everything (. . .) I liked school, (. . .) So this space for the construction of identity that would be acceptable to the system was very confusing to me, because, on the one hand, I constantly felt like a traitor. I would read very well, for example, and since I read well they would ask me to read in school assemblies. So, more than once, I found myself reading things at the military parades. I would read texts, things about Chilean soldiers during a school ceremony. And that duality, I wasn't that conscious of it, but my family would point it out to me, very directly, they weren't very subtle about it.

Column 1 A Soundtrack	Column 2 Onstage action	Column 3 B Soundtrack
Daniela	**Pelegri's bottle**	**Daniela**
I would say that by the end of the morning I'm not sure if the school makes an announcement or if it's something my mom tells me later, when she goes to pick me up, because they started to pick up the kids at school. And I remember, vividly, when my mom comes to school to get us and we're going home, it was a long way, we were listening to Cooperativa radio and they announced the news; in fact, in the horror of the brutality of what was going on, you knew terrible things were going on. I had a relationship with José Manuel, with Javiera's family. . . and the brutality, in a school, it's like they were breaking all boundaries, in the end, the military's brutality. Two days later, they find them. I remember, then, the images of the place where they found them in Quilicura: images of the cathedral, the big mass where all hell broke loose: I remember, we were inside and these water cannons, I don't know how they didn't break the glass vitraux because you could feel the water on the glass windows; I remember visiting the Vicary, of going over there and seeing lots of people.	*Pelegri has a water bottle in her hand. She takes out a packet of red powdered juice and pours it into the bottle. She shakes the bottle to dissolve the juice. She looks up, hears helicopters. She, desperately, drinks all of the juice, spilling on to her white shirt. She smiles mischieviously. She walks towards the audience. She sits down. Pours red powder into her right hand. She licks it, seductively. She laughs. She places her head on her right hand as she looks to the sky. A bomb is heard. Her cheek bears the mark of her red stained fingers.*	I would say that by the end of the morning I'm not sure if the school makes an announcement or if it's something my mom tells me later, when she goes to pick me up, because they started to pick up the kids at school. And I remember, vividly, when my mom comes to school to get us and we're going home, it was a long way, we were listening to Cooperativa radio and they announced the news; in fact, in the horror of the brutality of what was going on, you knew terrible things were going on. I had a relationship with José Manuel, with Javiera's family. . . and the brutality, in a school, it's like they were breaking all boundaries, in the end, the military's brutality. Two days later, they find them. I remember, then, the images of the place where they found them in Quilicura: images of the cathedral, the big mass where all hell broke loose: I remember, we were inside and these water cannons, I don't know how they didn't break the glass vitraux because you could feel the water on the glass windows; I remember visiting the Vicary, of going over there and seeing lots of people.

Column 1 A Soundtrack	Column 2 Onstage action	Column 3 B Soundtrack
Emilio	**The day of the coup**	**Genaro**
My dad doesn't really like to talk much, all he said that night. . . I have this image in my head where he said that very hard times were coming, and I have this image of him lying in bed, he called us to his room, my brother and me, my mom was standing next to him and he said 'boys, sons, very hard times are going to fall on the country.' We asked him why and he said because there were some military in government and, before, when they had been in government with Carlos Ibáñez del Campo, it had been very rough. That's all he said. He remembered Carlos Ibánez del Campo because he was young, my dad is 84 now, and he could remember that it had been a military government and that many people had died and that they had beaten the poor. Later, he told is that he had this image of policemen on horseback chasing people with a lance when they got together to protest. That the police would charge on to the people with their horses, there aren't horses now but they charge at them with trucks or jeeps.	*Everyone has a little battery powered radio. They're all listening to Cooperativa Radio.* EDICT N 1 'From this moment on, we will transmit a provincial and national broadcast from the Armed Forces. We invite all free radio stations to connect to this radio network:' Santiago, September 11, 1973. Considering: 1. The extremely grave economic, social and moral crisis that is destroying the country. 2. The Government's incapacity to adopt measures that will detain the further development of this situation. 3. The constant rise of paramilitary groups, organized and trained by the Popular Unity's political parties that are leading the Chilean people into an unavoidable civil war, the Chilean Armed Forces and Police Force do declare: • That the President of the Republic must immediately surrender his office to the Armed Forces and the Chilean Police Force.	And then I have some images of the coup itself, I don't know is that was eve before the coup or the day of the coup itself that I remember coming back from playing and coming into the apartment and seeing all of my uncles together- the uncles are my parents' friends, they must have been party members at that time- My father was the president of the Popular Unity of the north, he was a MAPU member and so was my mother; What I remember was this scene of coming home and that it was a bit of a mess, I remember my uncles burning and tearing documents and, a sort of dramatic scene; my uncle's kind of nervous, throwing things, breaking and getting rid of things. I remember that, and the day of the coup, this scene where the military are raiding the house and I'm this scrawny kid and I spit at a military during the raid; they put us in this place, I don't remember the scene very well, it's very blurry, in fact, all I remember is the sun, this typical northern thing. Like a burnt photo, like a camera flash fixed on your eyes.

Column 1 A Soundtrack	Column 2 Onstage action	Column 3 B Soundtrack
Ivan My aunt took me to La Moneda and showed me the place where they had taken out Allende. We stood by the Morandé door for a while and she told me several things. She had told me things before, she had named people, so. . . look, this is where they were lying. She knew quite a lot about what was going on, she was very involved, lots of people she knew died, some got away but, in general, she heard a lot of stories of what happened that day, so she was also imagining (. . .). I could, also, see she was very nervous as she told me, she would get emotional and cry, and that made it get to me even more.	• That the Armed Forces and the Chilean Police Forces have been united, to give way to a historical and responsible mission in the fight for the Homeland's liberation from the Marxist yoke and the restoration of order and institutionality. • The Chilean workers can rest assured that the social and economic achievements they have reached thus far will not be fundamentally affected. • The press, radio networks and television channels adhered to the Popular Unity must suspend their informative activities from this instant onwards. If they deny, they shall receive punishment from areal and land forces. • The people of Santiago must remain in their homes in order to avoid the injury of innocent victims. Signed: Augusto Pinochet Ugarte, General Commander in Chief of the Army; Toribio Merino Castro, Admiral; Gustavo Leigh Guzmán, Air Force General, Commander in Chief of the Chilean Air Force; and César Mendoza Durán, General, Commissioner of the Chilean Police Force.	**Leo** And my dad lifted me onto his shoulders and, from where we lived, you could see a column of smoke from afar and that was the fire from La Moneda. They commented on the dead they had seen on the streets. I remember that. . . years later, I understood what all those dead meant. It's because, back then, children didn't matter much. You were there, things happened; you would listen in. The adults didn't hesitate to speak of these things in front of children because children didn't exist. You could hear everything about everything and that was amazing because they were talking about dead people; I had never seen a corpse. But if you can imagine, they were talking about corpses in the Mapocho, on the streets. . .

| Column 1 | Column 2 | Column 3 |
A Soundtrack	Onstage action	B Soundtrack
	Luis	
I was, practically, born with the dictatorship.	I was, practically, born with the dictatorship.	I was, practically, born with the dictatorship.
	Caro	
The devil is always the devil.	The devil is always the devil.	The devil is always the devil.
	Andrea	
My mom always tried for us not to have those memories.	My mom always tried for us not to have those memories.	My mom always tried for us not to have those memories.
	Pablo	
I feel like my parents couldn't deal with it, it was so strong for them that they couldn't deal with explaining it to us.	I feel like my parents couldn't deal with it, it was so strong for them that they couldn't deal with explaining it to us.	I feel like my parents couldn't deal with it, it was so strong for them that they couldn't deal with explaining it to us.
	Vicente	
I have the feeling that there wasn't a limit to evil.	I have the feeling that there wasn't a limit to evil.	I have the feeling that there wasn't a limit to evil.
	Pelegri	
Ghost people, in the end.	Ghost people, in the end.	Ghost people, in the end.
	Caro	
I never asked.	I never asked.	I never asked.
	Andrea	
I've tried to relive that moment asking questions but no one has been able to answer.	I've tried to relive that moment asking questions but no one has been able to answer.	I've tried to relive that moment asking questions but no one has been able to answer.
	Pablo	
Things you can't explain.	Things you can't explain.	Things you can't explain.
	Everyone	
Pig ears.	Pig ears.	Pig ears.
	Vicente	
Whenever my grandfather had a drink he would start screaming on the street 'the military . . .' and he would start swearing, so they would go and get him because they could kill him.	Whenever my grandfather had a drink he would start screaming on the street 'the military. . .' and he would start swearing, so they would go and get him because they could kill him.	Whenever my grandfather had a drink he would start screaming on the street 'the military. . .' and he would start swearing, so they would go and get him because they could kill him.

Column 1 A Soundtrack	Column 2 Onstage action	Column 3 B Soundtrack
	Luis	
At that age you don't assimilate, you have no political consciousness.	At that age, you don't assimilate, you have no political consciousness.	At that age you don't assimilate, you have no political consciousness.
	Caro	
There weren't many answers.	There weren't many answers.	There weren't many answers.
	Pablo	
I asked my mom why the other kids didn't have presents, I think she told me but I never understood.	I asked my mom why the other kids didn't have presents, I think she told me but I never understood.	I asked my mom why the other kids didn't have presents, I think she told me but I never understood.
	Andrea	
All of a sudden the cartoon would get crooked.	All of a sudden the cartoon would get crooked.	All of a sudden the cartoon would get crooked.
	Caro	
My parents' smell, of my absent parents.	My parents' smell, of my absent parents.	My parents' smell, of my absent parents.
	Luis	
But you can't sleep because you hear things.	But you can't sleep because you hear things.	But you can't sleep because you hear things.
	Andrea	
But he never talks about that.	But he never talks about that.	But he never talks about that.
	Pelegri	
We are the daughters of repression.	We are the daughters of repression.	We are the daughters of repression.
	Luis	
I, somehow, feel like I played a lead role in something.	I, somehow, feel like I played a lead role in something.	I, somehow, feel like I played a lead role in something.
	Luis	
I lived a little paranoid.	I lived a little paranoid.	I lived a little paranoid.
	Andrea	
Just shut up, Roberto.	Just shut up, Roberto.	Just shut up, Roberto.
	Pelegri	
The violence at my house was the silence.	The violence at my house was the silence.	The violence at my house was the silence.
	Pablo	
A little girl knows and doesn't know what's going on.	A little girl knows and doesn't know what's going on.	A little girl knows and doesn't know what's going on.

Column 1 A Soundtrack	Column 2 Onstage action	Column 3 B Soundtrack
	Caro	
I was a monkey up a tree.	I was a monkey up a tree.	I was a monkey up a tree.
	Pablo	
I was all into eating chicken.	I was all into eating chicken.	I was all into eating chicken.
	Everyone	
It's funny, I hadn't thought about this for a long time.	It's funny, I hadn't thought about this for a long time.	It's funny, I hadn't thought about this for a long time.
	Andrea	
You're stained with blood.	You're stained with blood.	You're stained with blood.
(*Music*)	**Walking**	(*Music*)
	Pablo and Pelegri take off their clothes on stage. They hold hands. They walk slowly, fragile.	

Permissions